Make Movies
That Make Mon

Make Movies That Make Money!

The Low-Budget Filmmaker's Guide to Commercial Success

Philip R. Cable

McFarland & Company, Inc., Publishers
Jefferson, North Carolina, and London

Library of Congress Cataloguing-in-Publication Data

Cable, Philip R., 1952–
    Make movies that make money! : the low-budget filmmaker's
guide to commercial success / Philip R. Cable.
        p.   cm.
    Includes bibliographical references and index.

    ISBN 978-0-7864-4163-1
    softcover : 50# alkaline paper ∞

    1. Motion pictures— Production and direction.
    2. Low-budget films.   I. Title.
PN1995.9.P7C248   2009
791.4302'32023 — dc22   2009005010

British Library cataloguing data are available

Cover photograph ©2009 Shutterstock

Manufactured in the United States of America

*McFarland & Company, Inc., Publishers
  Box 611, Jefferson, North Carolina 28640
    www.mcfarlandpub.com*

To the two most important women in my life:
my mother, who protected me from evil,
and my lovely wife, who has always believed in me.

Also to my dear friends
Chuck Dichiera, Lori Lovelady, Steve Ross, and Ed Savage,
who were there for me during times of great trial.

Acknowledgments

I would like to thank the following people, without whose help the writing of this book would have been much more time consuming.

Gabriel Campisi for his valuable insight when I was seeking a publisher.

Mervin Fulton for supplying me with some technical data and release form information.

The Adventures of Superman Message Board for helping supply me with information about television pioneer Whitney Ellsworth.

Genie Williams and Kalor Marche for permitting me to use a Marche-Williams Productions business proposal in this book.

Anthony Castillo for information on non-union contracts.

I would also like to thank Lewis Insurance for supplying me with details on various types of insurance.

Table of Contents

III. PRODUCTION

IV. POST-PRODUCTION

V. DISTRIBUTION

Preface

There are a thousand and one reasons that some eager beaver might want to direct and produce a movie. Some are film students wanting to prove themselves. Some are seasoned professionals who want to be in charge of their own destinies. Some are actors who want to have a showcase for their talents. Some are control freaks with delusions of grandeur. Some are merely dreamers with fantasies of fame and riches. There are as many reasons as there are stars in the eyes of a "wannabe" actress getting on a bus headed for Hollywood. The only thing they all have in common is their burning desire to make something happen for themselves by making their own movie. Did I say only one thing? Oops, my mistake. They have another thing in common: they don't have the millions of dollars it takes to make their filmmaking dream come true. What few, if any of them, realize is that millions of dollars is not needed to make their dream come true.

Allow me to paraphrase the great director John Ford and say, "My name is Philip R. Cable; I make low-budget movies." Currently, I am the Chief of Production for Marche-Williams Productions, a movie company which might be described as a mini-major studio. It is my responsibility to oversee our company's big-budget movies as well as those made on small budgets. I was hired because of my background and experience in making — yes, you guessed it — low-budget movies. The term "low-budget" can mean just about anything nowadays. It can refer to movies made for under seven million, under a million, under a hundred thousand, or, for that matter, movies made with no money at all. This book is for the *would-be* filmmaker who has little or no money to make a movie. It's not only designed to show them how to get their movie made and distributed, but also how to maximize their movie's potential for profit.

This book, and its 104 individual points, is a practical, no-nonsense blueprint of how to make a good, as well as successful, movie. It does not present theory or opinion disguised as fact. The information stated herein is based upon my years of experience in the film business; and if you follow it, point for point, your chance of making a successful movie will be greatly increased. If you don't ... well, don't quit your day job.

As for those skeptics out there who refuse to believe that low-budget movies can make money (don't bother hiding, I can see your pointed heads out there), I can only say: "DO YOUR HOMEWORK!" Why *should* filmmaking have to cost so much? Each year movies made for next to nothing make fortunes. Or perhaps I should say the *right kinds of movies* make fortunes. What constitutes the right kinds of movies? The kinds of movies that I'm talking about are well made and tailored for financial success. In these pages you'll learn everything from commercially viable genres, to how to attract investors, to the ins and outs of movie distribution. All this plus a whole lot more. Information that the next Steven Spielberg needs to learn before he shoots a single frame of his next film.

What this book does not do is present the same redundant information that has been printed in every other book on filmmaking. If you want to learn what a gaffer is (in laborious detail), or how the Blue Screen process works, then find that information at the local library. This book is for the filmmaker who can't afford a large crew (which might not even have a gaffer) or expensive effects (which might include the Blue Screen process). This is for the filmmaker who wants to make a good movie, with little or no money, that is also commercial.

You may be asking yourself, "If money-making movies can be made on a low budget, then why isn't everyone doing it?" The answer is simple. It's because it's *hard. Very hard.* It takes imagination, skill, determination, and an awful lot of hard work to make a good low-budget movie; whereas incompetence or indifference can be masked with a *big* budget. Bad direction and technical ineptitude can sometimes be fixed in post production if you have the millions to allot to it, but the low-budget filmmaker cannot afford that luxury. The low-budget filmmaker has to be better trained, demonstrate more imagination, and have more moxie than his or her big-budget counterpart. When this kind of filmmaker finishes their movie they earn a reward beyond the financial. The movie of such a filmmaker is a true creation of that filmmaker's style, brain, heart, and spirit. It reflects their artistic soul and business acumen. The collective demands and/or input from committees, or studio executives, or a huge film crew cannot produce this reflection.

Oh all right, I'll tell you what a gaffer is. Basically, he (or she) is a technician whose job it is to work with the lights on the set in accordance with the requirements of the director of photography. I'll let you look up the involved explanation of the workings of the Blue Screen process. Now that your curiosity has been partially satisfied, what are you waiting for? Start reading and start making movies.

I. Getting Started

The DARK at the Beginning of the Tunnel

1. REALISTIC EXPECTATIONS

- You want to film an epic and you need a ton of money.
- You want to make an intimate drama about a boy and a flower, and you're sure that everyone will want to see it.
- You want to shoot an art film that will change the world.
- You want to star yourself in a movie that will win you an Oscar.
- You want to make anything that will make you rich.
- You want a lot, don't you?

Let's get real for a minute. I fully admit that just about anything is possible in the film business. After all, it's a world where a movie about a talking mule can become a hit and *Citizen Kane* can lose the Academy Award for Best Picture. Miracles happen every day ... but don't count on them.

It's very important to have a realistic idea of what you can accomplish artistically, as well as financially, with your movie. Some of this will be covered in specific detail elsewhere in this book, but let's take a minute or two to consider the story of Tony X. Tony X was an actor I met after a lecture I'd given at the American Film Institute on behalf of a Screen Actors Guild summer program.

Tony X was a rather ordinary-looking man in his mid-thirties whose acting career had never really taken off. He firmly believed in his talent and believed that if he could play the lead in a movie just once, he could become a star. Tony X decided that he would make his dream come true by producing his own film in which he would naturally be the star. After the lecture, Tony X bombarded me with questions about filmmaking. I answered his questions, and he wanted to know if he could meet with me to discuss a movie that he wanted to make. I agreed, and a couple of weeks later Tony X met me on a sound stage where I was doing some preliminary work for a film I was planning to shoot. I took a break, and Tony X made his pitch. He had been a successful businessman before the acting bug had bitten him, and, due to that success, Tony X had a hundred thousand dollars to finance a film. I waited for the catch. There's always a catch. Tony X stated that he wanted to star in the movie. That catch wasn't too outrageous a demand. I had seen him act, and while Tony was not a great actor, he was at least adequate. Sadly, his demands didn't end there. Tony X was also certain that he was a great screenwriter and he had written the perfect script to turn into a movie. He was absolutely certain that his movie would make millions. My stomach began to churn. I knew that he was headed for disaster. I also knew that Tony wouldn't listen to any advice that might burst his bubble, but I figured I'd give it a shot. Fool that I am, I always try to prevent a train wreck, even when that train is aching to become scrap metal. First of all, I told Tony X that he had picked a genre for his screenplay that was five years out of date. The public was no longer interested in such films. Equally important was the fact that the overseas buyers wouldn't buy the theatrical, video, or television rights to such a film. Losing them would mean death for any low-budget motion picture hoping for a profit. Tony seemed unaffected by anything so unimportant as logic. He tried to defend his position by quoting the huge amount of money made by a film similar to his. I explained that the movie he was referring to was made twenty years earlier and had half a dozen major stars in it. I tried to talk him into making a different film. Tony X wasn't crazy about the idea, but he listened attentively. Ultimately, he agreed that it was more practical to make a movie that would have at least a chance for an audience. Tony X reasoned that with a hit or two under his belt, perhaps he could then afford to risk his savings on the impractical movie which he had originally approached me about. He decided to meet with me in a few weeks to discuss more commercially viable genres. I was genuinely surprised. It's difficult to be practical about a dream, but Tony X was acting like a professional by using his brain instead of just following the dictates of his ego. I felt proud of him.

Many months went by and Tony X had still not met with me. Out of the blue he gave me a call to brag about a public access TV talk show that he was doing. He had directed an episode and was now convinced he was a great director. I sighed and quietly listened as he proceeded to tell me that he was going to direct the movie he had *originally* wanted to do. Tony X was one hundred percent certain that with the combination of his brilliant script, his fine acting, and his inspired directing, his movie would be a sure-fire hit. He then asked if I would produce it for him. I declined and explained why, which was merely a repeat of what I had told him months earlier. Tony X was surprised but took my refusal in stride. He would produce the movie himself if he had to. After all, how hard could it be?

Nearly two years later I happened to come across Tony X. He had finished the movie he'd so desperately wanted to make, but things hadn't turned out the way he had hoped. Instead of the movie costing one hundred thousand dollars, it had cost him four hundred thousand. He was also utterly confused over the fact that no distributor had picked up his movie. He had offered his movie to everybody, but no one was even remotely interested. Tony X said that he wasn't very worried about it because he knew that he had a great film that would soon net him millions. I waited for the question that I knew was coming. Using a very bad poker face, he asked if I would be interested in distributing his film for him. I told him that I didn't know of any way to sell it. Tony X forced a phony smile on his face and told me that my decision was probably for the best because he was thinking that he should distribute his movie himself. All he had to do was to get a booth at one of the film markets and sell his movie to all of the overseas buyers who were just dying for a film like his. I asked Tony X if he knew anything about distribution. Tony X's response was that he knew what he wanted to make from his movie, and that's all he needed to know. I wished him good luck. I knew that he would need it. Filmmakers like Tony X always do.

Several months later, Tony X spent a small fortune getting a booth at a film market where buyers for overseas theater chains, video companies, and TV stations gather each year to buy movies for their countries. Did any country buy Tony X's movie? No buyer I know did. Also, his movie never played in an American theater, never came out on video, and never played on television. What became of Tony X? I have no idea. I haven't heard from him in nearly a decade. I probably never will.

The whole point of this story is: "Don't let your ego get in the way of your good judgment." Tony X did, and he paid a heavy price for his immaturity. Don't get so caught up in your dream that you end up traveling the same path as Tony X. Remember this: Being a good filmmaker doesn't just mean that you have talent; it also means that you act responsibly and with intelligence.

2. Is There a Need for Your Movie?

Thomas Edison supposedly said that he had never invented anything there wasn't already a demand for. This adage is applicable to all forms of business, including motion pictures. For example, several years ago some producers decided to create a new daytime TV talk show, so they looked into the market. They learned that the public was inundated with *Oprah* clones, and what was really wanted was a talk show akin to the *Tonight Show* but with a stronger appeal to a female audience. The result was the *Rosie O'Donnell Show*, which became a huge hit.

Back in the eighties a network executive told a producer that he wanted him to create a stylish detective show that would appeal to the growing youth market. Since he didn't have a concept, the executive referred to it as MTV cops. It ended up being called *Miami Vice*, one of the biggest hits of that decade.

In the seventies a producer and his son searched for a picture that would be a sure-fire hit. Checking the market, they learned that there had been a fictional character that had been a huge success on radio, in cartoons, in movie serials, and on television. They immediately bought the rights to the character and produced one of the most successful movies of all time. The name of that movie: *Superman: The Movie*.

You'll find story after story of such successes. The question is, what does this mean to you? It means that you shouldn't try to fit a *square* movie into a *round* marketplace. Try to tailor your film to what is already in demand. By doing this, your chances for a good financial return will increase sharply. Even with limited resources you can do your homework and see if there is a large enough audience for your movie to justify the cost and effort of making it. How? Find out what the grosses are on all the recent hit movies, while paying particular attention to how much money the *low-budget* films made. Another solution is to check out what genres are currently popular with audiences and distributors. What are those genres? The answer to that question leads us to point 3.

3. What Kind of Movie Makes Money?

Almost any kind of movie can make a profit, and occasionally does. However there are genres that tend to make money and there are those that don't. Dramas generally do not make much money because there is such a small market for them domestically, as well as overseas. Comedies can do better domestically, but there is virtually no market for them overseas due to the varying senses of humor from country to country. However, there are certain genres that traditionally make money year after year. The popularity of each of these genres may change with the times, but they are generally a safe bet.

These genres are as follows, albeit in no particular order.

(a) ACTION. Action movies are extremely popular domestically and overseas. As such, it is the genre that is *most* in demand throughout the world.

(b) SCI-FI. Science fiction movies are only slightly less popular than action, but overseas buyers who want such movies are willing to pay a little more for these films, and, as such, they can make more money than an action movie. They are particularly successful if the science fiction film abounds with action, becoming a hybrid of the two genres.

(c) EROTIC THRILLER. The worldwide value of the erotic thriller has diminished a bit over the years, but it is still very much in demand thanks to cable TV and changing censorship standards in international television.

(d) MARTIAL ARTS. Just like the action genre, martial arts movies have a good international appeal. Some distributors refer to them as bread-and-butter movies. Inexpensive to film, they tend to make a decent profit.

(e) HORROR. While low-budget horror movies are not as successful as they were during the 1970s and '80s, there is still a good worldwide market for them, assuming that the movie has excellent production values.

(f) T AND A. There has always been a demand, both domestically and abroad, for lighthearted, simple sex comedies featuring pretty young women, in various stages of undress, falling in love and lust with handsome young men.

(g) WESTERN. At one point in cinematic history the Western was America's most popular movie genre, but things change. Due to the over-saturation of the market with movie and TV westerns, the popularity of the Western became compromised. Currently the domestic market is rather indifferent, with the exception of certain cable channels. However, there is still a market for Westerns throughout Europe, Asia, Central and South America — enough so that a Western movie can still be profitable.

(h) CHRISTIAN. The appeal of Christian films has always been somewhat limited, but due to the growing number of Christian bookstores, and through them an escalating video market, the profit potential for films and videos of faith has risen sharply. One of the advantages of this genre is that there is far less competition in nonsecular moviemaking.

4. What Sells Each Genre?

Each genre has unique ingredients which make it marketable. These ingredients are as follows.

(a) *Action* films are sold by the amount of action scenes. *There must be a lot of action.* Overseas buyers will not buy an action film unless there is a major action sequence every five to ten minutes. Fights, gun battles, and explosions are an absolute necessity for success.

(b) *Sci-Fi* movies are sold by the quantity, and type, of special effects. Nowadays there *has* to be special effects in a science fiction movie that are either computer generated or at least have the appearance of computer animation.

(c) *Erotic thrillers* always have an extremely beautiful heroine, living in an expensive home, who is seduced by a mysterious stranger only to then find her life endangered in some manner. The love scenes need to be more sensual than sexual because a major portion of the audience for erotic thrillers are women. There has to be an overall feeling of forbidden passion and subtle suspense. The love scenes *have* to occur every five to ten minutes.

(d) *Martial arts* are sold by the quality, and frequency, of the stunt fight choreography. Similar to the action film and the erotic thriller insofar as its timing requirements, the martial arts fights scenes *have* to occur often. Usually, a fight every five to seven minutes is needed to make the film marketable.

(e) *Horror* films are sold by the quality of the special effects make-up and the suspenseful photography. In today's market there *has to be a monster* in each horror film. The monster is needed for advertising later on; but, more importantly, very few, if any, overseas buyers would buy a horror film without a monster. In addition, few domestic distributors could promote such a film without the selling point of the monster. Since the predominant audience for horror movies is quite young, the monster is vital. This is because the typical horror movie viewer (teenagers) doesn't care for subtlety.

(f) *T and A* movies traditionally have a pretty girl, or girls, in the nude every five to seven minutes. The stories are always simple, designed to cater to the youth market, centering on the principal characters' preoccupation with the opposite sex. Upon occasion the stories will center on a group of young men and their juvenile antics pursuing beautiful young women. Apart from the obvious differences in gender, the male-oriented stories tend to be pretty much the same as the female-oriented tales.

(g) *Western* movies are at their most commercial when they are simple in style and packed with action. This means minimal dialogue, clearly defined characters, easily understood storylines, and lots of gun battles and fistfights.

(h) *Christian* movies have to be spiritually inspiring, and be biblically accurate. In order to be competitive with all the other Christian films and videos, it is necessary to present a unique premise without straying from the expected spirituality of the genre.

And while I don't recommend the following two genres, here are the selling points for each of them.

(i) *Dramas* are sold by the box office appeal of the movie stars that appear in them. The bigger the star, the more likely the drama will be marketed.

(j) *Comedies* are sold by the universal nature of their humor. The greater the number of people who would probably find the movie funny, the greater the chance of it selling tickets, videos, or DVDs. The more specific the type of humor, the less likely a distributor will pick it up. For example, an urban comedy probably won't be funny to people living in a small town in middle America, and ghetto humor will be lost on a fisherman in Thailand. The ideal comedy is a visual one because it translates more easily to foreign audiences.

Once again, it's important to note that both of these genres can be very hard to sell and are not the best choice for a newcomer's first film.

5. Contact a Distributor *Now*!

Okay, you've settled on the commercial genre that you want to use, but you want to check on its current popularity. As I said earlier, things change, so checking to verify a genre's current market value is important. To do that you need to do some serious research. Get a list of movie distributors and start calling them. You will find such a list in Appendix F. Be sure to ask for whomever is in charge of acquisitions. Once you get the person in charge, tell them that their company was recommended to you (company executives love to hear that), and you would like to know if there is a good market for the kind of movie you want to make. You will probably receive a variety of opinions since no two distributors sell the same types of films. The consensus should give you a much more informed idea as to what to do next. If just about everyone tells you that they cannot currently sell the particular genre you are interested in, you should seriously reconsider doing your project. If they say there's a good market, then you know that you are on track. In addition, you will find that later on, when dealing with potential investors, it will pay to have a list of distributors who stated that your movie was potentially profitable. If possible, find out from the distributor how well movie genres, like yours, did in domestic video and on cable. Also, find out which overseas markets want a movie like the one you are going to make. Are the major buyers hungry for it, or would the smaller third world countries be the only ones interested? If the major buyers want it, then your film is far more likely to make some serious money. The only exception to this would be if a great many of those small counties were interested. Collectively they can be a very lucrative market, even if the major buyers aren't involved. Don't get discouraged if a distributor won't reveal this information to you. There are plenty of distributors who will. Why? Because distributors are hungry for movies. They have on ongoing need for well-made movies that they can sell. If by giving you a little information the odds are increased that you will produce the kind of movie that they need, then they would be foolish not to advise you. Please take note! Don't abuse their courtesy by pestering them constantly with questions. They are busy people who have more to concern themselves with than a filmmaker who has yet to make a film. Try not to phone them more than once, and when you do, make sure that you ask all the questions that you will need answered.

Now you should have a clear picture of the kind of movie that you are going to make. Your next step is to obtain a Letter of Intent. Just what is such a letter? Read on....

6. LETTERS OF INTENT CAN MAKE, OR BREAK, YOUR MOVIE

What exactly is a Letter of Intent? Is it a contract or dealer memo? Not quite. To put it simply, it is a letter from an individual, or company, stating that they have an interest in being connected with your movie. This does not constitute a binding agreement between you and the other party. It merely states that the other party *may* be interested in doing business with you, either during production or upon completion of your film.

"So what good does that do me?" you may be asking. The value of a Letter of Intent lay in how you plan to raise the money for your movie. If you hope to interest investors, it will help enormously if you can demonstrate that the *right* people are potentially involved. Those *right people* being a distributor and/or a star. When a distributor, or star, demonstrates interest in your movie it can help motivate an investor to become financially involved. It also helps in other ways. Since you have so little money to work with, a Letter of Intent can aid in gathering the cast and crew that you want for your movie. People are far more likely to want to be a part of the film once they know that your project is "real" and not just a pipe dream.

Since there is no standard form for a Letter of Intent, each letter will vary in style and content. Make certain that whoever sends you a Letter of Intent stresses the following points: that *they* are interested in doing business, *when* they are interested in doing business, and *why* they are interested in doing business. The reason behind knowing *who* wants to do business has already been discussed. *When* sets an artificial deadline that helps motivate people to get things done in a timely fashion. *Why* explains the value of your project to people who might otherwise not see its potential.

Letters of Intent are easy to get ... if you are diligent. Once you find a distributor who is interested in the concept of your movie, ask them for a Letter of Intent. If they say no then keep calling distributors until one finally says yes. Once again, please keep in mind that this isn't a binding contract, and, as such, either side can ultimately choose not to do business with each another should they wish. The Letter of Intent's sole purpose is to prove that doing business with each other may be *possible* under the right circumstances.

Getting a Letter of Intent from a star is much more complex, but basically involves the same procedure as obtaining one from a distributor. I will go into more detail on this subject in point 33: *HOW DO YOU GET A STAR?* Since you will probably be negotiating with a third party for the services of this star, it will often be more difficult to get all the specific points you need for your letter. In this particular case, however, the most important point is that *they* are interested. If the distributor has stressed all three points in their letter, then the when and why of the star's letter won't be quite as important.

You can, of course, make a movie without a Letter of Intent. It has been done, and, upon occasion, these movies have been successful. However, it is a lot easier if you do have such a letter to use when, and if, you need it. The question you need to ask yourself is, "Can I get the job done, *the way I want it done*, without the advantage of a Letter of Intent"?

7. Show Me the Money!

Okay, let's get down to brass tacks. To make a movie you need money. At least enough money to cover the cost of tape, (or film), food for actors and crew, and any props that are not in your possession. If you are shooting on film then you will also need enough money to cover processing. As in every business, there are two ways you can finance that business. Self-financing and financing coming from another source (i.e. a partner or investors). Let's examine the pros and cons of self-financing first.

You have probably figured out the conventional ways to come up with the money for your movie by yourself, such as tapping into your personal savings, taking out a loan, selling and/or pawning everything you own, maxing out your credit cards, etc. Before we go any further, let's shoot down a couple of those ideas. Taking out a loan or using credit cards can be financially disastrous. It could conceivably take up to two years *after* your movie is distributed before you see any sort of profit. By that time you could be living out of a cardboard box. If you aren't independently wealthy, and you are determined to finance your movie yourself, figure out how much you can realistically afford to risk, also taking into consideration the probable delay in getting a financial return on that risk. Whether it is five hundred dollars or five thousand or five hundred thousand, you will have to tailor your movie around the limits of that budget. We will discuss this concept more thoroughly in point 14.

If the money is coming from another source, it is probably coming from a partner, investor, or investors. A partner is probably the simplest to deal with. You will note that I said "simplest," not "easiest"; I also said *probably*. A partner is the simplest because you tend to know their agenda before you go into business together. The arrangement is just what you would expect. You make the film, they finance the film, and both of you share in the profits. It would be nice to believe that this is all there is to it, but the reality is rarely that simple. Usually a partner wants to take an active role in the filmmaking process, often as a producer, sometimes as an actor as well. If they can do these respective jobs with a professional level of competence, then everything may work out. If they can't, then you will undoubtedly have problems. There can also be problems if the two of you don't share a common vision for the movie. It is also important to remember that the partner's financial responsibility does not end with the completion of the movie. There are ongoing costs, such as making video copies for distributors to watch, designing poster art if it is needed, and producing a trailer. There is always a need for a few extra dollars, as there is in all businesses. If your partner isn't willing to (continually) hold up their end of the deal, perhaps you should reconsider having them as a partner.

If a partnership is what you want, then head down to the nearest county courthouse to find out which type of partnership best suits your needs. You should be able to locate what you need in the office where licenses are issued. There, you should also be able to find explanations of each type of partnership available. It's a good idea to come up with several different names for your business just in case the one you want has been taken. There should be a computer at the courthouse, which can tell you whether or not another company is using the name you want. Once you have selected your type of partnership and have settled on a name for your business, you will need to pay for the business license and place a classified ad in a local newspaper declaring that you are now in business. If you need help with this ad, the office issuing you the license, or the newspaper printing the ad, will explain what you need to do.

On the other hand, if you don't want a partner and would rather have investors, then you will need to form a corporation or a limited partnership, which is covered in point 8.

8. CORPORATION OR LIMITED PARTNERSHIP: WHICH IS RIGHT FOR YOU?

When discussing investors, it is important to understand that investors *do not* invest in a movie. They invest in the *business* that makes the movie. This may sound like splitting hairs, but it isn't. A partnership in a *business* means that the heads of the company can sell the ownership of the film outright to someone else should it be in the best interest of that corporation or limited partnership and its investors. This business practice is called a negative pickup and will be discussed in greater detail in point 91. Even if all rights to the film or video have been sold, the company still remains intact and is fully capable of doing business in the future, if need be.

Basically, the difference between a corporation and a limited partnership is the amount of investors that you can have, along with the complexity of setting up each type of business. The amount of investors, or stockholders, in a corporation is limited only by the amount of percentage points that you can legally sell. You can have thousands of investors if you like. Naturally, you have to know what percentage of your company you wish to sell, and what each share an investor buys will be equal to in relation to that percentage. For example, let us say you want to sell 50 percent of your company. Let us also say that the budget for your movie is approximately one hundred thousand dollars. Then you could sell fifty shares, collectively equaling fifty percent, at two thousand dollars each. You may, of course, choose a variation of this. Each variation, however, would still have to equal fifty percent. One hundred shares at one thousand dollars per share, two hundred shares at five hundred dollars, or even one hundred thousand shares at one dollar each. The variations are almost endless. You may also sell a different percentage, but, again, the collective shares made available for sale must equal that percentage.

Forming a corporation will ultimately become expensive, at least to someone trying to make a low-budget movie. However, doing the paperwork to get the ball rolling is rather easy and inexpensive. You only have to go to a stationary store and purchase the paperwork for a few dollars. It is advisable that you also pick up one of the books that stationary stores will have for sale, usually for around twenty dollars, which will explain, in detail, how to get your corporation off the ground. Eventually, stockbrokers and the SEC (Securities and Exchange Commission) will have to become part of the process once you start selling your stock to potential investors. It is at this point that things will become complex, so it's advisable that a lawyer handle the legalities of incorporating your company for you. Of course, once a lawyer gets involved, things become expensive. It is due to these reasons that I recommend you consider a limited partnership instead.

Just like a corporation, the forms for a limited partnership can be purchased at your local stationary store at a cost of two to ten dollars. The limited partnership is divided into two parts: the general partners and the limited partners. The general partners would be you and whomever would be acting as your vice-president and/or treasurer. Like a conventional business, you will also need to go to your county courthouse and file papers for it, which will cost you a small sum of money, usually under fifty dollars. Your business name will have to be printed in the classified ads of a local paper. This will also cost you a few dollars (the amount dependent upon where you have it published). Unlike forming a corporation, this will constitute your primary costs. In a limited partnership, you cannot have more than thirty-five investors in your company. Therefore, you will need to divide your budget into thirty-five parts. Figure out the percentages that you wish to sell, and then do the math. As a rule, it is best not to sell more than 49 percent of your business. In this way you will always retain control. The primary advantage of a limited partnership is that it's not complicated. Anyone can easily form one. Your questions can also be easily answered at the courthouse where you pick up the filing forms. It is important to remember that if you give away points (another word for a percentage) of your movie to any member of the cast or crew, they would qualify as a limited partner. It is important to know that there cannot be more than thirty-five limited partners in a limited partnership; otherwise, you are in violation of the law. Therefore, whatever the combination of investors, actors, or crew, their total must not be greater than thirty-five. To have a number greater than thirty-five you have to form a corporation.

Once you have selected which of these types of businesses suits your needs, you will have to start beating the bushes for investors. How do you find them or convince them to invest? That's where salesmanship comes into play. The question is, are you a good salesperson? If the answer is "no," you will have to become one. To do that, read on.

9. Selling Yourself Isn't Selling Out

Now it's time to start selling potential investors on the moneymaking opportunity that you are offering. To accomplish this, you have to transform yourself into a businessperson. This is where filmmakers often fail. They, understandably, resent the shifting of gears from artist to salesperson. Understandable or not, it's necessary. Art cannot exist without some form of patronage — or, in this case, investors. It is not a matter of jumping through hoops to satisfy the taste of some fat cat. It is a matter of you demonstrating to someone that, by parting with his or her hard-earned cash, both of you will get something you want. In other words, to achieve your goal you have to be someone who can help others achieve theirs. To accomplish this you have to change the way you think when it comes to motivating people. You have to truly *listen* to what people say to you. If you pay attention to people, you will not only hear their words but you will also understand what they *really* want. No two investors are exactly alike. Each will have unique personal likes and dislikes, which influences their decisions. Perhaps they want to get rich off one investment. Perhaps they like the idea of an investment that has a glamorous side to it. Perhaps they want a screen credit that they can point to in front of their friends. Maybe they want to take a chance on a business venture that is totally different from anything they have ever tried before. Whatever their reason, you need to learn what they secretly want so you can help them achieve that goal. When you meet them, take a few minutes to talk to them and get a sense of what they "really want." If business were only about making money then no one would ever make deals over a hole of golf or at a mixer. Business is often as much about relationships as it is about potential profits. Does the other person respect you or merely like you? Do you hold their interest or do you bore them? Do your ideas spark their imagination or leave them unmoved? One makes deals happen; the other causes them to fail.

Always be prepared at a business meeting. Know your facts and be prepared to explain them simply and clearly. Most important of all, make sure that the following points are addressed.

(a). **Your name and your company's name.** Make certain that any potential investor is well aware of both your name and your company's name. It is quite common for people to lose sight of this point during conversation, but it is vital that the potential investor remembers with whom they are doing business.

(b). **What is your idea?** Your idea, obviously, is that there is a profit to be made by your company producing a movie. Explain the premise of your movie in dramatically compelling yet simple terms.

(c). **Why will this venture make money?** Briefly explain how low-budget genre films are traditionally successful, then state the value of your movie's particular genre.

(d). **How much will this cost?** This is often quite difficult because your potential investor isn't going to understand how a low-budget movie can make money when Hollywood is producing films for a hundred million dollars or more. The simplest way to answer the question is to make a specific comparison with a low-budget film that is also a big hit. One example that you might use is, "Our budget is the same as *The Blair Witch Project*." You could just as easily substitute *Blair Witch* with *El Mariachi* or any other well-known low-budget movie success story. An investor can't argue with the success of a hit film, so your proposal is put in a more attractive light.

(e). **Why should they invest in your venture instead of someone else's?** This is always a very tough question to answer because there is no *good* answer. How can you possibly compare your business venture with someone else's without sounding pompous? Turn the question around and state that similar ventures to yours have traditionally made a good profit. Let others needing investors match that record.

(f). **What is the timeline involved?** In other words, "When do you need to start production, and when can you expect to be completely finished?" The long length of time involved may surprise them, so explain that a major film's production and post-production can take up to a year. Because of your efficiency, you will do the same amount of work in far less time.

(g). **When can they expect to see a return on their investment?** Generally, it's safe to assume that four months to two years after the distribution process has begun, profit can be expected (assuming that there is any).

(h). **Who else is connected with the venture?** Remember the Letter of Intent discussed in point 6? Here is where it pays off. It clearly demonstrates that others are interested in your venture, which makes it much more attractive to potential investors.

(i). **Who else has invested?** This is a very tricky question because no investor wants to be first. One way to answer it is to say that it would be unethical to discuss the details of your business with other investors, just as it would be unethical to reveal the details of your business meeting with *this* person to another potential investor. A different tack is to say that you are approaching a large number of investors at the same time. Only the first thirty-five who sign contracts will be allowed to invest. Unfortunately, this only works if you have already formed a limited partnership. You can also be forthright and admit that you have no investors because you have just started approaching them. If you take this route then it is very important to quickly add that you are confident that you will *soon* have all the investors you need because you are offering such a great deal. The suggestion here, like the previous approach, is that if the potential investor doesn't act fast they will miss out on a great deal.

(j). **What will this mean to them personally?** The answer to this question depends upon whether or not you were listening to the potential investor earlier. If you have a strong sense of where the potential investor's personal interests lay, then you can let them know that these interests can be addressed. If they have a big ego (or even a small ego), then an associate producer's credit may be in order. If they like to drop names, then let them hobnob with the stars. If they have ideas about production, let them tell you. You don't have to use their ideas, but they will appreciate the respectful attention. If they object later because their ideas weren't employed, then remind them that you have also rejected cast members' ideas. These rejections were all for the same reason — it would have made the production more complicated and therefore more costly. You are working in the best interest of your investors, and if the budget were to increase, the profits would diminish. It's hard for an investor to argue this point.

(k). **Any guarantees?** The answer to this is always the same: there are no guarantees in business ... except that when you are ready to produce your *next* movie you will only deal with investors from this venture.

10. Investors Buy the Sizzle, Not Just the Steak

Before investors can put up the money of your movie, you have to do two things: (1) find them and (2) convince them that shelling out their cash is a good idea. Both are very hard to do. *Extremely* hard.

Would-be filmmakers use several methods to find investors. These include classified ads, TV spots, asking family members and friends, word of mouth, going to business mixers, and the internet. Let's discuss the merits of these ideas, one by one.

(a). Classified ads. Theoretically, an ad should work, but for some reason it doesn't. At least I have never heard of a documented example of it succeeding. Mostly, what you end up getting are people who call you, very curious about your film, and waste your time. Strangely, many people don't read ads very closely and far too often don't fully understand what they are reading or contacting you about. Some may think that you are advertising for partners in a new video store. Others may think that you are promoting a local video business to tape weddings. Their confusion is in direct proportion to their limited frame of reference. In other words, this method of contacting investors doesn't have much chance of working. If you are bound and determined to try it, then make sure that you advertise in a widely read newspaper in a large nearby city. Also, do not place an ad in a paper that caters to people looking for bargains. The paper may be widely read, but it targets the wrong audience. You are looking for people who want to invest money, not save pennies.

(b). TV spots. Apart from the fact that a commercial asking for investors currently violates FCC government regulations, TV spots suffer from the same problem as the classified ad. True, more people see them, but you also have to come up with the money to make a twenty to thirty second commercial. As I said, a commercial asking for money violates FCC regulations; at least it does at the time of this writing, so check with your local TV station to make sure that this is still the case. The only possible way to avoid this problem is to make a commercial that is dramatic while also being non-specific. The commercial announces that a company has been formed to produce "low-budget, highly profitable motion pictures. Those interested in learning how they can become a part of this unique experience can call us at...." If nothing else, you will get a list of potential actors and crew from the commercial. If you are bound and determined to do a TV spot, which, in case you haven't figured it out, I do not recommend, check the Internet and see where you can get the best deal. You may find a service on the web which offers discount TV spots on some of the smaller stations in your area. If not, then check your local cable company. They often offer great deals on commercial airtime if you buy blocks of ten commercial airings or more. If you do this, then you have to make sure that your commercial will air at a time that it will be seen by your target audience. Are you making a sci-fi or horror film? If so, have your commercial air during the local horror movie. Are you doing an action film? If so, then have your commercial air during the local broadcast of Action Theater. You get the idea: aim your commercial at the very audience who might like the genre film you are making. An alternative to this is to have your commercial air during a show which features financial reports, real estate deals, or other forms of moneymaking opportunities. The people likely to watch this kind programming might also be likely to invest in a potentially profitable movie. As for the commercial itself, it may be necessary to have the local station do the commercial in order to get the good deal on the cost of airtime. If you can make the commercial yourself, all the better. Just remember that you only have twenty to thirty seconds to motivate your audience. Also, keep in mind that, depending on the policies of your local stations, it may not be possible to place a commercial promoting your project, no matter how non-specific it is, over the airwaves.

(c). Asking family members and friends. This is actually a pretty good method, which often works, so long as the budget isn't too high. If anyone is going to believe in you, it will probably be friends and family. At first, it will seem to many of them as a pipe dream of yours, but as you present your facts and a good proposal it will seem more logical. Most people reject this method out of hand because they figure that their family and friends will get mad if they are approached for investment. This is quite true. *Some,* but not all, will get mad. It's important to remember one very important thing, though: if you don't ask them, and your movie makes other people a lot of money, *all* of them will get mad because they weren't given the opportunity to invest. That being the case, you might as well ask.

(d). Word of mouth. This can also be a very good method to try. Have all the people involved in your film ask everyone they know if they are interested in investing. Then have those people ask everyone they know. Soon you will start getting inquiries from interested parties. Don't forget family and friends, however.

(e). Going to business mixers. If you merely attend other people's business mixers, odds are that your attempts to find investors will meet with failure. Why? Because most of the people there will be the wrong type for your business venture. Simply because someone is at a mixer to advance their career does not mean that they would have the slightest interest in investing in a movie company. On the other hand, if the mixer is one that *you* have organized, then you have a decent chance of achieving your goal. Using methods c and d, gather all of your potential investors together and make your business presentation, your pitch, in a party-like setting. Typically, a few of the possible investors attending will decide to invest. Be prepared for the fact that it may take several mixers to obtain the budget you need.

(f). The internet. Putting up a web page or website can be fine if you are simply promoting your film, but it is frequently ineffective when it comes to raising money. This is mainly due to the fact that there is no reason for anyone to go to your web page or website unless you spend a lot of money promoting the web page/site itself. This, naturally, defeats the purpose. There are filmmaking message boards where filmmakers can ask for investors, but these pleas are largely ignored. However, having a web page/site can be of help insofar as informing potential investors (who you have gotten interested by using methods c, d, and possibly e) of what you have in mind. Once again, this reinforces the "reality" of your venture and can be additionally appealing to potential investors.

(g). Self-promotion. This is a particularly effective method which most people don't think of. First, you phone the entertainment editor of your local paper and let them know that you are going to be shooting a movie later that year. You don't need to tell them that you haven't gotten your necessary budget yet. Odds are that the editor will probably do an article about you. This article will let the community know that the project is going forward. At this point, asking family and friends, word of mouth, and business mixers have a far greater chance to succeed.

Let's now address the second problem. How do you convince a potential investor to invest? Some of this is discussed in point 9, so if you haven't read that point, go back and do so before you read any further. To begin with, dress for success. Do not over-dress or wear jeans and flashy jewelry. Either extreme creates the bad impression of you being a fish out of water. Wear the suit of a successful businessperson. Dark, classic, simple but stylish. Truly successful business people dress well but do not show off their wealth. Your intent is to project the look of someone who is businesslike and comfortable around money. Next, meet your potential investors in an impressive location, such as a posh restaurant, a hotel meeting room, a fancy home, etc. Probably the easiest one of these locations to get is the fancy home. Just about everyone knows at least one person who lives in an impressive house. See if you can borrow it for one evening. Give the owner screen credit if you have to, but get access to it. Once you have it, throw a mixer for a large batch of investors. The catering for this isn't as hard, or as expensive, as you might think. With a little thought and planning, it shouldn't cost you more than two hundred dollars. Probably less if you are careful. Give yourself some time to organize this. It is far too important to be tossed together at the last second. The extra time also saves you money. Let's say that you have a month to organize this mixer. During that time, start looking for food bargains in the local paper. Are wine, champagne, soft drinks, coffee and tea on sale? If so, buy a ton of the stuff. Finger food is expensive, but the ingredients aren't. Buy the breads, meats, and condiments you need for finger sandwiches and make them yourself. Buy flavored crackers and vegetables for vegetarians. Remember that some people attending might be on a diet, so offer a sugar substitute and diet drinks. Get some fancy-looking (but cheap) plastic glasses, plates, and flatware. Buy some cocktail wienies at a discount supermarket and make your own sauce or fondue. If you don't know how, find someone who does. If you can't find anyone, then look up a recipe at the library. If you can't do that (lord knows why you couldn't), then get some barbecue sauce and simmer the cocktail wienies in it. Or buy some frozen buffalo wings at a discount store and cook them shortly before the mixer. Or get a recipe for Swedish meatballs and make some. All these kinds of foods are cheap, taste good, and are popular at parties and mixers. Get some soft instrumental music CDs to play in the background. You always want to play music that is pleasant to hear but doesn't become a distraction to the listener. Always keep in mind that the focus of the mixer is conversation, not entertainment. For this reason, do not employ a live band. They will become the focal point of the mixer, which is the last thing you want.

Now that you have your potential investors on hand and they've been put in a good mood by food and drink, what do you do next? Do you rush over to one, shake his or her hand, and start making your pitch? Nope. Take some time to know your guests so that you will have a better sense of who they are. There is an old gambling term called "charting the table." It refers to a professional gambler's technique of watching a table where he is interested in placing his bets. He may study that table for ten to fifteen minutes before he begins gambling. Why? Because that gambler can then enter the game with a more informed sense of what is going on at that table. Perhaps red is coming up a lot at the roulette wheel. Or perhaps seven is being constantly rolled at the craps table. Or perhaps all the cards are coming up tens, jacks, queens, kings, and aces at the blackjack table. This information gives the gambler a slight edge because it tells him how to place his bets. The same logic applies to a mixer. Take a little time to "chart the room." Stroll around without mingling. Pay attention to the conversations you hear as you pass by people. What are they discussing? Who is saying what to whom? Try to keep the respective conversations in mind for later. Once you have a sense of everyone's likes, dislikes, and tastes, you can begin your presentation. Gather everyone together and explain who you are and what you have in mind. Stress all the things discussed in point 9. Answer everyone's questions courteously and with brevity. If you have an Investment Proposal, go over it, answering questions at the end of your talk. Stress the positive aspects of your business venture and play down the negative. Be in charge of the moment without becoming domineering. If you seem indecisive, no one will take you seriously. You have to conduct yourself as if you know what you are talking about. Your confidence has as much to do with motivating people to invest as the facts do. However, you must not appear to be rude, curt, or a know-it-all with delusions of grandeur. This is a tricky tightrope to walk for people who are not used to public speaking. A good way to master this high-wire act is to practice your spiel before a video camera until it feels, and looks, natural. Have people that you trust critique you. Evaluate their ideas and use them to eliminate the flaws in your presentation. Soon, an effective presentation will be second nature to you.

  If you have made a feature film before, or worked on one in some capacity, then a nice way to begin — or end — an evening is to show that movie. A major studio has been known to employ this technique with possible investors. It often works because the audience gets caught up in the glamour of the idea. They reflect on how much they could have made if only they had invested in that movie. The taste of the steak may be fine, but the anticipation of the steak, its *sizzle*, is what gets people interested in the dinner. If the potential investors are motivated by the drama of moviemaking, they will be much more likely to invest. If you haven't made a film before, then show a film starring one of the actors committed to your film. You must always keep in mind, though, that your project will be judged by the merits of the movie shown to your potential investors. If it isn't very good, then that's how *you* will be perceived as a filmmaker, even if you didn't make the movie.

Another possibility is to show a trailer of the movie you plan to make. You do this by selecting the visual high points from your story, each lasting only a few seconds, then filming, or videotaping, these high points. Edit them together with some dynamic music and put some titles at the beginning and end. The advantage to this is that you give your audience a flavor of the movie that you want to make without the majority of the cost. If you don't know how to put together a trailer, use a theatrical trailer as your blueprint. If you do this type of presentation then it's very important to explain that what you are showing is only meant to give the potential investors an idea of what you will do with the movie. There are pros and cons to this kind of presentation. The "pro" is that it might help motivate people to invest in your film. The "con" is that if you are dealing with people who have no imagination, they will never truly see the movie that *could* be. If you have no film of any sort to present, then show trailers of recent low-budget hit movies. At their conclusion, explain how much profit was made by each movie. Point out to your audience that if they had invested in any of these movies they would have made a fortune. A chance to invest in a moneymaking movie is now theirs if they are fast enough to seize the opportunity.

Some will seize the opportunity that you are offering. Some will not. Some will waste your time and energy. The latter category of possible investors will be discussed next.

11. SIZING UP AN INVESTOR

You will periodically run into potential investors who waste your time and never come through. Sometimes what they really want is to get a part in your movie, and aren't above pretending that they want to invest in your movie in order to secure that role. Sometimes these people keep asking for information to relay to their partners. Asking and asking and asking. It never ends. Sometimes they are people who feel special because you are *their* connection to the film business. Sometimes they are jerks who think it's funny to string you along for as long as they can. Sometimes they are indecisive people who cannot make up their minds. There are a million different kinds of time-wasters. These kinds of people can be emotionally and financially draining. Since they are all so different, how can you spot them and not be taken in by them? There is no particularly good answer to this question. You need to treat each possible investor as if they might come through for you. And, unfortunately, following up with these potential investors is a necessary part of doing business. Generally speaking, anyone, no mater how eccentric, may end up investing. As a result, you should never count anyone out from the start as someone to avoid. Having said that, here are a few things to watch out for that might be of help when you are exposed to such time-wasters.

There is usually something that doesn't ring true about these people. Nothing concrete, just an uncomfortable feeling that they are not what they seem. They seem odd, out of place, no matter where they are. When asked questions, they answer a little too quickly or much too slowly. They never seem to specify how much they would like to invest. They act as if they have all the time in the world to sign a contract with you. The most trivial things impress them, as if they don't truly understand what is important. They like to talk a lot, but never say anything of consequence. They might never talk at all, even to ask questions. You have to explain things repeatedly to them as if they were children. They often have someone with them that they are trying to impress. They continually speak of their partners but never name them. They tell you that they have invested in other motion pictures, but they don't have the slightest idea how the investment process works. If you meet with them, one on one, at a restaurant they never pick up the check. They don't dress as well as someone with money should dress. They are confusing to listen to. They constantly interrupt you. They always want answers but are too impatient to listen. They act as if you are trying to put something over on them when they don't immediately grasp your answers. They demand personal meetings with you for things that could easily be discussed over the phone. They start repeating the same questions after a few weeks. They react insulted that you can't drop everything just to talk with them at a moment's notice. A meeting that would take ten minutes with anyone else takes an hour and a half with him or her. The questions they ask are often quite childish, naïve, or downright stupid. It takes them forever to come to the point. They talk an awful lot about people that they don't like. They continually mention a friend or family member who told them that if they were to invest in a movie they would be cheated. Their attitude is often very negative. They argue a lot. They tend to be rude. They tend to be a little too nice, as if they are trying to seduce you. They talk about how they are devout churchgoers, but don't act as a godly person would. They ask about your sex life or the sex life of the stars you know. They contradict themselves a lot. They don't trust anyone. There is an indefinable sense of cheapness about them.

When you see any of these signs, give yourself a *short* time table to deal with this possible investor. If they don't sign contracts quickly, assume that they aren't going to and cut them loose.

Most of us have an innate sense that tells us when not to do business with someone. A little voice that tells us to avoid them. Unfortunately, may people tend to ignore this voice because their needs, or desires, overshadow their instincts. Pay attention to your instincts because they are often right.

12. AN INVESTORS PROPOSAL THAT MAKES SENSE

In point 10 I refer to an Investors Proposal. An Investors Proposal is a written presentation of your business venture. Far too many of the proposals presented, for investing in a movie company, are huge affairs that are nearly the size of a phone book. This is often a mistake. For one reason, it's too large for a potential investor to read at one sitting, so they often set it aside and never get around to reading it. There's also a good chance that they may just turn it over to their financial advisor or lawyer who, not wanting to take a risk on anything that they are professionally unfamiliar with, advise their client to turn down the investment. For another reason, large Investment Proposals are often too complicated for a layman to fully understand. This confusion can sour people on your business venture. Make your Investment Proposal simple and to the point. A length that is somewhere between seven to thirty pages, depending upon how much data you wish to include, can be effective. Any shorter and you won't cover the information properly. Any longer and you'll begin to bore the reader.

If you are offering shares in a corporation, then you should have a proposal, or business plan, put together by an expert trained in such things. Possibly an attorney. If you don't have the money to hire someone, then borrow a proposal, sometimes called an Investment Package, from a stockbroker. On the other hand, if you are forming a limited partnership, the following generic template of an Investors Proposal could be used. You can also find many business proposal or business plan templates on the Internet. Simply choose the one that best serves your business needs.

Investment Proposal Template

The front cover should be eye catching, yet not so busy that it's confusing. It should have something to do with the theme of the movie. Please note: if you are doing a horror film, don't put something grisly or bloody on the cover. It will undoubtedly turn off a lot of potential investors.

At the top of page one, in large print, will be the words: **OFFERING MEMORANDUM**

Below the heading for **OFFERING MEMORANDUM**, should be the name of your limited partnership in equally large print.

Below your limited partnership's company name you need to put your business address, phone number, and the date that the proposal was offered. The print size on this is approximately half as large as those above.

Near the bottom of the page, in bold type, print the following:

> This memorandum has been submitted on a confidential basis solely for the benefit of highly qualified investors in connection with the private placement of limited partnership interests and is not for use by any other persons, nor may it be reproduced. By accepting delivery of this memorandum, the recipient agrees to return this copy to the Partnership at the address listed above if the recipient does not undertake to invest in the Partnership.

> Confidential plan Number_____
> Delivered to_____

On the top of the next page, in large bold print is the following heading: **TABLE OF CONTENTS**

Below the **TABLE OF CONTENTS**, and to the left is the word **SUMMARY**. This should be in smaller bold print than the heading above.

Below the **SUMMARY**, we see the following smaller headings, which are numbered:

1. **The Project**
2. **The Production and the Production Team**
3. **Marketing and Distribution**
4. **Budget**
5. **Structure of Partnership**
6. **Bio's on Producers**
7. **Synopsis of Screenplay**
8. **Other Participants**
9. **Miscellaneous Notes of Interest**
10. **Limited Partnership Agreement**

At the top of the next page, in large bold print, is a repeat of the heading **SUMMARY**.

In the following paragraph you should discuss the following points: the name of your company, what kind of partnership it is, and its purpose.

The second paragraph should explain that this investment concerns a low-budget movie and how it can be competitive in a marketplace full of films that are more expensive.

In the third paragraph, explain how you can make a quality film on such a small budget.

In the fourth paragraph, explain how the investor will receive 100 percent of all profits received by the General Partners until the investment is recouped. In this way there are none of the usual risks associated with an investment. For legal reasons it is very important to have the following in writing: *"Nevertheless, all investments in a motion picture carries a genuine risk, and no investor should consider this undertaking who lacks the financial strength to risk the amount of his or her investment in the pursuit of a successful project."* Placing this in your proposal informs the investor of the possibility that the movie could conceivable fail. This helps protect you if the film doesn't turn a profit.

On the top of the next page, in large bold print, is the heading: **1. THE PROJECT.**

On this page you explain what kind of genre your film belongs to and why there is a strong market for this specific film.

On the next page, in large bold print, is the heading: **2. THE PRODUCTION and the PRODUCTION TEAM.**

In the first paragraph, explain where you intend to film your movie. Also, include any additional information which is important and not printed elsewhere.

On the rest of the page, briefly explain who your producers are and their credentials and experience. Do the same for any other members of the production team who have committed themselves.

Atop the next page, in large bold print, is the heading: **3. MARKETING and DISTRIBUTION**

In the first paragraph, give an estimate of how much money your movie can expect to make. Get the information from a distributor. If you cannot obtain such information, go on the Internet and find the domestic and overseas grosses for a movie similar to yours. Mentioning more than one movie would be good, assuming that the grosses are similar. If you do not supply this information, it will appear to possible investors that you have no idea how much *your* movie might make. This could prove disastrous.

If you have a Letter of Intent from a distributor, be sure to put some information about their distribution company in the next paragraph.

In the following paragraph, mention any other moneymaking possibilities that would be tied into your business venture. For example, toys, books, posters, etc.

On the remainder of the page, under the heading Targeted Markets, write the names of countries, obtained from distributors, who would be interested in purchasing rights to your film. For example, the potential markets could include the following countries and regions, grouped by continents:

• **Asia, Europe, Africa, South America.** Hong Kong, Belgium, North Africa, Argentina, Indonesia, France, South Africa, Brazil, Japan, Germany, West Africa, Central America, Korea, Greece, Chile, Malaysia, Italy, Colombia, Philippines, Netherlands, Mexico, Singapore, Scandinavia, Peru, Taiwan, Spain, West Indies, Thailand, Turkey.

• **Additional.** America, Australia, Canada, India, Pakistan.

These MARKETS entail all media — THEATRICAL, VIDEO, and TELEVISION.

Atop the next page, in large bold print, is the heading: **4. THE BUDGET.**

In the first paragraph you explain that the budget reflects only the "hard costs" of the film and do not include what would normally be paid to you and your associates. Your payment will come, in part or in totality, from your share of the profits.

Above the next paragraph, in large bold print, is the following heading, centered on the page: **SUMMARY BUDGET — (YOUR MOVIE'S TITLE).**

Just below this heading, also centered, is: **Based upon** 2 Weeks of Filming (Or however long a shooting schedule you deem necessary).

Next is listed the actual summary budget. I have included a brief explanation for some of the terms for your, and the investor's, benefit:

<u>Above-the-Line</u> (*This refers to the costs of artistic elements needing to be paid before the production begins.*)

Story and Screenplay	(The amount)
Producers	(The amount)
Director	(The amount)
Stars	(The amount)
Total Above-the-Line	(The total amount)
<u>Below-the-Line</u>	
Cast	(The amount)
Stunts	(The amount)
Extras...	(The amount)
Sound	(The amount)
Director of Photography/Cameraperson	(The amount)
Gaffer	(The amount)
Make-up Artist	(The amount)
Hairdresser	(The amount)

Costumes/Wardrobe	(The amount)
Locations/Sets	(The amount)
Production Assistant...	(The amount)
Props	(The amount)
Special Effects	(The amount)
Meals/Craft Services	(The amount)
Hotels	(The amount)
Sound Technician	(The amount)
Negative	(The amount)
Editing	(The amount)
Conformation of Negative	(The amount)
Raw Stock (Negative Film) or Video Tape...	(The amount)
Video	(The amount)
Processing and Print (Film only)	(The amount)
Film Transfer	(The amount)
Titles/Optical Effects	(The amount)
Credits	(The amount)
Insurance	(The amount)
Music	(The amount)
Total Below-the-Line	(The total)
Finder's Fees	(The amount)
GRAND TOTAL	**(The budget's total)**

Atop the next page of the Proposal, in large bold print, is the heading: **5. STRUCTURE OF PARTNERSHIP.**

Below the heading, in slightly smaller bold print, is the heading **THE PARTNERSHIP.**

The remainder of the page is a slightly more detailed explanation of what has previously been said. It clearly states the kind of partnership it will be, and the names of all the general partners. It states who the producers are. It explains how the profits will be divided. It explains how many percentage points are collectively being sold to the investors.

Atop the next page, in large bold print, is the heading: **6. BIOGRA-PHIES of PRODUCERS.**

Below the heading, and centered, is the name of one of the producers in bold print.

Below that is detailed all the pertinent accomplishments of that producer. Make certain to list all of his or her credits. It's quite important that this short bio be written in a fashion which makes the producer seem impressive.

You repeat the process for each of the producers. Try not to use more than two pages on these bios; otherwise, it will become boring to the reader.

Atop the next page, in large bold print, is the heading: **7. SYNOPSIS OF SCREENPLAY.**

Below this you present a one-page synopsis of your movie's story. It should include all the dramatic highlights. It must be written so that it's exciting to read.

Atop the next page, in large bold print, is the heading: **8. OTHER PARTICIPANTS.**

Below the heading you write: "Among those who have expressed interest in this project are: [the name, or names, of those who have expressed interest]."

Below that you write the name of a participant, or star, in **<u>bold underlined</u>** type. It is followed, in normal type, by a list of their credits and/or accomplishments. The titles of all **films** should be printed in bold type to catch the reader's eye.

You repeat this process until your list of important participants is completed.

Atop the next page, in large bold print, is the heading: **9. MISCELLANEOUS NOTES of INTEREST.**

The first paragraph should say: "The following [whatever films you choose to include] and statistics relate additional information concerning [title of movie], the producers' previous work, and financial data on the commercially viable genre of [name of genre]-based movies.

Over the next few pages you can include the grosses of similar low-budget movies; posters of the participants' previous film, TV, or stage work; newspaper or magazine articles; etc.

Atop the next page, in large bold print, is the heading: **10. LIMITED PARTNESHIP AGREEMENT.**

Over the next several pages you present your contract. This contract will be discussed in greater detail in point 13.

On the back inside cover it's a good idea to make a closing comment. It can be almost anything, so long as it is catchy and lingers in the memory. For example:

[Your Movie's Title in Large Bold Print]
A Dynamite Script...
Soon to Be a Hit Movie...
A Sure Investment!

At the bottom of the page write: "For further information, **call**: [place your business phone number here]."

It is very possible that some potential investors will want to see a business proposal before they look at your Investment Proposal. Contrary to what some people may believe, these two proposals are not the same thing. Wanting to see a business proposal is common practice when dealing with people or institutions who invest in other people's projects on a regular basis. As such, you may want to have on hand a proposal for your proposal. More simply, you may need to show them a business proposal similar to the one presented in this book before you will be permitted to show them an Investment Proposal like the one previously presented in this point. You might be wondering what a business proposal is. A fair question if you have never come across one. Basically, it's similar to the Investors Proposal except that it (usually) focuses more on your company and is phrased in a very businesslike language. It is also very similar to a business plan, except that it is less detailed regarding graphics and future business projections of gross and/or net profits. The following is a business proposal that was used to help Marche-Williams Productions generate tens of millions of dollars from an overseas investment group. Study it, and use it as a template for your own proposal, should you need one.

MARCHE-WILLIAMS PRODUCTIONS
Sample Business Proposal

Table of Contents

MARCHE-WILLIAMS PRODUCTIONS

1.0 Executive Summary

Marche-Williams Productions will be formed as a motion picture company specializing in the producing and marketing of theatrical movies, direct-to-video movies, television movies, and television series, and other related media, for sale in the worldwide market. Its founders include movie producers and international movie distributors, each an expert in motion picture production, post-production, and distribution in all international markets.

They are forming Marche-Williams Productions to make greater use of their individual resources, which include their considerable moviemaking knowledge, along with a wealth of contacts in the film business, both domestically and overseas.

1.1 Objectives

1. To make highly commercial and financially successful motion pictures.
2. To make motion pictures of superior quality.
3. To make motion pictures efficiently.

1.2 Mission

Marche-Williams Productions will offer major movie distributors a reliable, high-quality alternative to in-house productions developed for a worldwide market. Marche-Williams Productions will also be able to offer major distributors motion pictures that will be superior to other independent movies in budget, in marketing value, and in production values. As a true alternative to in-house and other independent productions, Marche-Williams Productions will offer these major distributors a very high level of practical experience, knowledge, contacts, and confidentiality to each motion picture. Each movie studio will know that by working with Marche-Williams Productions that they can expect a more professional, less financially risky motion picture project than they could receive from anyone else. Marche-Williams Productions will also be able to maintain financial balance, charging a high value for its productions, and delivering an even higher value to all companies and/or individuals with which it does business.

1.3 Keys to Success

1. Excellence in fulfilling our promise to employ our completely professional, reliable, trustworthy expertise to create successful motion pictures made on schedule and on budget.
2. Developing additional business leads and contacts in both domestic and in overseas markets.
3. Exploiting potential markets for motion pictures such as the internet, as well as exploring potential motion pictures originating from theater, books, stories, comic books, etc.

2.0 Company Summary

Marche-Williams Productions is a new company providing high-level expertise in international film and video production, post-production, distribution strategies, and the marketing of high concept movies. It will focus initially on providing two kinds of international triangles: (1) Providing United States clients with productions created with the lucrative European, Latin American and Asian markets in mind; and (2) providing European, Latin American and Asian movie consumers with the best possible motion pictures from the United States.

2.1 Company Ownership

Marche-Williams Productions will be created as a California corporation based in Los Angeles County, owned by its principal investor(s) and principal operators. As of this writing, it has not been chartered yet and is still considering alternatives of legal formation.

2.2 Company Locations and Facilities

The initial office will be established in a quality office space in Los Angeles County (the "Hollywood" area of California), the heart of the world's movie capital.

2.3 Company Executives

The executives of Marche-Williams Productions will include **Genie Williams** and **Kalor Marche,** who will be the **Co-CEO's.** Ms. Williams is a former Fox TV network executive, and Ms. Marche is a prime mover in the music business. Each will bring their contacts and years of experience to negotiate deals with distributors and above-the-line talent. **Philip R. Cable** will be **Chief of Production.** Mister Cable is the producer, director, and screenwriter of a multitude of movies, and an acknowledged expert in film and video production. **Belinda P. Cable** will be Mister Cable's **Executive Assistant**, while also serving as a company **Consultant**. Mrs. Cable is a former movie distributor, a producer of documentaries, and has decades of experience in both sales and office management.

3.0 Competitive Comparison

The competition comes in two forms:

1. The most significant competition is a major studio production. Our key advantage over this competition is the fact that the incredibly high overhead of a major studio motion picture make potential profits extremely unlikely. It is also for this reason that major studios will be eager to distribute our films due to their greater likelihood of financial success.
2. The second kind of competitor is the independent producer who makes one or two films a year. Such producers will not be able to match the output that Marche-Williams Productions will be able to, nor can they provide the kind of high-level diverse understanding of worldwide distribution and marketing that Marche-Williams Productions will provide.

4.0 Sourcing

1. The key fulfillment and delivery of each film will be provided by the principals of the business, realized through their professional expertise, provided by a combination of experience, hard work, industry contacts, and knowledge.

2. To provide additional assistance we will turn to qualified professionals for any talent which is needed in front of the camera or behind it. We will hire the best writers, directors, technicians, box-office stars, and additional producers to achieve our twofold goal of quality at a price designed to maximize profit potential.

5.0 Market Analysis Summary

Our most important group of potential customers is large companies who either distribute or purchase the rights to our motion pictures. They include distributors of domestic theatrical movies; sell-through video wholesalers; video rental providers; cable; satellite channels; network television; and overseas buyers of theatrical, video, and television rights. Unlike our competition, we will tailor our movies to the needs of these marketplaces, thereby assuring a need for anything that we produce.

5.1 Industry Analysis

The "movie industry," while one of the most successful industries in the world (annually making between 33 and 42 billion dollars), is far too often unnecessarily wasteful. This is typically the result of executives in charge who have little or no understanding of film production, post-production, or distribution. Because of this, the collective knowledge of the executives of Marche-Williams Productions in these areas give this company a competitive edge that is second to none.

6.0 Production Strategy for Enhanced Profit

Marche-Williams Productions will increase its already great chances for financial success by making movies on two separate budgetary levels: the larger-budgeted films, to be released by major studios; and low-budget direct-to-video movies. The low-budget movies will finance the day-to-day operations of the company while also serving as a proving ground for talent, which may later be used in our larger-budget movies. These low-budget movies will be made in commercially proven genres that have a history of being enormously profitable, playing to ready-made audiences.

7.0 Investment Advantage

Because of § 181 of the Internal Revenue Code there are currently great tax incentives for investors to invest in a Marche-Williams Production. These deductions include the *Income-Forecast Method*. Under this approach, the ratio of: (a) the film's total net revenues for the given tax year, to (b) its lifetime projected revenues, is calculated. This fraction is then applied to the film's total capitalized costs to determine the allowable depreciation deduction for the given tax year. There is also the *Straight-Line Depreciation*. Under this less common method, the cost of the film is deducted in equal annual amounts over the film's useful life. These tax deductions make a motion picture investment most advantageous. Plus, given that the ceiling limit for §

181 is 20 million, no major studio can compete with Marche-Williams Productions insofar as offering this great investment opportunity and tax incentive to investors.

8.0 Strategic Alliances

At this writing, strategic alliances with several major studios and video companies are either in the process of being arranged or are in the contractual stage.

9.0 Organizational Structure

Marche-Williams Productions will be managed by working partners. The organization will be very lean in the beginning, with each of the founders responsible for his or her own work and management. Added to this team periodically will be independent contractors who will be responsible for individual projects, which will include producers, advisors, and other experts in their respective fields.

10.0 In Conclusion

Given the facts stated throughout this proposal, Marche-Williams Productions fully expects to have a healthy growth of net worth, and a strong financial position resulting from a number of commercially profitable motion pictures produced over the course of the coming year.

As mentioned earlier, there are several ways to attract investors. Sometimes, however, it may not be you who finds the investor because it may instead be the investor who finds you. You may discover that, in dealing with people or companies wishing to invest large amounts of money in a motion picture, you might be approached by someone acting as an agent for an unknown third party who has expressed an interest in possibly funding your movie. This agent may make it a requirement of the negotiation process that you never disclose any of the particulars of your potential deal with them. To achieve this protection, the agent, or the unknown investor, will almost certainly ask you to sign a Non-Disclosure Agreement. A Non-Disclosure Agreement is, basically, a mutual agreement stating that under the right circumstances, a possible financial agreement might result. Normally, signing a Non-Disclosure agreement means that you will not tell anyone the name of this possible investor or the specifics of your business dealings with said possible investor. If the deal takes place, the agent will then collect a negotiated fee for having brought you and the investor together. This is one of the reasons that the agent wants all negotiations to be private. If other people were to know how to contact and deal with the investor directly, the agent would be out of the loop and would, of course, lose money.

The following is an example of such an agreement.

Sample Overall Mutual Non-Circumvention
and Non-Disclosure Agreement

[INVESTMENT COMPANY NAME] & [Your Company Name]

This agreement (the "Agreement") is entered into by and between _____, represented by _____ and [Company Name], represented by [Name(s)], and relating to the subject matter hereof, and the full understanding of the parties is embraced herein, in which hereinafter shall collectively be referred to as "Party" or "Parties."

The Parties wish to enter into this agreement to define certain parameters of their legal obligation and whereas the undersigned desire to enter into a business relationship for mutual and common benefit of the Parties hereto, whereby each Party acknowledges that they may learn from one another the names and telephone numbers of investors, borrowers, lenders, agents, brokers, banks, lending corporations, individuals and/or trusts, or buyers and sellers hereinafter referred to as "Contacts." Now therefore in consideration of the mutual promise, assertion and covenants herein and other good and valuable consideration, the receipt of which is acknowledged hereby, the Parties hereto agree as follows.

(1) The Parties will not in any way whatsoever circumvent or attempt to circumvent, avoid, bypass or obviate each other, directly or indirectly, to avoid payment of fees, commissions or any other form of compensation in any transaction with any corporation or individual, revealed by either Party to the other, or any of the Parties involved in any of the transaction the Parties are desirous of entering into and do. Parties will also refrain from soliciting business and contracts from sources not their own which have been made available to them through the other party, and that they will not enter into direct negotiation or transactions with such contacts revealed by the other Party without the express permission and knowledge of the party who made the original introduction.

(2) Parties will maintain complete confidentiality regarding the other's business source and/or Contacts, that they each recognize such Contacts as the exclusive property of the respective Parties, and will disclose such business sources only to named Parties pursuant to the express permission of Party who made available the source.

(3) Each party acknowledges and agrees that it may have access to Confidential Information and Materials of the other party. The Receiving Party agrees (i) that the Confidential Information and Materials shall remain the sole and exclusive property of the Disclosing Party; (ii) to use the Confidential Information and Materials only for the purposes described in this agreement; (iii) to hold the Confidential Information and Materials in strict confidence; (iv) to exercise the same degree of care as it uses to pro-

tect its own confidential information of like importance, but in no event with less than reasonable care, to safeguard the Confidential Information and Materials against disclosure, loss, theft or discovery; and (v) to take such steps as are reasonably necessary to insure and maintain such confidentiality.

(4) "Confidential Information and Materials" means any and all information which is now or at any time hereafter in the possession of either Parties, including, without limitation, know-how; files; names; addresses; telephone numbers; fax numbers; e-mail addresses; e-mail correspondence; transaction details or transaction codes; banks; bank officers; bank coordinates; tenders; borrowers; fees; commissions; data relating to stocks, securities or shares; all financial information relating to both Parties, their clients and affiliates, employees or associate companies; and any other material bearing or incorporating any information that may be disclosed either directly or indirectly to either Parties or any of their employees, associates, advisors, agents or assigns, whether orally, electronically, or in writing, and irrespective of whether such information is expressly marked as private and confidential.

(5) If either Party, through their own effort, is already in contact, working with or involved in negotiations, directly or indirectly, with the Contacts introduced by the other, then the Parties have to immediately notify one another.

(6) That in the event of the circumvention by either Party, directly or indirectly, if proven to be intentional and commissions have been lost, the circumvented Party shall be entitled to a legal monetary penalty equal to twice the maximum service fee it would realize from such a transaction, plus expenses, including, but not limited to, legal expenses that may later be incurred while attempting to recover lost revenue.

(7) This document shall in no way be construed as being an agreement of partnership in such a way that any of the individual Parties to this agreement shall have any claim against any separate dealings, ventures, or assets of any other Party, nor shall any Party be liable for any other Party's commitments or liabilities in business or personal dealings or situations.

(8) This agreement may be executed manually, by electronic mail or by facsimile transmission signature in any number of counterparts. Each of such counterparts shall be deemed, for all purposes, an original, and all such counterparts shall together constitute but one and the same instrument. It is further agreed that faxed copies of this instrument are deemed as legally binding as the original.

(9) This agreement is valid for any and all transactions brought by the herein mentioned Parties, to their mutual business benefit. This agreement shall not be modified except by a written document executed by both Par-

ties. Signatories to this agreement acknowledge having full legal authority to execute the document in the name of the Party for which they have given their signature. The duration of this agreement shall perpetuate for two (2) years from the date signed.

IN WITNESS WHEREOF, the undersigned have read, understand and agree to the terms stated above without change.

Investor/company name. Month/day/year
Represented by: [Name]_____

[**Your Company Name**] Month/day/year
Represented by: [Name(s)]_____

13. Investor Contracts: Keep It Simple

The simpler the contract, the easier it is for an investor to understand what is involved. Some people prefer a complicated contract because they think that potential investors will be impressed by it. I have never known a case where this has proven to be true. A simple contract avoids an endless parade of complicated questions. A simple contract is less likely to intimidate a reader. A complex contract usually results in the potential investor turning over the Investor Proposal to a lawyer or accountant for their evaluation. Needless to say, such financial professionals will be negative about the idea because it might reflect badly on them if the project were to fail. Given this situation, using a simple contract means that it is more like to be read and, therefore, signed.

If you have formed a corporation you will need to talk to a lawyer about coming up with a contract. Tell him that you don't want it to be complicated. Emphasize to the lawyer that it has to be written in a manner which can easily be understood by a layman. The lawyer may protest, but stand your ground and get what you want.

The following is an example of a simple agreement designed for those who have formed a limited partnership.

Sample Limited Partnership Agreement

By this agreement the signers form a limited partnership under the laws of [name of your state] as of [the exact date goes here] and agree to the following terms and conditions of this agreement:

1. MEMBERS.
The general partners are

_____, _____,
_____, _____.

The limited partners' names and addresses are set forth on EXHIBIT A, attached hereto.

2. NAME OF PARTNERSHIP.
The name of the partnership shall be: [name of your movie company].

3. PLACE OF BUSINESS.

_____

The partnership's principal place of business shall be at [business street address, city, state, and zip code], or other such place as the general partners determine in the future.

4. PURPOSE.
The purpose of the partnership shall be to produce and distribute [name of movie], and to engage in all activities reasonably incidental thereto.

5. TERM.
The partnership shall begin as of the date of this agreement and shall continue until the first of the following events:
A. The distribution, sale or abandonment of all partnership properties and assets.
B. The election by the general partners to terminate the partnership.
At which time it shall dissolve, the contributions and assets of the partnership shall be returned and divided as set hereto.

6. CONTRIBUTIONS AND RETURN OF LIMITED PARTNERS' CAPITAL/EXHIBIT B.
Contribution to capital shall be in units of—[written amount of money per unit, then, in parentheses, the numbered amount. For example: five thousand five hundred dollars ($5,500.00)]; the minimum permitted contribution shall be one unit.

Each of the limited partners has contributed the amount of cash set forth opposite her/his name in EXHIBIT B, attached hereto.

For each [the amount per unit] contribution the limited partner shall receive [the amount of the percentage in relation to the units paid for] percent of the film's net profits.

After the initial investment of [the amount of one unit] has been recouped, and all payments and deferments incurred during production have been paid, subsequent net profits from the film shall be divided between the limited partners and the general partners; proportional to the percentage owned by each limited and general partner. Limited partners shall not be required to contribute any additional capital to the partnership. [This section of the agreement is VERY important. The reason for its importance will be explained at the conclusion of this point.]

7. CAPITAL ACCOUNTS AND REPORTS

All money taken into the limited partnership will be handled through a special account, and supervised by an accountant acceptable to both general and limited partners. General partners agree to provide limited partners a quarterly report on the activities and progress of the project.

IN WITNESS THEREOF, the parties of the limited partnership have executed it effective as of the day and first above written.

GENERAL PARTNERS [typed, or printed by hand]

NAME	ADDRESS	PHONE #	DATE

LIMITED PARTNERS [typed, or printed by hand]

NAME	ADDRESS	PHONE #	DATE

EXHIBIT A [handwritten signature]

LIMITED PARTNERS NAME AND ADDRESS:

EXHIBIT B [handwritten signature]

AMOUNT OF INVESTMENT:

The section of the contract (section 6) which explains recouping the investment is extremely important because it serves as a tool to convince possible investors to invest in your movie project. This particular contract states that the investors receive *one hundred percent of all profits* made by the company until their investment is recouped. After this, any debts and/or deferments are then paid. It's only after this point that the general partners begin to receive their proportionate share of the profits. The value of this is that the potential investor realizes that no loophole exists. If any profits are made, those profits will go back to the investor first. This is a very attractive contractual arrangement to a possible investor. It makes them feel much more secure about the business venture and may conceivably close the deal for you. Normally, investors get whatever is left over from net profits after everything else is taken care of. An unscrupulous filmmaker can create "debts" that eat up the profits so that the investor never sees any money. By stating that the investor receives all monies before anyone else, you assure your potential investors that you won't try to cheat them somewhere down the line. You may, of course, modify this contract so that the investor receives a return on their investment in a more conventional manner, but I have found that this contract, as presented, is more convincing to potential backers.

14. THE BUDGET DICTATES THE MOVIE YOU MAKE AND YOUR PROFIT POTENTIAL

Okay, now you have your budget, or do you? Just because you approached some people about investing does not mean that you received the budget you wanted. What do you do if you have only collected a portion of the money you need? What if the best you could do was to raise a few thousand dollars? Maybe you only raised a few hundred. What do you do now? Give what money you have back to the investors and crawl in a hole? If you believed that, then you wouldn't be reading this book.

If you have no money to speak of, then you will have to save up a few hundred dollars to get the ball rolling. This should be enough to buy some videotape and pay for the meals for your cast and crew. You will need to borrow a video camera from a friend. Promise him or her a percentage of your movie's profits if they will loan it to you for a month or two. See if you can borrow a few lights and a microphone while you're at it. If you can't borrow lights and a microphone, then save up some more money, buy some makeshift lights from the hardware store, and purchase a cheap intercom microphone. See points 63 and 64 to understand how to do this. Take a week to familiarize yourself with the camera so you will be experienced in its use when you actually begin filming. Gather together your cast and crew, then, when everyone's schedules permit, shoot your movie. Schedule it so that you use the equivalent of twelve to fourteen shooting days. A schedule lasting longer than that will make it too difficult to pull together all the needed resources over the course of filming. Whether you have a few hundred dollars or a few thousand, this method of filming won't change very much. You won't have enough elasticity in your budget to do much more than the following. You will need to use any free and available locations instead of sets. The script will probably require rewriting to accommodate your film's financial limitations. Streamline the script to make it simpler. And I mean as simple as possible. This will make it easier to film when you finally start shooting. Costuming should be limited to outfits that are donated to the project, or those outfits belonging to you. Ask everyone you know for any props that you need but don't have. Will people work for screen credit and a copy of the film? If you don't know, ask. Will some wannabe special effects man be willing to do some work for you in exchange for a percentage of the net profits? It can't hurt to ask.

If you have four to eight thousand you should be able to buy a decent video camera, some lights, and a microphone. This will give you more flexibility insofar as you will not be dependent upon someone else for the use of this equipment. Apart from this advantage, you will still need to pull in a lot of favors, and people will still need to work on the project for free.

If you have ten thousand dollars or more, it may be possible to shoot a movie in 16-millimeter. Ask a company that sells 16-millimeter raw stock if they have discounts for student (or independent) filmmakers. If they don't, find out about short ends. Short ends are the portions of raw stock unused during a production that are sold back to a company that sells negative film. If you buy short ends in bulk, you will save a lot of money. Make sure you buy the right kind of film stock, though; otherwise, you will be wasting your money. Ask a film teacher or your director of photography what you will need. After you shoot your film, have it transferred to tape and edit the tape.

If you have twenty or more thousand you might be able to edit your 16-millimeter negative instead of transferring it to video.

If you have seventy-five thousand or more, it may be possible to shoot your movie in 35-millimeter. The amount of your production budget will dictate how much money will be allotted to your post-production. The amount will determine whether you edit the negative or whether you have that negative transferred to tape to be edited in that format.

If you have *no* money to spend on your production, any profit you make off your video sales will be gravy. You may not be able to find a video distributor for your movie, but you might be able to sell some copies by taking ads in some appropriate magazines or via an internet site. Having said that, you should still try to interest a video distribution company in your movie. You never know, you might just get lucky.

Naturally, it is impossible to accurately predict how much profit a movie will make, no matter what budget you have to work with. There are too many considerations that factor into a movie's success or failure. However, the following can be regarded as a conservative estimate of profit potentials based upon your movie's budget.

If you have a few thousand, and the production values are good, then you may be able to get a video distributor to pick it up. You might be able to make ten to twenty thousand dollars profit over the course of its distribution.

A twenty to thirty thousand dollar budget might make twenty-five to forty thousand dollars profit, depending on whether or not it was shot on film.

If you have a fifty to seventy-five thousand dollar budget, and your movie is shot on 35-millimeter, it could make somewhere between one hundred thousand and two hundred thousand, depending upon whether it was edited on video or film.

Anything over a hundred thousand can potentially be a bit of a risk in the current market, and there is no way to know exactly how well the movie will do in the domestic and overseas marketplaces. Its success will almost certainly be based upon the skill of the distributor and the worldwide market's interest in your movie at the specific time of its release.

15. In What Format Should You Shoot Your Movie?

There are eleven basic formats that can be used to make your feature. These formats are VHS tape, ¾-inch tape, Super VHS, High-Band 8, Beta SP,

M2, Mini-DV, High Definition video, Super 8-millimeter, 16-millimeter, and 35-millimeter. Let's look at the advantages and disadvantages of each of these formats.

VHS. There is very little you can do with VHS. Its resolution is low and doesn't work well when it comes to editing. It is possible to use, but VHS will always result in a video which is second rate and looks it.

¾ Inch Tape. This is a particularly bad format. It is more expensive than VHS but has only slightly better resolution. As such, it suffers from the same problems as VHS.

Super-VHS (S-VHS). This is a pretty good format. It has almost twice the resolution of VHS, and it isn't as costly as ¾-inch tape. The cameras tend to come in one- and three-chip formats. The three-chip cameras give a very sharp image. Unfortunately, at the time of this writing it is getting harder and harder to find good Super-VHS cameras and tapes.

High-Band 8. Many video experts consider this to be a superior analog tape format to Super-VHS. Some don't. Whoever is right, the resolution of High-Band 8 is at least as good as Super-VHS, and it holds onto the integrity of its video resolution exceptionally well during the editing process. However, due to its small size, it is much more fragile than Super-VHS. As a result, it may suffer from some form of video distortion. Like the Super-VHS camera, the High-Band 8 camera is available in one- and three-chips. It is currently available to purchase in more stores than Super-VHS, and it costs approximately the same.

Beta SP. This is an especially superior format. Many professional videographers traditionally shoot their videos on Beta SP or Beta Digital. Unfortunately, it is terribly expensive, and editing with it can be somewhat cost-prohibitive. There are video experts who believe that the image recorded by a Beta SP camera is no better than the image recorded by a three-chip High-Band 8 camera.

M2. This is a rarely seen video format that is superior to Beta-SP. Unfortunately, most of the M2 video equipment is used on the East Coast, so if you live anywhere else you are generally out of luck trying to locate it. This format is designed especially for editing, not photography. It is also rather expensive; so if you are working on a very limited budget, it is not a practical format to use.

Mini-DV. This is an extremely good format. It offers high resolution, and the cameras are often equipped with wide-angle lenses, which can be of great help if you have to film in cramped locations. Cameras have dropped to affordable prices over the years, and the tapes are not very costly. Mini-DV works especially well when you edit on a computer. Unfortunately, the tapes, like High-Band 8, are very fragile and can bunch up in the camera or break.

High Definition video. This is the format of choice of the professional videographer. It offers extremely high resolution, and the cost of the tapes is no worse than buying M2. It is designed to have high enough resolution to transfer to 35-millimeter film and show in theaters. As of this writing, there are now affordable consumer High Definition cameras. The primary difference between these cameras and their more expensive counterparts (to which they are supposedly comparable) is that the recorded image is stored on an internal, and non-removable, hard drive rather than on a tape. This can make the transfer of the video difficult. At this point it is unknown if these cameras can meet the necessary requirements to make a professional movie.

Super 8-millimeter. This was, at one time, a great alternative to shooting on the more expensive film formats. The slower-speed film stocks were not grainy and offered good detail. In the past, it was often transferred to tape and edited in that format. The end results were very difficult to distinguish from 16-millimeter. Sadly, the quality of processing Super 8 film has sharply declined in recent years to the point where it is no longer a practical format to use for professional work.

16-millimeter. A very good film format to work with if your goal is to transfer it to video and do your editing there. It is less expensive that 35-millimeter and, if transferred to video properly, looks the same.

35-millimeter. The film format of choice. It possesses very high resolution, and is somewhat easier to edit than 16-millimeter due to its larger frame size. It also has a major advantage in that it can be shown in more theaters worldwide than any other format. It is also more ideally suited for doing optical effects than any other film format due to its superior resolution. It is, however, quite expensive. If you have very little money, it is probably not the format you should work with.

Needless to say, the format you use will be dictated, in part, by your budget. If you choose to use a more expensive format than your budget would normally allow, then you will need to take money away from other parts of your budget to accommodate this decision. Practicality suggests that you should use Mini-DV, Super-VHS, or High-Band 8 since these video formats offer excellent quality at an affordable price.

16. Dangerous People to Watch Out For

There are many kinds of dangerous people in this world, but for the filmmaker there are two in particular to be on the lookout for. If you have the slightest inkling that you might be dealing with one of them, start running.

I'll start with the most obvious: those who are dishonest. They might be investors, distributors, video company executives, other producers, anyone. They offer the moon and give you a pocket full of nothing. You can usually spot them via such telltale signs as: they never seem to give you a straight answer; they don't have references that are verifiable; they brag an awful lot; they are self-absorbed and often rude in public; they dress much too flashy; they drop names too much, but they won't tell you the names of people they have done business with; they continually talk about the expensive car that they drive; they are late to important meetings; they never seem to be able to deliver on their side of the deal; they generally act like a jerk. Any one of these signs should make you wary. Naturally, someone might have one of these flaws and be a perfectly legitimate businessperson. However, if they display several of these traits then it would be a good time to back off because you are either going to be cheated or, at the very least, have your time wasted.

The second kind of dangerous person is the worse of the two because they aren't dishonest and therefore are much, much harder to detect. They are the self-deluded. They really believe everything they say, even though they don't have the means to make it happen. They truly believe that they can get you all the money that you need for your movie. They truly believe that they can make a deal to get your movie picked up by a major studio. They truly believe that a big star will do them a favor. They truly believe they can accomplish everything they tell you ... but they just can't do it today. Maybe tomorrow or the day after. Certainly by next week. They truly *believe* because they really *want* to believe that they can do it. Unfortunately, they eat up your time. It's possible to lose months because the self-deluded can't deliver on their promises. Since they aren't truly lying, at least not in their own mind, it is quite difficult to discover what they really are. Sadly, there is no good method by which to make such a discovery. All I can recommend is that you pay close attention and become suspicious if you notice any of the following: they never explain in detail how they will accomplish the things they talk about. They continually say that they need one more thing from you, such as information, another meeting, etc. Their promises seem too good to be true. They sidestep specific questions. They don't seem as knowledgeable as they should be. The credentials they offer do not seem as impressive to you as they are to them. They don't have a web page, or e-mail address, or fax number, or even a business card. They seem much more interested in the fantasy of making movies than the reality. They never seem to worry about anything. They demonstrate a lack of intelligence. They always dismiss your concerns. They talk a little too much about movie stars and not enough about filmmaking. They have an empty personal life. They talk in grandiose terms about what they can accomplish. All their friends or family seem like misfits. They seem socially awkward at dinner meetings. They dress several years out of date. They dwell too much on things like premieres, interviews with the press, and fan letters rather than on how to make the movie. They make you feel uncomfortable no matter what they say or do. Whenever you spend time with them, you feel inexplicably depressed. There are many quirks unique to these people, but overall I would have to say that there is probably one trait that is common to nearly all of the self-deluded: a lack of maturity. They demonstrate a childlike quality that can be very endearing. It's because of this quality that people often trust them when they shouldn't. Of course, as I mentioned earlier, one or more of these traits doesn't mean much. However, if they are demonstrating too many of these flaws, you should be careful.

So there you are. Two dangers, one solution: keep your eyes open for trouble.

17. YOU'RE NOT READY UNTIL *YOU'RE* READY

At this point, some filmmakers will begin to have some serious doubts about their movie. Doubts that can paralyze them creatively and spiritually. These doubts have nothing to do with talent, money, skill, experience, or resources. It has to do with resolve and confidence. Have you ever met someone with an abundance of confidence? Such people appear to be almost superhuman at times. Whatever they try, they seem able to do. The world is theirs to conquer. They may not be any smarter or more physically competent than you are, but they still succeed when you, and others, fail. Why? What's the difference that makes such a huge difference? The answer is simple: they believe in themselves and what they are doing. Then again, perhaps it's not so simple, because even if these people falter, they get up and keep trying until they eventually succeed. Ultimately, they succeed because they have great faith in what they are doing, and they refuse to accept defeat.

What about you? Do you believe in yourself? Do you believe in what you are doing? At this point, others believe in you. Others have trusted you with their money. People's futures depend on what you do next. If you aren't truly ready to start the next phase of filmmaking then you will undoubtedly fail. The question you should be asking yourself is "Why wouldn't I succeed?" You have read and digested the contents of this book, haven't you? The money for your movie is there, isn't it? You have prepared yourself, and your movie, haven't you? Why don't you feel that you are ready? Is it the burden of being in charge? Is it a fear of failure? Do you even have a reason? In each thing you do in life, a lack of confidence can be very destructive if you allow it to overwhelm you. It is relatively simple to make yourself intellectually ready to make a movie, but it can be extremely hard to make yourself emotionally ready. You have to believe that you can accomplish what you have set out to do. If you don't believe in yourself then no one will believe in you. Fear is a natural instinct when you tackle something that you have never done before, but you cannot let it control what you do. Conquer the fear, the lack of confidence, the self-doubt by understanding that nearly every new filmmaker feels some anxiety before beginning a movie. In spite of this, they continue on, and, in the process of working on their movie, the negative feelings diminish. Moreover, with each film the anxiety gets smaller.

In the end, you need to remember that there are people around you who want you to succeed. If you have no faith in yourself, then trust in those around you who have faith in you.

18. TEN HARD LESSONS ABOUT GETTING READY

Before you move on to the next chapter, let's quickly go over these 10 lessons, which will aid you in **GETTING READY**.

1. There's an old expression: "You can make movies or make money to make movies, but you can't make both." This is an overstatement, of course, but it is basically true. If you decide to seek out investors, then be prepared to spend a lot of time getting the capital that you need to make your movie. *A lot of time*!

2. There's another old expression: "You can makes *good* movies *cheaply*, and you can make *good* movies *quickly*, but you can't make *good* movies *quickly*, and *cheaply*." Something has to give — quality, time, or the budget. Since an increase of budget is unlikely, give yourself time to plan a good movie. One reason that movies often cost so much is because not enough time was taken to plan things out properly. Take as much time as possible to put your movie together. You will save money and make a much better film.

3. Don't let your ego sway your common sense. Take a rational approach to each creative or financial decision. Greed or pride can ruin things faster than you can say "No, really, I almost made a movie."

4. List all the advantages that you possess which you are certain can be brought to the project. For example, locations, costumes, props, actors available to you, anything and everything. And when I say "certain," I mean *certain*. Don't *assume* that this advantage will be available when you need it. Be absolutely positive! When you get around to writing your script, make sure that you incorporate these advantages into it. They will enhance your production values and thereby make your film more desirable to both distributors and the public alike.

5. Always check out the commercial viability of the genre that interests you before you settle on a particular project. The only thing that never changes is that things always change. A particular type of film may be popular one year but not the next. Don't just ask the clerk at the local video store about the genre that you are considering. Ask questions of a lot of distributors. It will save you a great deal of grief.

6. If the answer you get from someone is not straightforward, whether they are a distributor, investor, or whatever, then either they don't truly know what they are talking about or they are hiding something. Whatever their reason, do not do business with them.

7. Whenever possible, make your pitch for financing to many potential investors at an investment gathering instead of pitching it to just one potential investor. Remember, it takes as much effort to sell a dozen people on your business venture as it does to convince one person.

8. *Always* treat investors with respect and fairness. When your movie makes money, they'll stand in line to invest in your next one. If, for some reason, it doesn't turn a profit, the investors will be far less likely to ride you out of town on a rail.

9. Write down every possible reason that an investor might not want to invest in your film project. Once you have done that, think up an intelligent comeback that will shoot down each point. By doing this you will be able to deal with possible investors with far greater ease.

10. I'm sure that you heard the biblical expression that no man is a prophet in his own hometown. Take that expression to heart because you will face the same problem. You will probably find that it is much easier to make deals with people who are not in, or from, your hometown. Why? Just because someone likes you doesn't mean that they trust your business acumen. You will also find that many people will be turned off by your belief in yourself and your film. There's a great many reasons for this, but most of them boil down to one thing: a lack of faith. Not a lack of faith in

what you can accomplish, but in themselves. If they know someone who succeeds in life where they haven't, what does that say about them? It is much easier to put down you and what you are doing than to try and make their own goals come true.

19. Flashback, Part One

Well over a hundred years ago a French magician was experimenting with a movie camera by filming on a city street when suddenly his camera jammed. With a momentary adjustment he resumed filming, and all was well. After the magician had the film processed, he noticed something remarkable while viewing it. A carriage on the screen seemingly vanished. He had just witnessed a moment of magic that was far more impressive than any trick he had ever performed on stage. The question was, "How did this miracle take place?" He quickly realized that, in the second it took to fix the camera, the carriage had moved on but the camera hadn't recorded it. When the film was projected, it looked as if the carriage had vanished. The magician's brain was on fire with the possibilities suggested by what he had just seen. With some experimentation he discovered that he could make things suddenly appear or change shape. With further experimentation he found that he could accomplish ghostly effects with a form of superimposition. Soon he could create giants, flying creatures, and countless other effects. The magician could now do illusions that were heretofore impossible to perform live on stage. The question was, what would he do with this knowledge? That magician's name was Georges Méliès, and his answer would change movies forever.

Méliès wisely reasoned that his discovery was much too important to ignore. He could have simply dismissed his discovery because he was a making a good living as a professional magician. The movie business was in its embryonic stage, and few people knew what to make of it. Those who gave the new medium any thought whatsoever regarded it as a curious fad and nothing more. There was little reason to think of it as anything other than that. Most movies were under ten minutes long and often displayed the most mundane matters of everyday life. Trolley cars, married couples kissing, trains en route were all filmed and projected on sheets hung up on walls throughout the world. Eventually these types of films would give way to tepid dramas or comedies that had some semblance of a story. These short subjects were, more accurately, skits for the screen. Méliès saw that there were commercial possibilities to explore in the brand new enterprise called "the cinema." He could offer the public something they had never seen before — trick pictures! His movies would be outrageous and magical, crammed full of special effects. He felt certain that there would be a huge audience for such movies ... if he planned things properly.

Before Méliès did anything else, he had to be certain that there was a demand for his type of films. Méliès was well aware of the fact that there was a terrible prejudice against movies, so he decided to photograph his films like staged events. His movies would employ the familiar stylized painted sets, and overly dramatic acting style of the theater, with which his audience felt more comfortable. Méliès would make certain that his movies would be simple enough for anyone to understand. He would include pretty showgirls in his films to spice up the stories as often as he could. Whenever possible, he would base his films on well-known stories that had a ready-made market. Each of his films would be loaded with as many special effects as he could devise so that his audience would leave the theater dazzled. By doing all of these things, Méliès believed that he could create a strong demand for his films, and he was right. Soon his special effects extravaganzas were hits all over the world. He was so successful that competitors began to make illegal dupes of Méliès' movies. Méliès countered by making sure that his name could be plainly read in scenes that were so crucial to the movie that they could not be cut out. Time and again the French magician's success was the direct result of his time spent getting things ready before he shot one second of film. Every trick shot had to be planned; every market had to be explored. For years Méliès was the king of the special effect film. It was only when Méliès ignored his own rule about planning and marketing that things changed for him. By the second decade of the twentieth century, film styles were changing. Directing became more cinematic and less reminiscent of theater. Acting became much more naturalistic. Filming in real locations became more common, and sets were designed to look more realistic. Méliès refused to adapt his film style to the needs of the marketplace, and soon there was no audience for his movies. As a result, Méliès went out of business.

Like Méliès, many filmmakers achieve success because they think things out before they make their movie; and, like Méliès, many filmmakers ultimately fail because they refuse to adapt. Every few years the marketplace for movies changes. Talkies are invented. Color movies become the standard. Video became an alternative to theaters. The direct-to-video boom peaks and plummets. Things change, and the modern filmmaker has to change with them. You have to "get ready" in order to make your movie a success in the marketplace, and part of being ready is being flexible. Have you done all your homework? Have you prepared yourself for the next step? If things change, will you go with the flow and make it work to your advantage, or will you refuse to change and watch your dream slip from your fingers? Are you positive that you have made yourself and your project ready for the next step? If so, then get ready for some long hours and sleepless nights because it's time for pre-production.

II. Pre-Production

20. THE BUDGET: IS THERE
EVER ENOUGH MONEY?

The answer to this is a resounding "No!" No matter what size the budget, there never seems to be enough money to do the film that you're working on. This forces you to be creative. Make every dollar count. For that matter, make every dime count.

You make a budget by breaking down your movie's various financial needs into individual categories. Point 12 includes a sample summary budget breakdown that can act as your guide. This not an example of the kind of budget a "Big" movie would use. It is streamlined for use by a low-budget filmmaker like yourself. Start making phone calls and get the prices of everything needed for your movie. This will tell you what you need to allot to each category. Never — I repeat, *never*— assume that you know what the price is before checking. Never rely on your personal judgment to guide you when you don't have the experience to back you up. I once knew a would-be producer/director who, in planning to make a 35-millimeter action film, allotted $50,000 dollars for catering and only $10,000 dollars for all his post-production needs. Why such ridiculous amounts? Quite simply, he was so certain of his estimates that he never took to the time to check the actual price of things. Needless to say, he never got the movie off the ground.

Once you have broken down your movie's needs into a budget, be sure to allot a little extra in each category to give you a little breathing room. Prices for things change periodically, and you can find your movie put on *hold* because you didn't have a few extra dollars to pay for something important.

Once you have made your budget, stick to it or you will find yourself stuck.

21. Over-Ambition +
Inexperience = Failure

It is possible to make a good movie, even though you are inexperienced. It may also be possible to make a *reasonably* lavish movie with the meager funds that you have available to you. It is not, however, possible to do both. You may have noticed that I italicized the word "reasonably" in the second sentence. It is there to emphasize that there are limits to what imagination and hard work can accomplish. It takes time and (once again) experience to learn what you can materialize on a small budget.

The movies of Ed Wood are typical, if somewhat amusing, examples of this problem. Wood had rather grandiose dreams for his low-budget movies. As a result, Wood's movies never truly materialized what he had in mind. In his movie *Plan 9 from Outer Space*, he has a script full of alien spaceship interiors, airplane interiors, flying saucers battling the army, miniature landscapes and space stations. All of these things were executed very badly. Even if Wood had been a competent director, he would have had a difficult time filming a movie like *Plan 9 from Outer Space* with his limited financial resources. In contrast to Wood, filmmaker Roger Corman, making less complicated movies with comparable budgets, produced exploitation classics like *It Conquered the World* and *Little Shop of Horrors*.

The entire point here is this: Keep things simple. Making your movie will be hard enough without you making matters more complicated than they have to be.

There are many companies that you can draw upon to supply you with a service or resource needed to make your movie. Nearly all of them can be found in a Los Angeles or New York City phone directory, or on the internet. However, if you want to save yourself hours, or perhaps days, of research, you should go to the following website: http://www.la411.com. This website is an internet directory of countless movie-related services and resources.

22. Write a Script That Helps
Your Movie, Not Hinders It

Let's get down to basics. If you don't have a good script then you cannot make a good movie. It's just that simple. I will be addressing specifics about proper plot structure and dialogue in points 23 and 24. The technical aspects of putting the script together are also very important. Unless you know what you are doing, you will certainly fail, so let's go through the process, step by step.

(a). YOUR STORY. Write your story in synopsis form first. Don't worry about dialogue at this point. Try to keep your story as visual as possible.

(b). YOUR OUTLINE. A good way to write an outline, also called a treatment, is to take a deck of index cards and write down each scene of your story on each card. Once you are done, lay out all the cards in sequence so you can read them at a glance. By doing this you have a much better sense of any problems with the structure of your scenes. Is there too much of this or not enough of that? Are too many of your more interesting scenes lumped together at the beginning, the middle, or the end? Does a particular character disappear for too many scenes? Does the dramatic conflict take too long to get underway? Does the pace of the story fluctuate from quick to slow? If so, then change some scenes around, if need be, to make the story flow more smoothly. Once you are certain that the outline is as good as you can make it, then you can use it as your blueprint when you start writing the screenplay. Once you are done with the screenplay it will then be time to set the script aside for a week or so to enable you, or another person, to reread your script objectively. Then you can begin to rewrite your script. Ouch! Rewriting may hurt, but it's absolutely necessary to make certain that your screenplay is good.

(c). REWRITING. This is where the real writing is done. It takes a *professional* to look at their script objectively and see its flaws. It also takes a professional to correct those flaws. Anything that isn't truly necessary should be edited out. Anything that doesn't advance character or plot should be cut without mercy. Any scene that can't be filmed on the budget you have available has to either be rewritten to accommodate your budget or edited out. Once this has been accomplished, go through the script and see if you can make the transitions between the scenes smoother. One of the most common things wrong with many low-budget movies is that each scene doesn't "flow" well into the next. Sometimes transitions can be aided through the use of "transitional shots." This refers to the insertion of a scene, or shot, which acts as a bridge to make the cut from one scene to another less jarring. For example, between the interior scene of the protagonist talking to a detective at the police station, and the interior scene where he is asleep in a motel, you place a transitional shot of the exterior of that motel. Such shots can also save you money in post-production. Dissolves between scenes can be expensive, at least when it comes to film, but you can eliminate them by employing a transitional shot as your bridge.

(d). TYPING YOUR SCRIPT. How you type your script is *extremely* important. The kind of font and tabulator stops used will tell you approximately how long your movie will be. If it has been correctly typed, then you can reasonably assume that your movie will run approximately one minute per page after the post-production is completed. Pages of action may time out to be longer or shorter than a minute, depending on how densely detailed the scenes are described. Without being verbose, write the description with sufficient information to clearly explain what is going on. If you are using a typewriter to type your screenplay, be sure to use Pica style, not Elite. The Elite has smaller type and is unsuitable for your script. This smaller type was used mostly for business mail and isn't employed too often today because it is currently out of fashion. If you are using a computer, use a Courier style font or the Prestige Pica font; and the size should be 12. These two fonts are preferred because they more closely resemble the typewriter Pica font than other fonts, and therefore can be estimated to run approximately one minute per page. The tabulator stops for typewriters are listed on the next page. There should be a cover page listing your MOVIE TITLE. Below the title, type Screenplay by. Below that, type the name of the screenwriter. Below that, you should put the month and year. This will become important later when you need to establish your ownership of the script by copyrighting it or registering it with the Writers Guild of America. Each rewritten draft of your script should have a retyped cover page and the number of this particular draft (i.e., second, third, etc.).

Until the advent of the computer, the tabulator stops for typing a screenplay on a Pica typewriter (presented in the next paragraph) were the standard.

TYPEWRITER TABULATOR STOPS

15. (Scene #)

(Scene #) 75.

20. (Interior or Exterior. Location of Scene. Day
    or Night.)

20. (Description of the action begins).

(Description of action ends) 61.

40. (Name of Character)

35. (Character's Reaction)

30. (Dialogue margin begins)

(Dialogue margin ends).   63.

(Cut To: Dissolve To: Fade In: Fade Out.) 60.

The following margins are the standard for computers:

> Dialogue has a left margin of 2.7" and a right margin of 2.4".
> Names of character have a left margin of 4.1".
> Character's reaction has a left margin of 3.4" and a right margin of 3.1".
> Stage direction has a margin of 1.7" on the left and 1.1" on the right.
> Scenes transitions have a left margin of 6.0".
> Left scene number has left margin of 1.0". The right scene number has a
>   margin of 7.4".

There are additional script terms and information that should be mentioned before we move on. They are:

> (VO). This stands for Voice Over. It refers to dialogue that is not spoken on the set. These words are often placed on the soundtrack during post-production. It is most often used in a movie during phone conversations. The parenthesized initials are placed in the space normally reserved for reactions.
>
> (CONTD). When a character is speaking and the dialogue "continues" onto the next page, the abbreviation CONTD is used in parentheses next to the character's name. When this occurs there should be no interruption of the line to be spoken. The line should be finished and the remaining line(s) continued on the following page. To the right, on the bottom of the interrupted page, capped and in parentheses, should be the word (CONTINUED). On the left, at the top of the next page, capped with a colon at the end, is a repeat of the word CONTINUED. The word "continuing" is employed, in parentheses, in the reaction space when a character needs to continue speaking after a necessary script direction has interrupted their dialogue.
>
> INSERT. An insert is a brief close shot of something that is "inserted" into the wider shot so that a particular detail is properly accentuated. For example, a killer pulls a pistol from his pocket but accidentally drops his car keys as he does so. The dropping of the killer's car keys could be an insert.

All descriptions of camera movements or angles, or sound effects, should be CAPITALIZED.

Transitional directions, such as CUT TO, DISSOLVE TO, etc., are not required but may be included at the discretion of the screenwriter.

The names of characters important to the story are normally CAPITALIZED when they are first introduced to the reader, thereby helping establish their importance.

These characters of importance should also have a brief description of their appearance when they first appear, so as to aid the reader in understanding the physical nature of that character, as well as helping the casting director form an idea of what kind of actor should be cast in that role.

When a specific piece of business directly affects the way an actor must *physically* deliver a line, that description may be placed in your script in one of two ways: as a scene description, or in the character reaction space. An example of the latter might be what the character is speaking into, i.e. (Into microphone), or as a clarification of which of the other characters present is being spoken to, i.e. (To George).

It is not necessary to write every camera angle because the decision of where the camera is placed will be decided by the director. However, each definitive and obviously separate piece of action needing to be visually independent of each other should be placed on separate lines to illustrate that the scene must have those particular cinematic actions filmed as individual shots. If a specific camera angle is necessary in order for that scene to work properly, then, and only then, write that camera angle into your script.

Contrary to what many writers think, there is no set standard for spacing. The rules vary from expert to expert. However, you will be safe if you work within the following parameters. On the line describing the location and time of day (known as a slug line, for some reason) put one to three spaces between each of the three descriptions. For example: INT. KITCHEN OF JOHN SMITH. DAY. The slug line or camera angles, a.k.a. shot headings, a.k.a. camera directions, should be preceded by two blank lines. It can be followed by either one blank line or two blank lines. Some writers put two blank lines before and after each description of action, while others only put one blank line after. The choice is yours. For whatever it's worth, I prefer to use one blank line after a shot heading or slug line, and only one line between descriptions of action, because it keeps the timing of the script closer to one minute per page.

There are additional details to script formatting that could be discussed further, but since you are writing a script for your own use, such information is of little consequence and therefore inappropriate here. If you wish to learn more about movie script formatting (to submit a script to a movie studio, for example), you can easily find those details on the internet. There are also computer programs called Final Draft and Movie Magic Screenwriter, which automatically formats your script as you type it. However, these programs tend to be rather expensive. One source for a free screenwriting format can be found at www.Scriptbuddy.com.

The Three Act Screenplay

It has become fashionable to refer to a screenplay as having three acts. This is hardly a new observation. All good stories have always had (1) a beginning, (2) a middle, and (3) an end. It is, however, important to make certain that each "act" is clearly delineated from the act that precedes it or follows it. In other words, act two must take us in a new and exciting direction from what was presented in act one. And act three's road to the movie's conclusion must differ in its dramatic course from either act one or two.

For example, in act one the hero of the story sees a murder being committed and tries to help save the victim. He doesn't succeed, but in the process of trying to help he finds himself mistaken by the police as the murderer. In act two he tries to find the real killer in order to clear himself and learns that he has been framed by a local mob boss. In act three he finds evidence proving his innocence but now has to find a way to get that proof to the police without being killed by a hit man hired by the mob boss.

And there you have it — three separate plot paths, or acts, within the same story.

One thing that is important for all forms of dramatic storytelling is conflict. Conflict has been described as existing whenever there are two opposing forces and compromise is impossible. In a movie script, dramatic conflict is vital in order to maintain the interest of your audience, as well as executing your premise properly. The following is an example of a scene without conflict.

> Two scientists hear thunderous pounding on their laboratory door! Both of them are terrified!

SCIENTIST 1
(Scared)
It's the mutant! It'll break through
that door any second!

SCIENTIST 2
(Urgently)
Wait! The stasis beam! That'll stop
it!

> The mutant bursts through the door and Scientist 2 fires the stasis beam at it!

Yeah, I know, the scene is corny. Okay, let's be honest — it's extremely corny. More importantly, however, it is boring. I am aware of the fact that the attacking mutant could constitute a mild form of conflict. Why mild? Since the beam will stop the mutant, there is nothing truly at stake. Let's try the scene once more, but with an important difference.

Two scientists hear thunderous pounding on their laboratory door! Both of them are terrified!

> SCIENTIST 1
> (Scared)
> It's the mutant! It'll break through that door any second!

> SCIENTIST 2
> (Urgently)
> Wait! The stasis beam! That'll stop it!

> SCIENTIST 1
> (Stunned)
> Are you crazy! You can't use that! It's untested. It could blow up this whole block!

> SCIENTIST 2
> What difference does it make? When that thing gets us, we'll die anyway.

> SCIENTIST 1
> Yeah, "we'll die"! Use that beam and a lot of innocent people could die with us!

Scientist 1 takes a step toward Scientist 2. Scientist 2 quickly picks up the stasis beam, turns on the power, and aims it at Scientist 1.

> SCIENTIST 2
> (Desperately)
> Keep away!

The mutant bursts through the door and Scientist 2 fires the stasis beam at it!

This time there is something at risk. Will Scientist 2 use the beam or will Scientist 1 stop him? If scientist 2 uses the beam, will it blow up and kill everyone in the building or will the mutant be stopped? Corny as the scene still is, we now have a greater emotional investment in the outcome of the scene than we did in the previous version.

Still not convinced? Okay, let's try something less fantastic. A young man wants to marry a woman whom he is hopelessly in love with and who also is in love with him. The problem is she won't marry the young man unless he gets permission from her father who regards him as a useless dreamer. The young man asks the girl's father for permission to marry her, but the father refuses the request and belittles the young man in the process. The young man nods meekly and leaves.

There it is. There is no conflict because the young man accepts the decision. Conflict would arise if the boy were to argue with the woman's father.

He could become angry and refuse to accept the father's decision, and the father could arrogantly refuse to consider what the young man has to say. This would help keep the outcome of the scene in doubt. Better still, if there were to be a risk inherent in the conflict, the drama would be much more compelling. What kind of risk? Perhaps something bad could happen if the young man doesn't win the argument. As it is, there is nothing to prevent the young man from trying to convince his lady love that she doesn't need her dad's permission. More to the point, if she is willing to lose the young man because of her father's unreasonable demands, then the young man would probably be better off without her.

How about this? What if the young woman has very low self-esteem and desperately seeks her father's love and approval. She can never be happy without it. The young man is worried what the woman might do if her father says no. Would she have a nervous breakdown? Would she take an overdose of sleeping pills? The young man is scared to death that the father's refusal would result in something terrible happening to the young woman. Also, what if the young man has a chance to advance himself in his career if he moves to a new job in another state. He's afraid that if he takes the job he will lose the young woman because her father is pressuring her to marry someone else. Because of these factors, the young man has to get the father to agree, otherwise he will definitely lose the woman he loves. Now something is at stake. What happens during the argument with the father will dictate the outcome of the young man's future. If the young man can't get the father's permission, then the young man will have to choose between losing the woman or his career. His life will change drastically, depending upon the outcome of this argument. Now something is really at risk. The young man is highly motivated to win the argument, and we are rooting for him because we know what could be lost if he doesn't succeed. Conflict — it's a very valuable literary tool. Use it!

The Title of Your Movie

Let's talk about the title of your movie. Your title has to be catchy enough to get the attention of you audience and a distributor, be memorable, and yet also explain the premise of your movie. For example, *Night of the Living Dead*. The title tells us right off the bat that this is a horror movie. The "*Living Dead*" portion of the title lets us know that we are dealing with people, probably monsters of some sort, who are dead yet appear to be alive. The "*Night of*" portion of the title tells us that the story has a nighttime setting. The overall effect of the title suggests that the movie is about seemingly dead monsters doing something dramatic, and probably scary, at night. This title sells the movie to its audience.

Let me tell you about another movie title. It was to be called *Sleep No More*. What does that title tell you about the movie? The answer: nothing. It is poetic, even lyrical, but it failed in its purpose to be interesting and informative. When the movie came out it had been given the more commercial title of *Invasion of the Body Snatchers*. A lurid title, obviously, yet one that accomplished its purpose.

Your Screenplay's Opening Scenes

Let us now consider how your screenplay begins. There are two ways of beginning a movie. One way is to slowly allow the characters to develop before the plot gets underway. This works best for a major film with top-notch actors giving performances so compelling that the audience is caught up in the movie from the start. For a low-budget movie it's better not to be so dependant upon your actors. For this reason your movie should have something interesting happen right away to grab the attention of the audience. This not only appeals to today's audiences, who have short attention spans, but also helps sell your movie to a distributor, who, in turn, will more easily sell it to a theater, a video distributor, or an overseas buyer.

There are two types of openings that are effective for low-budget screenplays, especially if those screenplays are fantastic in nature. By fantastic I mean something that is, on some level, unreal. For example, if your screenplay were based upon an Arabian Nights story, or was about a secret agent who is invisible, or whose villain is a giant beast attacking a city. Get the idea? These two types of openings can also work for more reality-based stories. For example, a thriller about a cop who is haunted by the brutal gangland murder of his partner, or an intimate love story about a widow falling in love with the widower next door. How well these screenplay openings work depends upon how well these openings are employed. Over the next several pages you will find samples of the opening sequences from two completely different copyrighted screenplays, both of which are currently in pre-production at Marche-Williams Productions. These screenplays represent two completely different genres that have proven to be commercially successful. Note: In accommodation of the printing needs of this book, neither sample uses the script format previously discussed. We will discuss the whys and wherefores of each screenplay sample after each has been presented.

First up: the opening for a Horror movie.

(Script samples and screenplays copyright Philip R. Cable.)

SHADOW SQUAD
Screenplay by
Philip R. Cable

1. EXT. A DARK CITY STREET. NIGHT.   1.

The street is empty and dangerous looking. A young girl comes around the corner of a building and cautiously walks down the street. The woman is **RILEY COHEN**. Riley is an attractive, albeit quirky-looking, young girl of 19 or 20, who has a faintly sad look about her.

Riley pauses at a crosswalk and waits for the light to turn green. She impatiently checks her watch and notices something on the ground. She reacts strongly to what she sees.

INSERT OF THE PAGES OF A NEWSPAPER LAYING ON THE GROUND NEXT TO HER FOOT.

The newspaper flutters in the wind, but the headline can be plainly read. It says— SERIAL KILLER MURDERS ANOTHER YOUNG WOMAN!

Riley becomes uncomfortable and tries to ignore the frightening headline.

From nearby, a man watches her from an alley, its shadows shielding him from being seen.

The stoplight turns green and Riley crosses the street, then turns onto a cross street.

2. EXT. NEW STREET. NIGHT.   2.

Riley comes to a new corner. She is unsure of where she is heading. She takes a note from her pocket and checks what's written on it.

INSERT OF NOTE.

The note says— Phone booth on the corner of Pike and Santa

Fe. Ten PM.

Riley looks around but doesn't see the phone booth. She keeps on walking.

3. EXT. PHONE BOOTH. NIGHT.   3.

Riley walks past a building and sees a phone booth nearby. She rushes to it. She reaches the phone booth and checks her watch as she does.

INSERT OF RILEY'S WATCH.

The watch says that it is 9:59.

Riley impatiently looks around and sees a handsome man in his mid-thirties looking at some cameras in a store window down the street. He glances at Riley and fleetingly smiles at her. She curtly ignores him, so he returns to looking at the store cameras.

Riley looks the other way and sees a large, somewhat menacing-looking, man walking in her direction. She swallows hard and starts to get very concerned. Is this guy dangerous? He sure looks like he is.

The large man gets closer.

Riley gets a little more scared.

The large man gets closer still. He is almost at the booth. Riley holds her breath.

The large man passes by the booth and Riley starts to breathe easier. She looks in the opposite direction and notices that the man at the store window is gone.

RING! Abruptly, there is the loud ring of a phone! Riley reacts to the loud ring with a start, sighs with embarrassment, and then grabs thephone.

RILEY
(Into phone)

Hello.

Surprisingly, the ringing continues. She reacts confused. She hangs up and looks around the booth and finds a cell phone duct-taped to the top of the booth. She peels the phone off the booth and answers the cell phone.

DAVY
(VO)

Hello Riley. You're on time.

RILEY

I wanted to meet you, Davy.

DAVY

That's good. I'm glad to hear that. It's important for me to meet you too.

RILEY

Where, Davy?

DAVY

Keep walking down the street. You'll know when to stop.

The phone goes dead so Riley hangs up. She exits the phone booth and starts to walk down the street. She gets more and more nervous with each step.

4. EXT. ANOTHER STREET. NIGHT.   4.

Riley continues walking, looking for Davy, but doesn't see him anywhere.

She comes to an alley. She notices a derelict asleep in the doorway of a nearby store. She hesitates as she considers whether of not it might be Davy. Naw, couldn't be. She comes to the mouth of an alley and the cell phone rings again. She answers it.

DAVY
(VO)

You're almost there, Riley. Go into the alley and keep walking until I tell you it's time.

RILEY

Time for what?

There is no answer.

RILEY

Where am I going, Davy?

INSERT OF DAVEY IN DARKNESS.

Davy is nearby in the darkness. We watch Davy's lips as he speaks into his cell phone.

DAVY

To me. Just a little closer.

Riley gets more and more nervous as she turns into the alley.

RILEY

All right, Davy. Whatever you say.
I'm coming.

5. EXT. ALLEY. NIGHT.   5.

Riley walks slowly down the dead-end alley.

Davy is standing in the darkness somewhere close by. He is watching everything that Riley does. He is breathing heavily, as if the moment is almost sexual for him.

Riley passes by a large bedspring leaning against a warehouse wall and comes to the end of the alley. No one is around. There is a terribly dangerous feel to the alley now. The confined space is nearly claustrophobic.

CLANG! She hears the loud crash of metal, which whips her around in fright. She only sees a cat running from an open trash bin. Her cell phone rings again and she quickly answers it.

DAVY
(VO)

Back up to the bedspring. There's a
door behind it. Go inside, I'm waiting for you.

Davy hangs up and so does Riley.

Riley crosses to the bedsprings and looks behind it. Sure enough, there is a door hidden there. She squeezes between the door and the bedsprings and tries the knob. It's unlocked. She opens it and sees that it's very dark inside. She slowly enters.

6. EXT. ANOTHER STREET. NIGHT.   6.

The derelict is standing on the corner smoking a cigarette, watching the mouth of the alley with great interest. He no longer seems drunk or sleepy. Something odd is going on.

7. INT. WAREHOUSE. NIGHT.   7.

Riley is inside the dark warehouse trying to see something in the darkness. There are faint pools of light that she follows.

As she walks around, the sound of a door opening is heard. She turns around but doesn't see anything or anyone, so she heads in the direction she came.

8. EXT. ALLEY. NIGHT.   8.

The derelict steps into the mouth of the alley looking extremely concerned. The large menacing man and the man who was looking in the store window join him. The large man and the derelict both pull pistols from their back pockets, then start to walk into the alley. The "window" man, who we will learn later is named MATT, grabs the large man's arm to hold him back.

Matt points to the pistol in the large man's hand.

                        MATT

            That won't do any good.

                    LARGE MAN
                    (Annoyed)

            You're just an advisor, Taylor.
            Nothing more.

The large man pulls free of Matt's grip, then he and the derelict both head into the alley. Matt sighs in frustration and follows them.

9. INT. WAREHOUSE. NIGHT.   9.

Riley is still surrounded by near darkness. She stops walking, unsure of where she is in the pitch-black warehouse. She looks around, trying to figure out her next move.

There is a faint outline of movement as someone comes up behind her.

Riley senses this and is scared. As the man behind Riley gets close enough to grab her, he steps into her faint pool of light, allowing us to see him. It's her caller, DAVY. Davy is a morbid-looking boy in his early twenties, slim, with slicked-back black hair, and pale skin. He is wearing a black jumpsuit with an occult symbol on the pocket.

                        RILEY

            Hello, Davy.

Davy gives her an embrace, which, while sensuous, is also threatening.

                        DAVEY

            I'm glad you came here. It's due to
            the power.

                        RILEY

            Power?

                        DAVEY

            Of the internet. It brings people
            together that would never meet
            otherwise.

Davy kisses the back of her neck. Nibbling, almost biting it.

                        DAVY

            It's amazing how many women are
            willing to meet someone like me.

RILEY

How many?

DAVY
(Amused)

Jealous?

RILEY

Curious.

DAVY
(Meaningfully)

Curiosity killed the cat.

10. EXT. ALLEY. NIGHT.   10.

The large man is confused. He and the derelict look up and down the alley
frantically. Matt is also concerned but somehow seems more on top of the situation.

DERELICT
(Desperately)

I don't get it. She went in here. I
saw her!

As the derelict and the large man continue searching for Riley, Matt takes note
of the bedsprings.

11. INT. WAREHOUSE. NIGHT.   11.

Davy's fingers start to fondle Riley's throat. Riley reacts, repulsed by his touch.

DAVY

When I leave the house, all the
mundane little people on the street
stare at me because they know I'm
not like them. I never have been.
Never could be.

RILEY
(Knowingly)

Started in high school, didn't it?
Started when you first read Dracula.

DAVY
(Threatened)

You know too much.

Davy bares his fangs and tries to bite her. She screams and struggles with him.

The door to the alley bursts open and the large man, the derelict and Matt dash
in! Both the large man and the derelict aim their pistols directly at Davy.

LARGE MAN
(Firmly)

Police! Back away from her!

Davy's grip lessens from surprise, and Riley pulls away from him.

LARGE MAN

On the floor! Now!

Davy hisses at him like a furious cat and takes a step toward the undercover police.

LARGE MAN

I said NOW!

Davy reacts, unafraid of their guns. Davy charges them, and the large man fires his gun! The bullet hits Davy squarely in the chest! He screams in pain, then falls motionless to the floor.

Riley stumbles forward and Matt rushes to her.

The large man and the derelict turn around and look at the dark surroundings of the warehouse.

RILEY
(To Matt)

You sure took your time.

MATT
(Dryly)

Was there a hurry?

LARGE MAN
(To Derelict)

What the hell is this place?

DERELICT

A warehouse, I think.

Unexpectedly, Davy rises up slowly behind the two undercover cops. Silent as a ghost, Davy crosses to them, his eyes ablaze with insane hatred.

LARGE MAN

Musta used the place cuz it's abandoned.

DERELICT

Maybe. So, you calling H.Q., or am I?

Davy slams his fist hard on the back of the derelicts neck! The large man whips around, but before he can fire his gun Davy backhands him across the face, knocking him back into the darkness where he crashes onto the concrete floor. Davy starts running. All of a sudden a large crucifix is thrust in front of Davy's eyes. He is horrified by the image of the cross. At first Davy is completely paralyzed by the sight, but he manages to take a step back, despite his terror.

As Davy takes a second step, Riley grabs him and punches him in the face as hard as she can! Davy falls back into the arms of the large man, who is getting up. The large man holds Davy as the derelict forces himself to stand and handcuff Davy.

> LARGE MAN
> (To Matt)
>
> How'd ya know that the bullets wouldn't —
>
> MATT
> (With authority)
>
> He wanted people to think he's a vampire, and bullets can't kill vampires. Check his jumpsuit. I'm betting it has a Kevlar lining. All part of the illusion; just like the phony fangs.

Davy is furious. He spits out his fake vampire fangs, his own blood dripping from his lips, and struggles to rise. The cops hold him back.

> DAVY
> (Screaming at Matt and Riley)
>
> You're not cops! The cops can't stop me! Who are you?
>
> RILEY
>
> Don't you read the newspapers? They call us the Shadow Squad.

As Davy is handcuffed, Matt and Riley smile and leave the warehouse. The music starts to swell and we —

> CUT TO:

12. OPENING TITLE SEQUENCE.   12.

13. EXT. WOODS. DAWN.   13.

A terrified young woman frantically runs through some thick bushes and past several trees. She pauses for a moment to catch her breath but suddenly hears a savage inhuman wail in the distance. Hearing the hideous sound sends her off and running toward the dirt road just past the trees.

14. EXT. A DIRT ROAD. SUNRISE.

The terrified young woman comes to the dirt road. Her clothes are torn and her body spotted with fresh blood. Claw-like scratches are all over her arms and legs. She looks like she's about to drop from exhaustion, but somehow she finds the strength to continue running.

She stumbles down the road until she comes around a curve where she finds herself facing an onrushing car!

The car slams into her and she is violently flung to the side of the road!

The driver skids to a stop and gets out to see if the woman is still alive. The driver checks her and sees that she isn't moving. Is she dead? We can't tell.

> WINSTON
> (VO)
>
> Her name is Claire Beaumont.

15. EXT. OFFICE OF BEN WINSTON PRODUCTIONS. DAY.   15.

WINSTON
(VO. Continuing)

She's currently in a coma, due to
having been struck by a car two
days ago. The prognosis for her
recovery isn't good.

16. INT. OFFICE OF THE BEN WINSTON. DAY.   16.

The man, whose voice we heard over the previous scene, is speaking to another
man seated across the room. The man who is speaking is BEN WINSTON, a
wealthy looking man in his mid-fifties. Winston is obviously a man who is
used to having his own way. The man he is speaking to is Matt Taylor, who
we saw earlier. For the first time we are able to have a good look at Matt. Matt
is a ruggedly handsome man with intelligent eyes. Everything about him projects the fact that he is a leader. Seated near Winston is a frail looking man in
his late twenties who has the bland corporate look of an accountant. The name
of this "accountant" is BRIAN HOLLIS.

WINSTON
(Continuing)

Beaumont is a research assistant for
the Ghost Quest television series,
which is produced by my company.
I assume you've seen it.

MATT
(Unimpressed)

Once or twice. For a show that's
supposedly about the paranormal,
you spend a lot of time talking
about Elvis. Your show trivializes
paranormal investigation.

WINSTON

TV's all about numbers. And numbers are why I have three shows in
the top ten.

MATT
(Impatiently)

That's all fine and good, but why
did you want to see me?

WINSTON

Ms. Beaumont was one of the members of my staff putting together a
segment on the Bloodworth House.
Have you heard of it?

MATT

I know the stories. None of which
are authenticated, though.

                    HOLLIS

Once we'd filmed our segment on
the house that would have changed.
The network planned to show it
during sweeps week so it figured to
be a ratings blockbuster.

Matt glares at Hollis, obviously wondering who the little upstart is.

                    WINSTON

This is Brian Hollis, an associate
producer on the show. Four of my
people were doing a preliminary
investigation of the Bloodworth
House the night before last. A
writer, a director, Ms. Beaumont,
and my daughter Ashley, who is one
of the producers. Other than Ms.
Beaumont, none of them have been
seen since.

                    HOLLIS

The local police were notified
immediately but ... I guess they
think it's some kind of publicity
stunt because they're just going
through the motions.

                    MATT

You still haven't answered my question. Why am I here?

                    WINSTON

Ask anyone who's the best atpara-
normal investigation and the
answer's always the Shadow Squad.
I need you and your team to
findout what happened to my
daughter. If she's alive I want her
back, if not ... I need to know why?

                    HOLLIS

We don't know what we're dealing
with and we're not equipped to find
out, but you are. We're willing to
pay whatever you want to secure
your services.

                    MATT
                  (Quietly)

    I see.

Matt gives Hollis a cold stare.

MATT

My services aren't for hire. If you
knew anything about me you'd
know that.

HOLLIS
(Smugly)

I do, but then again ... I'm a great
believer in the old expression
"Everyone has a price." Mister Taylor, what's yours?

MATT
(Indignant)

You just said the wrong thing, Hollis.

Matt gets up to leave. As Matt heads for the door, Winston becomes desperate.

WINSTON
(Urgently)

Mister Taylor! If you've got a problem with Hollis or my show then
take it out on me, not my little girl.

MATT
(Firmly)

I appreciate your situation, butI'm
not interested in —

WINSTON
(Interrupting. Pleading)

Mister Taylor, I'm going to say
something that I've never said
before.... Please.

Matt debates whether or not he should help. This is not an easy decision for
him. He sighs and gives in.

MATT
(To Winston)

You'll have to fix things with the
police. My team isn't doing some
jail time because we messed around
in an open case.

WINSTON

It'll be taken care of.

MATT

And I'll need all the information
you have on the missing people.

WINSTON

Anything else?

MATT

Yeah, I want Hollis to be there with us. If something bad happens, I want him on the front lines.

Matt exits and Hollis reacts, shocked by what he has just gotten into.

Let's start with the title. The title *Shadow Squad* tells us that we are dealing with a team who combats things that are dark and probably mysterious. It also lets us know that this is most likely a horror movie about a team who deals with shadowy forces. This is exactly what we want — a catchy title that explains the genre and premise.

There are two ways to start a movie with a fantastic premise. One way is to start off with something visually impressive so that the audience is dazzled. The other way is to subtly manipulate the audience into believing that the impossible is actually possible. Shadow Squad falls into the second category. As its screenwriter, I felt that it would help a supernatural horror film like Shadow Squad to start with some semblance of reality. This would seduce the audience into believing that what they are watching could really happen. Then, bit by bit, things could become more fanciful until a monster in a haunted house would seem plausible.

In scenes 1 and 2 we are introduced to Riley Cohen in a manner that sets up both the genre and premise of the movie. Given that a serial killer is on the loose, we know that Riley could be in danger. Riley is heading somewhere specific yet seems confused. Why? What's going on? One page into the script and we find ourselves already wondering what's going to happen next.

In scenes 3 and 4 everything around Riley seems dangerous, thereby helping generate additional suspense, which is mandatory in a horror film.

In scenes 4 through 7 Riley is put in even greater danger. We know something bad is going to happen at any moment. The audience should be yelling at the screen, "Don't go in there!" The suspense keeps building and building.

In scene 8 we are also introduced to Matt Taylor, who will prove important to our story. The fact that there is conflict between Matt and the undercover cops also helps create a greater sense of drama. Also, the cops ignoring Matt's advice helps motivate his annoyance for Hollis, who demonstrates a similar a lack of respect later in Winston's office.

In scenes 8 through 11 the dramatic tension builds to a peak. When Matt and Riley stop the serial killer, it establishes how capable they are as well as their overall importance to the story.

In scenes 13 and 14 the screenplay becomes a bit more fanciful. These scenes also set up the main storyline of our movie.

Scenes 15 and 16 give us our exposition while also establishing the conflict between Matt and Hollis, which heightens the drama.

And so, via these opening scenes, we have established our movie's premise and presented our major characters while also whetting the appetite of our audience.

Let's consider the locations and sets for a minute. Could a filmmaker with little money afford them? It's easy. The exterior locations for the opening scenes are just city streets and alleys, and, as such, are easily accessible for a low-budget filmmaker. The warehouse interior could be a little more difficult to get ahold of, but, given the fact that it is supposed to be dark inside, you could use any large dark room in its place. The office of Mister Winston could easily be borrowed from any businessperson willing to loan you their office in order to see their name in your movie.

And now, from the fantasy-horror of the previous script we will jump to a new screenplay sample whose genre is science fiction/action, a genre considered to be the opposite of the genre we have just sampled.

STAR FORCE
Screenplay By
Philip R. Cable

1. EXT. OUTER SPACE.   1.

We can see a starship in the distance. From the design of the ship, it is obviously a military craft.

WE EMPHASIZE A WINDOW OF THE STARSHIP.

Someone is staring out the window. Someone grotesque and unearthly.

2. INT. STARSHIP CONFINMENT ROOM.   2.

The very large, grotesque alien turns away from the window and looks at the other two prisoners. One is another alien with blue skin wearing a high-tech helmet. The third prisoner is a beautiful (and human looking) woman dressed in a form-fitting, rust-colored uniform that is vaguely militaristic. The woman is using a sliver of metal to pry open the lock of the helmet worn by the blue-skinned alien. There's a click, and the lock pops open.

As the helmet is removed, the grotesque alien checks the door of the cell to see if anyone is in the corridor outside. No one is there.

The woman studies the wall next to the cell door for a moment. She motions for the blue alien to pay attention to a specific spot. The blue alien concentrates, and a bolt of psychic energy shoots from his eyes into the control panel. It explodes, exposing some wiring. The woman reaches inside and fiddles with the wiring. There's a whoosh, and the cell door is now unlocked. The grotesque alien tugs at the door until it opens a crack. He then forces it open wide enough for all three of them to rush out!

3. INT. STARSHIP CORRIDOR. 3.

The woman directs the other two down the corridor. She obviously has a plan, knows exactly where she's going and how to get there.

Abruptly some starship crewmembers race around a corner. The crewmembers see them and quickly draw and aim their laser pistols at them.

The grotesque alien is hit in the shoulder.

The blue alien concentrates and shoots a bolt from his eyes that hurls one of the crewmembers twenty feet away.

The other crewmember fires and hits the blue alien in the chest, dropping him to the floor! The woman instinctively reaches for the blue alien, but the grotesque alien stops her, then starts running down the corridor. Reluctantly the woman follows him.

The crewmember starts after them.

The dying blue alien forces himself to concentrate and hurls one final psychic bolt that explodes the crewmember's laser pistol and kills the crewmember.

The blue alien gasps, his head drops, and he dies.

4. INT. ENGINE ROOM. 4.

The two escaped prisoners quickly run into the Engine Room. The Engine Room is huge, with gigantic turbines used to help power the ship.

The escaped prisoners start running for the exit but find themselves chased by more crewmembers. Then additional crewmembers appear in front of them! The crewmembers blocking their way try to grab the prisoners, and a frantic fight starts.

Amazingly, the woman and the grotesque alien hold their own against superior odds. The woman throws off her attacker, hurling him hard to the floor and knocking him out.

The grotesque alien slams the heads of two crewmembers together, but another crewmember jumps on him from behind. The woman pulls the crewmember off the grotesque alien, then throws him over her shoulder. He holds tight onto her and they trade punches, but the woman delivers a savage kick to the crewmember's head, which ends the fight.

The escaped prisoners then race across the Engine Room, searching for a specific exit. They are unsure of its location at first, but then the woman sees it. They both race into the corridor beyond.

5. INT. CORRIDOR. 5.

The escaped prisoners rush down the corridor. They pause at the end of the corridor to enter the Computer Room.

6. INT. COMPUTER ROOM. 6.

The grotesque alien stands guard at the door while the woman rushes to a computer and types in some commands on the keyboard.

The monitor comes up, and planets suddenly appear on the screen. The woman looks for a specific world and, upon seeing the Earth, zooms in on it. More commands are typed, and a computer disc pops out of the computer.

As she shoves the disc into her pocket, the grotesque alien opens the Computer Room door.

Suddenly a monstrously large robotic arm reaches into the archway and grabs the grotesque alien by the throat! The grotesque alien's throat is effortlessly crushed! The grotesque alien is then tossed aside, and into the doorway steps a seven-foot robot aiming a laser pistol at the woman. Before it can fire, she dodges aside and jumps past the robot into the corridor!

7. INT. CORRIDOR.   7.

The woman tucks and rolls, then runs as fast as she can down the corridor toward the stairs.

The robot fires at her but misses because the woman quickly dives into a stairway.

8. INT. STAIRS.   8.

The woman races down the stairs but unexpectedly runs into a crewmember. The crewmember is young and rather immature in appearance, but is very determined to stop her. He takes a swing at her, but she blocks the punch and kicks him away. The crewmember slams hard onto the floor, but he quickly gets back up and chases after the woman.

The woman darts through a side door.

9. INT ESCAPE HATCH.   9.

The woman locks the door, then quickly hops onto a platform with a chair attached to it. She buckles herself in, then pushes a button on the console in the right arm of the chair. Immediately the chair is enveloped in a glowing red ball of energy. She then inserts the computer disc into the control console and types a launch sequence on the small keyboard.

10. INT. CORIDOR.   10.

The crewmember who fought with the woman on the stairs tries to enter the escape hatch but finds it locked. He tries to open it, but in vain. He tries to figure out what he should do next, then gets an idea. He runs back toward the computer room.

11. INT. ESCAPE HATCH.   11.

A section of the ceiling spirals open.

The "energy pod" whines with growing power, then the console on the arm of the chair flashes a yellow light. The woman pushes a launch button.

The energy pod shoots through the open hatch with lightning speed!

12. EXT. STARSHIP.   12.

The energy pod streaks away from the starship and soars into the distance, picking up speed with each moment!

13. INT. STARSHIP BRIDGE.   13.

A crewmember detects the energy pod on his sensor. His superior, COMMANDER MANOC, is also watching this. Commander Manoc is an impressive looking man in his late thirties. He has the physique of an athlete, yet projects the quiet intelligence of a leader.

COMMANDER MANOC
(Urgently)

Stop her before she goes into hyper-
drive!

The crewmember adjusts his controls on his console and gets the energy pod in his sights. He gets ready to fire.

14. INT. ENERGY POD.   14.

The woman is sweating bullets. She is well aware that she is a sitting duck. She looks down at her console. It's still flashing a yellow light. All of a sudden, it starts flashing a green light.

15. EXT. STARSHIP.   15.

The starship fires a laser beam at the energy pod!

16. INT. ENERGY POD.   16.

The woman urgently hits another button.

17. EXT. SPACE.   17.

The energy pod suddenly shoots across space at a faster-than-light speed, causing the laser beam to narrowly miss it.

18. EXT. DIFFERENT AREA OF SPACE.   18.

The energy pod flies faster and faster as it flies through our solar system.

19. INT. COMPUTER ROOM.   19.

The crewmember who was pounding on the escape hatch door rushes into the Computer Room and scans the records on the computer. He urgently types in a command.

On the screen appears a shot of the Earth.

Now the crewmember knows where the woman is going.

20. EXT. SPACE.   20.

The energy pod heads straight toward Earth.

21. EXT. EARTH'S ATMOSPHERE. NIGHT.   21.

The energy pod arcs in its course and heads toward the West Coast of America. It arcs again and heads for Central California.

22. EXT. WOODS. NIGHT.   22.

The energy pod slows down, then lands gently near some dead bushes.

The bubble of pulsing energy dissipates, and the woman gets out of the chair.

She quickly scans her surroundings and starts gathering bushes with which to cover the energy pod.

23. INT.STARSHIP. ADMIRAL'S CABIN.   23.

The crewmember we saw earlier in the Computer Room, along with Commander Manoc, are both facing an impressive alien military leader called ADMIRAL XON who is seated behind a desk. The tension is so thick you can taste it. The source of this tension is Xon, a heavyset bald man in his late fifties who has weary features. Xon looks briefly at both men, as if sizing them up.

XON
(Quietly upset)

So she managed to get away.

Commander Manoc and the crewmember glance at one another nervously. The situation is dangerous, and they know it.

CREWMEMBER
(Scared)

But, at least, we know where she's
headed.

MANOC
(To Admiral)

Do you want us to track her down?

XON

No. Call in an expert to do that.
Make sure that he has whatever
he needs. Technology, memory
implants, everything.

The crewmember and Commander Manoc start to leave, only to halt when they hear —

XON

It wouldn't be wise to fail again.

The Commander and the crewmember nod, then exit as Admiral Xon presses an intercom button on his desk console. There's a beep from the intercom.

ANOTHER CREWMAN
(V.O.)

Yes sir.

XON
(Meaningfully)

Connect me with Division Tachyon
of High Command.

24. INT. STARSHIP CORRIDOR.   24.

Both men walk down the corridor as if their lives depend on it ... which they do.

MANOC

We have an observation team on
that planet, don't we?

CREWMEMBER

We should. We do just about every-
where else.

MANOC
(Importantly)

Contact them.

They come to a corner, and each man heads in a different direction.

25. INT. A CAR. DAY. 25.

Sitting in the passenger's seat of a sports car is the woman who escaped from the spaceship. Her name is RAYNA, a lovely dark-haired woman of about 27 with a nice figure. Despite her stunning looks, she somehow projects a haunted quality. The car is being driven by a well-dressed man in his fifties. The man checks his speedometer, and it clocks the sports car at 80 miles per hour.

26. EXT. A COUNTRY ROAD. DAY. 25.

The quiet of the country road is interrupted by the sound of the onrushing sports car. It roars down the country road and disappears into the distance.

27. INT. THE CAR. DAY. 27.

Rayna seems indifferent to the high speed of the car. She wearily tries to relax but is unable to.

The driver glances at Rayna's shapely legs, then quickly looks straight ahead. A couple of seconds later he glances at her ample bosom and again looks quickly ahead. A couple of more second pass, then once again he glances at her and notices that there's some discoloring on the shoulder of her jumpsuit where a patch or emblem has been torn off.

Rayna realizes that he's looking at her and covers the discolored spot with her hand.

The driver sees her concerned reaction, so he quits his staring and looks back at the road.

Rayna becomes nervous, and her eyes dart around, as if looking for something. She catches sight of an upcoming crossroad and points it out to the driver.

RAYNA
(Urgently)

There's good.

The driver gives her a surprised look, then shrugs and turns the steering wheel to the right.

28. EXT. A CROSSROAD. DAY. 28.

The car slows and comes to a stop at the crossroad. Rayna quickly gets out. The driver leans toward her.

DRIVER

It's kinda lousy spot to hitch a ride. You're right in the middle of a whole lot of nowhere. You sure you don't want me to drop ya off a little closer to town?

She shakes her head. The driver sighs in defeat, starts up his engine and drives off.

Rayna studies the roads as she tries to decide which road to take. By her reaction, we can tell that this is an extremely important choice. She selects the road heading north and starts her long walk.

29. EXT. A DIRT ROAD. DAY.   29.

A bland-looking dark car drives up and parks on the side of the road. Three dark-suited and officious-looking men get out of the car and look around. From the way they are acting, we can tell that they are waiting for something, or someone, very important.

The first officious man looks across the road to the empty field beyond. There is nothing in the field for at least a mile. He looks at the trees on the opposite side of the road, and again there is no one.

The man reacts a little impatiently and looks back at the empty field he looked at earlier. Unexpectedly, there is now a man in a black leather trench coat standing there. The other two men realize that someone is in the field and also look at him.

The man in the field stares at them as if sizing them up. Each man waits for one of the other men to do something. None of them do.

The man across the street walks toward the three men.

The three men react with growing apprehension.

Each of the men takes something out of his pocket and places it on the hood of the car. One object appears to be a photograph of the woman they are searching for. Another is a small device about the size of a cell phone, with a large button on it. There is also a small crystal, approximately the size of a marble.

The man, who we will call the Slayer, crosses to the car and examines each item with a professional demeanor.

SLAYER
(Indifferently)

Number 1?

Number One steps forward obediently.

NUMBER 1

Sir?

The Slayer casually turns around and aims the cell phone–like device at Number One. A bolt of energy is fired from the device, which violently hits Number One in the chest! Number One reacts dumbfounded at first, then falls to his knees, dying. In shock, he painfully looks up at the Slayer, trying to fathom why this has just happened.

SLAYER

That's a personal message from
High Command.

Number One slumps to the ground dead.

The second and third dark-suited men are shocked by what has just happened. They are confused as what they should do, if anything.

The third man cautiously kneels beside the body of Number One and checks him for any sign of life. There isn't any. Number Three looks up at the Slayer, utterly confused.

NUMBER 3
(Bewildered)

What did he do?

SLAYER
(Indifferently)

I have no idea.

The Slayer returns to studying the three items. He looks at the photograph and touches a button on the frame. Alien writing shoots across the picture as if it were a computer screen.

The two officious men step up and look at the photo over the Slayer's shoulder.

NUMBER 2

We've estimated her arrival as two
and a half hours ago. She's probably
trying to—

SLAYER

I know why she's here.

Number Three leans in a little closer and stares at the photo in the Slayer's hands. Number three is very impressed by what he sees.

NUMBER 3

She's pretty. Too bad you have to
kill her.

The Slayer glares at Number Three briefly. Number Three becomes uncomfortable and quickly backs off, leaving the Slayer alone. The Slayer continues his work but this time takes note of the "pretty" woman's face. The pretty woman is Rayna.

30. EXT. SIDE ROAD. DAY.   30.

Rayna is a mile or so into her long walk on the road. With every step she becomes more and more lost in thought. Very deep and very personal thoughts.

RAYNA
(V.O.)

Sometimes you have to go even
when the logical thing to do is to
stay put. When you're young, the
idea of being a soldier sounds
vaguely romantic, but nine years on
the front line paints a different picture. A portrait colored blood red

and rubble gray without the confusion of black and white. Like everyone else, I'd heard the rumors of
people escaping to some world outside of Imperial rule. Of new iden-
tities ... better lives. At first I tried
to ignore the stories, but I couldn't.
So I ran; and now I'm here and I
don't really know why I did it ...
except that when you live in a
nightmare all you have left are your
dreams. If I've guessed right, this
road might lead me to my dream ...
but I don't hold out much hope for
that, though. Hope is a luxury I
gave up a long time ago. But you
never know, sometimes you get
lucky.

Once again, let's start with the title. *Star Force* is simple and easy to
remember. The "Star" portion of the title tells us that this is a science fiction
movie, while the word "Force" suggests some sort of violence or action is
involved. The title *Star Force* also conjures up an image of an extraterrestrial
military. All of these elements work well together, explaining to the audience
that the movie they can expect is a science fiction/action film.

Unlike with the horror movie, opening your movie in a visually impressive manner can work well for a science fiction film. For example, the opening in *Star Wars* has a small starship attacked by a huge battleship. This
establishes the movie's production values as well as catching the attention of
the audience.

There was a wonderful director by the name of William Witney who
once stated that movie serials were based on the following idea: "In a door,
into a fight. Out a door, into a chase." Action films follow the same formula
as serials. The hero chases after something or someone, or the villain chases
after the hero or something, or a mixture of the two takes place. One way or
another, an action film is a chase movie livened by ongoing physical battles.

In scenes 1 through 22 we establish the pace for the movie. Frantic action
and danger keeps building until Rayna manages to escape her captors.

Are you thinking that the spaceship interiors are too expensive for a low-
budget movie? If so, you lack imagination. I will discuss how to build a spaceship interior in point 39; but until we get to that point, let's consider the
following. This is not an Earth rocket or space shuttle, so it can look any way
you want it to. Get a few flats and make a short corridor. Paint it black and
put some flashing lights and alien-looking symbols on it, and *Alakazam*, you

have a spaceship interior! A spaceship doesn't have to be brightly lit, so adjust your contrast and lower the brightness in post-production, and the walls will seem dark and scary. Want to enhance your corridor? Position a paper cutout of a large spaceship corridor in front of the camera lens. A wide-angle lens could make that paper cutout look like it's part of the set. Do some tests. You'd be surprised at how effective this can be.

As for the space footage in scenes 1, 12, 15, 17, 18, 20, and 21; they could be accomplished in a variety of cost-effective ways. One is to make a deal with a computer technician to do a little computer animation for you. There are tons of them in computer classes and film schools all over the world. It's amazing how much can be done on a simple home computer when the footage doesn't last very long. After all, let's remember what we are talking about. The background of outer space is black with pinpricks of light scattered about. That's easy to reproduce. The spaceship exterior would take the most time to animate, but since it is seen in only a few shots it wouldn't be too difficult to produce. The shots of the energy pod is just a ball of light and could easily be created on a computer. These effects, while impressive to look at, are not that difficult to do. If you don't have enough money to pay the technician, then offer that technician a percentage of your movie. Another possibility is to use stock footage. There are hours of NASA footage you could use, some of which employ high-tech–looking spaceships. Or perhaps you could use stock footage of space and place computer animation on top of it. There is, of course, the old-fashioned method of doing the special effects yourself. This isn't as hard as it may sound. First, build a miniature of a space ship, or have one made by a good model builder. This can be done relatively cheaply by buying a lot of model kits and gluing them together in a creative way to form a completely new model. Next, find a room that you can paint black or cover with black cloth. Buy a lot of LED lights and place them on the walls to simulate stars. Then hang the spaceship miniature from the ceiling with a black thread or thin monofilament used for fishing. Now you have your spaceship. All the laser beams or energy pod footage could be added later by using video effects or cheap computer animation.

In scene 23 Rayna reaches her destination and our opening action sequence ends. At this point, the audience is wondering who Rayna is and therefore can't help but be involved in the story. Is she a criminal? Who are her captors?

In scene 24 the plot of our movie gets underway. We start to understand that Rayna is very important to her captors for some reason. The quiet threat inherent in the scene also suggests that Rayna's captors are potentially dangerous. From a production standpoint, opening our script in outer space has set the tone for our film. The science fiction basis for the movie has been established, whether or not any future scenes take place aboard the spaceship.

In scenes 25 through 28 we establish that Rayna is more than just an expert in hand-to-hand combat. She is also a very desirable woman. More to the point, it is established that she has a destination in mind. The question is—where? And why is she headed there? Since these, and subsequent scenes, are set on Earth, the budget is much easier to manage, making the rest of the production simpler and cheaper.

In scene 29 we introduce the Slayer. Through his introduction we establish that this will be a chase movie, with the Slayer tracking down Rayna. We also establish that he is very dangerous and unquestioning of his mission.

In scene 30 we learn who Rayna is and why she is running. The premise of *Star Force* is now firmly established, and we are now ready to be entertained by all the subsequent action that scenes 1 through 30 have led us to expect.

And so we accomplish our goal as a screenwriter: to create an opening for our movie that hooks our audience right away, while also establishing our premise and our principal characters quickly. This allows us to get deeply into our story with no wasted time.

Literary Sources for Scripts

How commercial your screenplay is will prove to be very important once it is made into a movie and sold throughout the international marketplace. One thing you can do to enhance the commercial aspects of your script is to base it on an existing literary property or character. Since you are making a low-budget movie, such an idea would seem impractical at first. However, there are many public domain books and stories available to you. If the books and stories themselves don't interest you, then one or more of the characters from those books and stories may inspire a story for you. Interestingly, a number of comic book superheroes from the nineteen-forties are now in the public domain.

If you want to make a horror movie then you might want to consider adapting one of the classic public domain stories written by the masters of horror: Edgar Allan Poe or H.P. Lovecraft. Such adaptations have proven to be very profitable. Edgar Allan Poe's tales and poetry can easily be found in your local library or on the Internet. I have included here a short list of stories by H.P. Lovecraft. The copyright status of much of Lovecraft's work has been in dispute for years; however, the stories listed below are understood to be in the public domain, and, as such, you may do as you wish with them.

Stories by H.P. Lovecraft (in chronological order)

"The Beast in the Cave" (1905)

"The Alchemist" (1908)

"A Reminiscence of Dr. Samuel Johnson" (1917)

"Dagon" (1917)

"The Tomb" (1917)

"Polaris" (1918)

"Beyond the Wall of Sleep" (1919)

"Memory" (1919)

"The White Ship" (1919)

"The Statement of Randolph Carter" (1919)

"The Doom That Came to Sarnath" (1919)

"Poetry and the Gods" (1920)

"The Cats of Ulthar" (1920)

"Nyarlathotep" (1920)

"The Street" (1920)

"Facts Concerning the Late Arthur Jermyn and His Family" (1920)

"The Terrible Old Man" (1920)

"The Picture in the House" (1920)

"The Tree" (1920)

"Celephaïs" (1920)

"Ex Oblivione" (1920/21)

"The Crawling Chaos" (1921)

"Herbert West–Reanimator" (1921)

"The Music of Erich Zann" (1921)

"Hypnos" (1922)

"What the Moon Brings" (1922)

"Azathoth" (1922)

"The Horror at Martin's Beach" (1922)

"The Hound" (1922)

"The Lurking Fear" (1922)

Not interested in horror? Fine. Luckily, there are thousands of public domain stories and books, in a wide variety of genres, to draw upon. The works of Lovecraft listed here represent only a very tiny portion of the popular genre–related public domain stories available for adaptation. Check your library and you will find a wealth of literary works waiting for you to turn into a screenplay.

Perhaps you aren't interested in a public domain story as much as you are interested in a character from that story. Okay, build a new story centered on that character. The following is a list of well-known literary characters, or characters from history or legend, who are not under copyright.

Public Domain Characters

Aladdin

Ali Baba

Alice (from the novel Alice's Adventures in Wonderland)

Allan Quatermain

Arabian Nights characters

Baby New Year

Biblical heroes and villains

Big Bad Wolf

Bigfoot

Black Beauty

Captain Nemo

Cinderella

Count Orlok (from the German film *Nosferatu*)

Doctor Dolittle

Doctor Jekyll and Mister Hyde

Don Quixote

Dorian Gray

Dracula

Easter Bunny
Ebenezer Scrooge
Fairy tale stock characters
Frankenstein's monster
Frog Prince
Golem (the man of clay)
Green Knight (fairy tale)
Grimm's Fairy Tales characters
Guinevere
Gulliver (from *Gulliver's Travels*)
Hansel and Gretel
Heidi
Hercules
Huckleberry Finn
Hunchback of Notre Dame
Ivanhoe
Jack and the Beanstalk
Jack Frost
Jack the Giant Killer
Jane Eyre (character)
King Arthur
Knights of the Round Table
The Little Mermaid
Little Red Riding Hood
Long John Silver
Merlin the Magician
Moby-Dick
Morgan le Fay (a.k.a. Morgana le Fey)
Mother Nature
Mowgli
Mythological characters from Greek mythology
Pinocchio
Prince Charming
Puss in Boots (fairy tale)
Rapunzel
Rebecca of Sunnybrook Farm
Rima the Jungle Girl (from the novel *Green Mansions: A Romance of the Tropical Forest*)
Robin Hood
Robinson Crusoe
Santa Claus
The Scarlet Pimpernel
Shakespearean characters
She (from the novel *She*)
Sinbad the sailor
Sleeping Beauty
Snow White
Thumbelina
Tom Sawyer
Tom Thumb
Tooth Fairy
Rip Van Winkle
Ulysses
Victor Frankenstein
The Wonderful Wizard of Oz

Public Domain Comic Book Superheroes

Airboy
Airman
Amazing Man
Doc Strange
Dynamo (from Fox Feature comics)
The Face
The Flame
Green Mask
Golden Arrow
Lady Justice
Lady Luck
Madame Fatale
Master Man
Miss Victory
Shock Gibson
The Targeteers

An excellent source for public domain books is Authorama-Public Domain Books, which has a great many free online books. Their internet website is: http://www.authorama.com/.

If you choose to make use of a preexisting story or character, I strongly suggest you ascertain the current copyright, or trademark, status of that story and/or character by checking with the Library of Congress.

Script Coverage

Once your screenplay is written, you may want to have its level of professionalism evaluated. There are companies who provide such a service. This script analysis is called script coverage. The price for this service varies from company to company, ranging from $75.00 to $500.00 dollars. The average price is about a dollar per page. The script analysis will detail the strengths and weaknesses of your screenplay, and, in doing so, give you a good idea of what you will need to do during your rewrite, assuming one is necessary.

Some script coverage companies are listed in Appendix A.

Please note that before you do business with any company on this list, or any other company listed in this book, do your homework and check out the company thoroughly. Nothing in this world remains the same. Addresses or phone numbers may change, company executives may be replaced, quality control may diminish, companies may even go out of business. Make certain that the company you deal with is the best possible company for your needs before you enter into any sort of business arrangement with them.

The value of coverage notwithstanding, let's not get too far ahead of ourselves. There's lots more to learn about writing before coverage can even be considered. First, let's delve into plot construction and how to do it properly.

23. PLOT STRUCTURE THAT WORKS

Somewhere along the line I developed the reputation of being able to write a good screenplay very fast. Generally, this is true. You see, making a movie is a bit like doing something in the army. Everything is "Hurry up and wait." Far too often, script writing is the "hurry up" portion of that process. The good and bad of that notwithstanding, I had to develop a means of writing a properly structured story quickly in order to make a living. How did I do this? By observation and deduction.

I happen to love reading. Books, stories, plays, just about anything. One day I realized that many great motion pictures scripts, as well as classic novels, had exactly the same plot structure. I wrote down this structure and discovered that I could then create my story plots much more rapidly because I now had a roadmap to proper story construction.

When you are structuring the plot for your script, try the following formula.

1. *An obvious problem arises.* It is important that the problem be established quickly so the audience can become emotionally involved in the plot from the start. It is equally important that the problem be sufficiently evident that everyone can understand its importance.
2. *Protagonist gets involved in the problem.* It is important that the protagonist has a stake in the resolution of the problem.
3. *The problem gets more complicated.* New twists and turns take place, making the resolution of the problem much more difficult.
4. *Protagonist has difficulty in trying to resolve problem.* The protagonist finds that the problem is extremely hard and complicated) to deal with.
5. *Protagonist gets into danger.* Something happens that endangers either the protagonist or the protagonist's goal.
6. *Protagonist gets out of danger.* The protagonist is able to resolve the immediate danger.
7. *Problem gets even worse.* Things get even more complicated, making it harder for the protagonist to resolve the overall problem.
8. *Protagonist gets into new danger.* Something even more dangerous happens, endangering the protagonist or the protagonist's goal.
9. *Protagonist gets out of new danger.* The protagonist resolves the new immediate danger.
10. *Problem advances to the point where it appears impossible to resolve.* Things become so difficult that it seem impossible for the protagonist to resolve the problem.
11. *Protagonist resolves problem.* The protagonist overcomes all the lesser problems and then resolves the main problem. Let's try out three seemingly different plots, using this formula, to see how well it works. First, we will try an action story, then a love story, and we'll end with a horror story.

Cool Million

1. Infamous criminal Derek Bain has stolen the prototype of a new super-weapon which can immobilize all technology. With such a weapon a handful of soldiers could destroy an army. He plans to sell this weapon to terrorists, but for the next two days he's going to hide out on New Hades. New Hades is an island whose territorial jurisdiction is in doubt. Because of this, criminals have flocked

to it and formed a city. The United States government has 48 hours to recover the weapon before Bain leaves the island and delivers it to the terrorists.

2. Due to an issue of jurisdiction, the government turns to a trouble-shooter named Kent Wilder for help. Kent, a champion martial artist and computer expert, was once a top government agent before retiring. The government hires Kent to retrieve the proto-type weapon for one million dollars.

3. Bain has the super-weapon taken from him by the big boss of New Hades, former syndicate kingpin Paul Martin. Martin places the weapon in the secret vault where he stores all his treasures. Martin then contacts the terrorist group, informing them that they are going to have to deal with him from now on.

4. Kent finds that it's just about impossible to reach the island without being seen by guards. He tries to hire a boat to approach it by night, but no one will go anywhere near it for fear of being killed. Eventually he finds one old sailor with a decrepit sailboat who is willing to take a gamble. He agrees to take Kent within ten miles of the shore of the island. Kent will have to swim the rest of the way. Kent doesn't know if he can accomplish his mission after the strain of such a long swim, but it's his only chance. At midnight Kent is taken ten miles off the New Hades shore. He puts on a "special" black skin diver's suit and gets ready to swim. Knowing that weight is his enemy during such a long swim, he only takes with him a small waterproof bag containing a knife and a pistol.

5. He swims to the shore and collapses on the beach, completely exhausted. As he catches his breath, Kent hears a sound in the distance. The sound of growling guard dogs! He forces himself to run but finds himself facing a sentry. He's trapped!

6. Kent begins to fight the sentry, then throws him into the guard dogs as he runs off. Kent makes his way into town, trying not to be noticed. Eventually he is able to get past the other sentries as he tries to locate Bain.

7. He discovers that Bain has been killed by Paul Martin. Kent has no idea what to do next. Suddenly, sirens are heard. He's been seen. The entire town is now searching for him! He eludes capture for a while but ultimately is caught.

8. Kent is taken before Paul Martin, who decides that Kent should be publicly executed. Kent is placed before a brick wall, and a firing squad aims their rifles at him!

9. The firing squad fires, and Kent crumples as the bullets hit him. Two guards take his body away and dig a grave for Kent. Abruptly, Kent jumps up and knocks both of them out. His "special" swimsuit is

made of a bulletproof Kevlar, which saved him from the impact of the bullets.

10. The terrorists arrive on the island to negotiate with Martin. He agrees to sell them the prototype for twice the price Bain wanted. They reluctantly agree to his terms. Once Martin is certain that his money has been transferred into his Swiss bank account he will then turn over the prototype. The transaction should be completed within fifteen minutes. The two unconscious gravediggers are discovered, and an alarm is sounded. The entire town is looking for Kent. Kent eludes them until he discovers two terrorists waiting outside Martin's office. He overhears one of them talking and learns that they will have the weapon in a matter of minutes. How can Kent possibly complete his mission?

11. Kent knocks out a terrorist and dresses in his clothes. Disguised as a terrorist, he makes his way past some guards and inside Martin's office. The money is transferred, and Martin opens his safe. The terrorists are about to take the prototype when Kent breaks in and steals the prototype. He leaps out the window, and the entire town starts chasing after him. He hops into a car, hot-wires it, and races toward the shore. Kent figures out how to turn on the prototype and aims it at those who are chasing him. Suddenly all their cars stop working. Kent makes it to the dock and tries to purloin a boat. Unexpectedly, Martin shows up and attacks him. Martin's men are only a minute behind him on foot. There's a terrific fight, which ends with Martin pulling his gun. Kent aims the prototype at Martin, and they both fire at the same time. Martin's gun explodes! As Martin screams in pain, Kent speeds off in the boat just as Martin's men show up. Kent, having completed his mission just in time, heads toward the mainland to return the prototype to the government and collect his million dollars.

Lost Love

1. Ally Evans is a successful executive in an advertising agency who feels that life is passing her by. At age 28 she has achieved pretty much everything in her career that she has ever wanted. Oddly, she now finds herself looking back on the things that she left behind in order to achieve her professional success. Unexpectedly, she gets a call from a high school friend who asks if Ally is coming to the class reunion next week. Ally isn't interested in attending until she learns that Matt Stevens has just gotten engaged. Ally grew up next door to Matt in a small town in Ohio. She loved him dearly and was even engaged to him at one point. Unfortunately, when she

was offered a job in New York they had a fight and broke up. Somehow, Ally always believed that she and Matt would end up together. Now she has lost him forever. Or has she?

2. Ally pretends to be sick so she can take time away from the important account that she's been working on. Ally then heads back to her home town to win Matt back. When she arrives, she is shocked to learn that Matt is engaged to Candy Wells. Candy was Ally's rival in high school. Candy is also a gold digger who has been married twice to wealthy old men.

3. Ally tries to reconcile with Matt. Matt still has feelings for Ally, but he refuses to hurt Candy, who acts devoted to him. Candy, suspecting that Ally might be trying to break up her engagement, convinces Matt to marry her right after the class reunion.

4. Ally wants to talk to Matt, but he constantly avoids her. Ally orchestrates a scenario in which she and Matt will "accidentally" bump into one another at the same restaurant, the one where Matt first proposed to her. She's hoping the location will bring back memories of better times.

5. Ally's plan seems to work. She bumps into Matt at the restaurant, and before they know it they are talking about the good old days. Matt nearly succumbs to the romance and nostalgia of the situation but soon realizes that Ally is manipulating him. He leaves the restaurant, angrily saying that he never wants to see her again.

6. Ally apologizes to Matt and offers to use her ad agency connections to arrange a free Hawaiian honeymoon for him and Candy if he'll forgive her. Matt agrees, but Candy is dubious.

7. As Ally arranges the details of the honeymoon with Matt, Matt breaks down and admits that he doesn't love Candy. Despite this, he still can't break up with Candy because she's pregnant with his baby. Ally is devastated by the news. She begins to wonder if she should keep trying to win Matt back. A little later Ally learns from a friend that Matt owns some land on which a local developer may want to build a mall. Ally suspects that Candy is only marrying Matt to get her hands on the money he might make off the sale of his land.

8. Candy doesn't trust Ally, so she contacts Ally's advertising agency and, upon learning that Ally is on sick leave, tells her bosses that Ally isn't sick. Ally's employers phone her and order her to come back to New York and finish her work on the account. If she isn't there by tomorrow morning, she will be fired. Ally faces a terrible dilemma. If she leaves, she will lose Matt. If she stays, she will lose everything she worked so hard to achieve.

9. Ally checks with her secretary and learns that it was Candy who called her superiors. Ally gets an idea and has her secretary check

her work history file. The secretary finds out that Ally hasn't taken a vacation in four years and has acquired over a month in accumulated vacation time. Ally then calls her lawyer and tells him to threaten to sue her bosses unless they let her take her vacation now. Her bosses cave.

10. Ally checks with the families of Candy's previous husbands and learns that Candy told each husband that she was pregnant, which proved to be a lie each time. Candy's last husband was planning to divorce her because he'd read a medical report proving that Candy was unable to bear children. Ally tries to find Matt to tell him what she's learned. She discovers that Matt and Candy have eloped, and no one knows where they went.

11. Ally remembers something told to her by the children of Candy's first husband. They were openly against their father's relationship with Candy, so he and Candy eloped and were married by a justice of the peace in the next town. Ally takes the chance that Candy might do the same thing again. Ally rushes to the same justice of the peace just as Matt and Candy are about to say "I do." Ally confronts Candy about her medical report, causing Candy to furiously attack Ally. The justice of the peace pries Candy off Ally, then has a local police officer arrest Candy for assault. Matt feels like a fool for trusting Candy and apologizes to Ally for putting her through so much trouble. Both of them then head back to their home town to enjoy a slow dance together at their high school reunion. Ally now knows that whatever the future has in store for her, she'll never turn her back on love again.

Spawn of Frankenstein

1. In 1943, brilliant young scientist Erik Frankenstein is facing death in a German concentration camp. He is about to be executed, along with other prisoners, when a Gestapo captain named Muller presents official papers to the commandant, stating that Erik is to come with him. Erik is taken to a large isolated house containing a secret lab where he is told to duplicate his ancestor's experiments in raising the dead. Hitler wants to create an unstoppable army of formally dead soldiers.

2. Erik refuses and is tortured. He still refuses. The Gestapo tries to force Erik to do what they want by finding Erik's finance, Ruth, and bringing her to the lab. Rather than let her be tortured, Erik agrees to do as the Gestapo demands.

3. Erik is brought mangled corpses of huge German soldiers. Erik knows that the experiment must not succeed, even though he

knows that if it doesn't both he and Ruth will be killed. He begins to construct a new body from pieces of the dead soldiers. An experiment is tried, and the monstrous creature comes to life but dies a few minutes later. The Nazis are angry but agree to let Erik try one more time.

4. Erik tells his captors that, in order to succeed, he needs the assistance of his old science professor, Dr. Kessler. Kessler is taken from a hospital bed where he is dying of cancer and is forced to work with Erik. Erik knows that Kessler has been working with the underground and hates the Nazis. He wants Kessler to contact the underground and arrange for them to help he and Ruth escape Germany. Despite his illness, Kessler is happy to help. Kessler is able to get a message out to the underground to meet them in the woods outside the lab at three o'clock in the morning. Erik creates a sleeping powder in his lab to incapacitate the guards, and then he, Ruth, and Kessler try to escape.

5. Erik and the others make it outside and meet with the underground. Just as Erik and the others are about to get away, German soldiers suddenly appear. Somehow they uncovered Erik's escape plan. The members of the underground are all gunned down! Erik, Ruth and Kessler run for their lives. A soldier runs after them but doesn't hear his captain's orders *not* to kill Frankenstein. Erik and the others find themselves facing a stone wall. They are trapped! The soldier runs up and aims his rifle at them. They surrender, but the soldier shoots Kessler anyway. As Kessler lay dying, the soldier aims his rifle at Erik and Ruth!

6. Just as the soldier is about to shoot Erik and Ruth, the captain runs up and stops the soldier from firing. Erik and Ruth are taken back to the lab. Erik has the bleeding body of Kessler also taken to the lab to be operated upon in the vain hope that it will save his life.

7. There seems to be very little chance for escape now. Erik prays that Kessler can live long enough to tell them how to contact other members of the underground, just in case they can get away from the lab. Under closer supervision than before, Erik is forced to try to create another undead creature. He patches together an even bigger body. The only thing left to do is to transplant a brain. Some soldiers bring in several dead bodies. One is Kessler's. Erik and Ruth now know that things are hopeless.

8. Kessler's brain is transplanted into the creature, and, after hours of work, it is brought to life. The huge monster, dazed and confused, snaps its bonds and starts attacking the soldiers. Bullets can't stop it! It turns its attention to Erik and grabs him as if it is going to tear Erik limb from limb!

9. Erik begins talking to the creature, which seems to calm it down. Deep in the recesses of the creature's memory, it faintly recalls that Erik is its friend. It releases Erik.

10. The Nazis test the creature and discover that it is as strong as ten men and cannot be killed. By using an experimental drug, they are able to control the mind of the creature. Unexpectedly, more members of the underground attack the lab. The Nazis send the creature out to kill the members of the underground. The creature is an unstoppable killing machine, slaughtering everyone it comes across. It is only when the creature has killed all the resistance fighters that it looks at each of the people that it has killed and feels remorse. Erik is ordered to create more undead soldiers.

11. Erik goes along with what the Nazis demand of him because he has a plan concerning the creature. During a free moment Erik tries out his idea. He injects the creature with a compound that counteracts the Nazi mind control drug. The Nazis see him with the creature and realize that Erik is up to something. The Gestapo, possessing Erik's notes and having studied his surgery, no longer feels the need to keep Erik alive. They are about to shoot Erik and Ruth when the creature goes berserk and attacks the Nazis. Erik destroys all his notes, then grabs a rifle and joins the fight. Ruth locks the front doors, keeping out the guards who were stationed outside. The creature and Erik mow down Nazis right and left. The captain races to the front door and tries to let in the guards. The captain takes out a grenade to hurl it at Erik when the creature grabs the captain's fist. The Nazi guards are battering down the front door. Any second the Nazis will be inside! The creature begins to remember its dedicated hatred of the Nazis. The creature motions for Erik and Ruth to get out while he holds the Nazis back. Erik and Ruth are able to get out the back way just as the Nazi guards break down the front door. The creature pulls the pin on the grenade, and the room blows up! Later, Erik and Ruth make their way to America where they hope to make a new life together. Still, they will never forget Kessler and the ultimate price he paid to save them.

Needless to say, none of these stories are fleshed out. They would need to be developed fully to qualify as good stories. They are, however, properly structured plots. Three *different* stories with the *same* plot structure. One thing that they all have in common is *conflict*. Without conflict, you have no drama. Without conflict, the audience is bored. If you use this plot structure formula and create conflict in every scene, you will have a script which will continually hold the interest of an audience.

Another thing that all these stories have in common is simplicity. The goals of the protagonist and the antagonist are clearly defined and understood. This simplicity also aids in the production. The locations, interiors, and props of *Cool Million* include seashore, some boats, a small town, Martin's office, some guns, and a prototype weapon. The locations and interiors are simple to gather. The guns can be borrowed from shooting enthusiasts. They don't even have to function. The flash of gunfire can be added in post-production. The prototype weapon can be made by gluing parts from various sci-fi model kits to a toy ray gun, which is then painted. *Lost Love* uses various offices, a restaurant, various homes, a motel room, and a hall for the class reunion. All of these locations and sets are easily obtained. A few phone calls to friends and family and you would likely have access to each necessary location. *Spawn of Frankenstein* has a concentration camp, a large home, a laboratory, some woods, Nazi uniforms, guns, a grenade, and some nineteen-forties furniture and set decorations. Of the three stories presented, this is probably the most complicated in terms of production requirements. This is why it was written to involve the least amount of locations, thereby making the overall pre-production process easier to deal with. The concentration camp can be a simple barrack or some shacks combined with a high fence. The large home can be any isolated country house that is not modern in appearance. The lab can be a large basement. Given the fact that it is set in the forties, none of the technology displayed has to look particularly advanced. Test tubes, beakers, some boxes with dials and electrical wires that can be attached to the creature would suffice. A lot of the gadgetry could be purchased cheaply during the Halloween season at a Halloween store. The uniforms could be rented from a costume shop or borrowed from World War Two collectors. The guns and grenade could also be borrowed from local gun groups. The forties furniture and set decorations could be purchased at thrift shops, then modified to fit the style of the period; or they could be borrowed from friends and family; or arrangements could be made with a local community theater.

So there you have it: proper plot structure, conflict, clearly defined goals, and simplicity. Four important elements for your movie's story.

24. DIALOGUE IS JUST WORDS, UNLESS...

Of all the elements that go into writing a screenplay, the writing of dialogue is the most difficult to get a handle on. Most people don't have a knack for it, and, unfortunately, it cannot be taught. It is possible to be taught plot structure, but no instructor in the world can teach you how to write dialogue that sounds dramatic as well as natural. Either you can write it or you can't.

Movie dialogue is not the same style of dialogue used in plays and books. It has to come to the point more quickly and sound more like the conversation of a "real" person. When it doesn't, the audience emotionally rejects what they are hearing. Everything seems false to them.

What this basically means is this: Don't write dialogue unless you can do it well. If you are bad at dialogue your movie will look ridiculous, no matter how good everything else in it looks.

If you have a good ear for dialogue, then remember these five points:

1. Dialogue has to be interesting enough to make the audience hang on each spoken word.
2. Each thing said should advance the movie's plot or the audience's understanding of the characters.
3. Each line should be written in the style of speech of the character who is speaking it.
4. If nothing else, learn this simple rule: Don't have anyone say anything unless it's important.
5. Don't write dialogue if your plot can be advanced through a character's actions. Remember, movies have to move. Use the dialogue to augment the action, not replace it.

25. What to Minimize

One of the other important things to know about movie dialogue is that it should always be used sparingly. Never be verbose. In a big-budget movie actors can talk and talk and talk, but not in a low-budget movie. Why? Because you aren't likely to get actors of *major movie caliber*. Actors of lesser skill and/or experience will always appear much better in a scene if the dramatic demands of that scene aren't placed entirely upon their shoulders. In this way, a good actor will shine and a lesser actor will look at least competent. Also, overseas buyers are far more likely to want to buy the rights to your movie if there isn't much dialogue. The reason for this is that the movie will have to be dubbed or subtitled. The greater the amount of dialogue, the greater the cost to that buyer.

After you write your script, start editing the dialogue. Keep only that dialogue which makes an important contribution to the advancement of the story. This is often very painful for a new writer, but doing it is the measure of a true professional. You will find that by paring away a lot of the dialogue, you have a much better screenplay.

26. Why Scene Length Is Vital

As stated in point 25, minimizing dialogue can make your script better and more commercial. The same logic also applies to scene length. There are four primary reasons for this.

1. Nowadays, most moviegoers have the attention span of a guppy. Long, drawn out scenes bore them. Short scenes don't. While I certainly don't advocate catering mindlessly to this audience, it is important to consider this fact because it will affect the success, or the lack thereof, of your movie.
2. If you don't have a lot of money to make a movie, it's a good idea to keep all your scenes short. Generally speaking, if a scene is brief the audience doesn't tend to notice its shortcomings. Also, if the scene is short, as well as good, it leaves the audience wanting more. On the other hand, if the audience doesn't like a scene, a better one is just around the corner.
3. Quicker paced stories are usually easier to film because they put less of a burden on the actors.
4. As a rule, it is a good idea not to write a scene that is longer than two pages unless it has a lot of action that will hold the interest of the audience. This is not always possible, but it is important to keep in mind as your script is being written.

27. Everybody's Got a Talented "Relative"

Once you announce that you are going to make a movie, you will constantly run into people who have a relative or friend who is "perfect" for your film. This is particularly true when you are soliciting investors or gathering some other resources for your movie. All of a sudden, an investor has a girlfriend who wants to be a star. The owner of a location that you need has a son who he believes is a better actor than Brando. A restaurant owner offers free lunches for the cast if he can play the lead. What do you do? Sadly, there is no one answer to this problem. No matter what you do, the solution is bound to make somebody unhappy.

The simplest way to deal with the situation is to take a professional approach. If someone wants to be in the movie, then let him or her know that they can audition. Who knows, they might actually be a good actor. If they aren't, then they at least had a chance to prove themselves. If this isn't an acceptable solution to the people that you are dealing with, then deal with someone else.

Another alternative is to point out that you will be filming for at least two weeks. Can this person be away from their job for that length of time? There would also be very little pay. Perhaps no pay. Will their financial needs suffer because they don't have a paycheck for two weeks? Sometimes these basic facts of reality will make a would-be actor shy away from an acting career.

There is one final alternative. If all else fails, cast them in a part that puts them in front of the camera for a few days but isn't artistically demanding. Does the crime lord in the script have henchmen around him a lot? Cast the investor, or whatever they are, as a henchman who is always in the forefront. Does one of the main characters surround himself with pretty women? Make the wannabe actress a groupie. Check your script for any parts that don't require talent but give the suggestion of prominence. If this person sees himself or herself on the screen a lot, they will normally be satisfied with the part.

28. Union Actors, Non-Union, and Financial Core

At some point you may start wondering if you should hire union actors or non-union. You may have also heard rumors of something called financial core status, but you aren't sure what it is. Here is some basic information on each of these subjects.

Simply put, a non-union movie actor is any actor who doesn't belong to SAG (Screen Actors Guild) or AFTRA (American Federation of Television and Radio Artists), or any other actors' union.

A union actor is any actor who is a member of either SAG or AFTRA (or EQUITY, the union for actors in the theater). It does not mean that they are better actors than non-union actors, nor does it mean that they are more professional in their conduct. It only means that they belong to a union, nothing more.

If you choose to make a union movie you need to know that there are four basic contractual agreements between producers and the Screen Actor's Guild. The reason SAG has four agreements is to make it easier for low-budget producers to hire actors belonging to SAG. Each agreement has a different budgetary range and different limits as to how SAG actors will benefit financially from their performance. Being as the particulars of these agreements, such as pay rates for actors, are subject to change, you would do well to contact SAG's Donna Sommers at (617) 742-2688 for current information.

These four low budget agreements are:

1. **Ultra-Low Budget Agreement**
2. **Modified Low-Budget Agreement.**
3. **Low-Budget Agreement.**
4. **SAG's Basic Theatrical Agreement.**

SAG's Ultra-Low Budget Agreement works within a budgetary ceiling of $200,000, and an actor's day-player rate of $100. This agreement allows professional and non-professional performers to work together.

SAG's **Modified Low-Budget Agreement** is specifically for movies having budgets less than $625,000, which are shot entirely in the USA and are intended for commercial release. The current day-player rate is $268, with a weekly rate of $933; and the producer is entitled to distribute the film with a full theatrical release. If the film makes a profit, each actor has to be paid additional money. The budgetary ceiling of this agreement may be raised to $937,500 if the movie's cast has a high proportion of women, performers of color, seniors, or performers with disabilities. If this happens, the agreement become a different agreement called the **Affirmative Action Low-Budget Agreement**.

SAG's **Low-Budget Agreement** has a ceiling limit of $2,500,000. The day-player rate is $504, and the weekly rate is $1,753. This agreement permits the producer full theatrical exhibition rights.

SAG's **Basic Theatrical Agreement** applies primarily to movies made by major studios and is designed for budgets that are quite high. The daily pay for an actor is $759, and the weekly rate is $2,634.

SAG would not allow me to include samples of the four types of low-budget agreements in this book, but these four agreements are available for anyone to read on SAG's internet website. The internet address for these SAG agreements is: http://www.sagindie.org/resources/contracts/.

If you would like to contact your local branch of SAG for additional information on contracts, or anything else relating to the Screen Actors Guild, you will find listed in Appendix B those branches and the states, or portion of a state, that they represent.

Right-to-Work States

Twenty-two of America's states have laws that allow union and non-union personnel to work together without fear of union interference or reprisal. For this reason, such states are very popular among filmmakers who need to keep their budgets low.

The following is a list of the 22 right-to-work states (established either by state constitution or by statute):

Alabama	Iowa	North Carolina	Texas
Arizona	Kansas	North Dakota	Utah
Arkansas	Louisiana	Oklahoma	Virginia
Florida	Mississippi	South Carolina	Wyoming
Georgia	Nebraska	South Dakota	
Idaho	Nevada	Tennessee	

Financial Core Status

In the late eighties the laws regarding unions changed because their practices were found to be in violation of anti-trust laws. Now no one can legally be compelled to join a union in order to gain employment. This resulted in something known as financial core status, (sometimes called fiscal core status or financial core membership). As a result, some union actors left their respective unions and declared themselves to be financial core, which allows them to work on both union and non-union projects. You can find out more about financial core status at the National Right to Work Legal Defense Foundation, Inc. Their phone numbers are (800) 366-3600 and (703) 321-8510, and their website address is http://nrtw.org. You can also go to the website of Mark McIntire, who has written extensively on the subject of financial core status. Mister McIntire's website address is http://www.markmcintire.com.

Insofar as a new filmmaker is concerned, their best bet is probably to do a non-union movie. It is simpler and much more practical financially. If you want to hire a union actor, you will need to refer to point 33 to learn how.

29. YOU CAN'T TRUST ACTORS' RESUMES

Now that your script is written and polished, it's time to think about actors. The biggest question that most new filmmakers have at this point is "Where am I going to find all the actors that I need?" You can go about locating them in several ways. Placing a notice in the local paper is one solution.

Another is to inform all the local community theater groups and college drama departments about your casting needs. You also can contact the various local talent agencies to find out what they have to offer in the way of actors. An ad for actors placed on http://www.craigslist.com can also be an effective means of finding actors or crewmembers.

There are publications in Los Angeles whose sole purpose is to advertise for actors and crew for your movie. Some charge for this service, some don't. The best known of these publications is *Backstage West.* Information on their services and prices can be found on the internet, or you can call them at 323-525-2358. If you go to their website at http://www.backstagewest.com, you can save yourself a little time by filling out some online paperwork and paying for the cost of your posting in just a few minutes. Basically, these various publications will require information, such as: What is the title of your movie? What is the name of the company making the movie? Who is the producer? Who is the director? Is it union or non-union? Is it a feature or a short subject? Is there pay? If there isn't pay, what are you offering? Is there nudity involved? When is the movie going to be shot? Where will it be shot? What genre is your movie? What is the movie about? What is the age range for the character to be cast? Is that character male or female? What kind of character is it? Where will the auditions be held? When will the auditions be held? Are auditions by appointment only? What should the actor bring, or have prepared, for the audition? Where should headshots and resumes be sent? What is the deadline for submissions? What phone number should be listed in the posting?

There are also a large number of internet casting services. These services are a little like talent agencies. You can rummage through their various photos and resumes to try to find the kind of actor you are looking for. Many of these sites' services are free. However, they are occasionally difficult to navigate. One of the websites that has worked well for me is http://www.therightcast.com. The Right Cast's internet format is simple enough that people who are not particularly computer proficient can easily post their casting needs. The questions that will need to be answered for any internet casting service will approximate the questions in the paragraph above. Generally, though, they are not as involved.

However you promote your requirements for actors, be a little bit wary once the headshots and resumes start to arrive. They don't always accurately represent the actor who sent them. Photos have been known to be retouched in order to make the actor look younger, and resume credits are occasionally exaggerated. Never ever hire someone because you are impressed by his or her photo and resume. *Always* call actors in for an audition.

You will also find that you cannot always trust the information you find posted on internet sites. One example would be the credits of actors and film crew technicians found on the *Internet Movie Database* (a.k.a. IMDb). Sometimes they are incorrect. Sometimes, as in the case of yours truly, the credits are nearly non-existent. Of the many movies I have produced or directed, only one is listed on their database, and its information is inaccurate. As such, the IMDb should be used only as one of *many* tools to research someone's body of work. For similar reasons you can't trust an actor's website or blog.

Most actors have demo tapes or DVDs showcasing samples of their film and television work. As a rule, a demo tape is a much more reliable indicator of their work than resumes or internet sites.

30. Auditions Don't Have to Be Agony

There are two types of acting auditions: the open audition and the kind where a specific actor is called in for a specific role. Most of the roles you will cast in your movie will probably be the result of an open audition, after which you should have a good idea of who to call back to audition for a specific role.

Auditions are often as tough on those doing the casting as it is on those hoping to be cast. Generally speaking, the open audition, sometimes known as a cattle call, is by far the most difficult kind of audition. They usually take a long time, can become tiring and boring, and you have to sit through tons of bad actors to find the handful that are competent.

Here are some things you can do to make an open audition easier for you.

(a) Hold the audition in a spacious hall or office that's readily available to you. This type of location projects a more professional image than someone's home. It also makes the actors feel more comfortable and looks better for interviews with attending members of the press.

(b) The audition script used by the actors doesn't have to be from the one that you are going to film. Instead, use an audition script that is relatively bland. If an actor's reading is good, then you can rest assured that it is coming from the actor and not the bland dialogue they are reading.

(c) Have your audition script's dialogue be between two or three people. This way several actors can audition at once. Besides saving time, you can get a sense of the chemistry between the actors.

(d) Make sure you video tape the auditions. After a while your memory of all the actors' faces will blur together, so you need a record of what each actor is capable of doing.

(e) Have each actor state their name clearly and also state the name of the character they are reading for.

(f) Have each actor fill out a form explaining what his or her name is, their address, their phone number, those days of the week that they would be available to act in your film, and their acting experience. If they have an actor's photo and resume, then attach it to the form they have filled out.

(g) Have an assistant whose job it is to hand out forms to all the aspiring actors, as well as keep order during the audition. This includes keeping everyone quiet so that those auditioning won't be disturbed.

(h) Keep some water and cups on hand. Actors may be waiting for a long time, and their nervousness might result in a dry throat. A sip or two of water can help relieve both the nervousness and the dry throat.

(i) Keep in mind that actors often look differently on tape than they do when they audition. Their performance may seem better, or worse, on the tape. Their looks may appear better or worse. As such, don't worry terribly about the live audition. Wait a day or so to view the tape so you can be more objective, then decide who might be right for each part.

(j) Make sure that you take a break every few hours, otherwise you will become emotionally exhausted. Your assistant can stand in for you during these points. After the first few hours your helper will have less to do, so they should be readily available to spell you without difficulty.

Here is a sample audition script to give you an idea of what you might use. It is designed to be read by either men or women, or a combination of both.

ACTOR 1

Good evening, everyone. At least, I trust it's good.

ACTOR 2

It is, if you think that the elimination of Carl Burns is good.

ACTOR 1

What about Maggie Burns? She knows more about our operation than her husband did.

ACTOR 3

I have my best men looking for her.
Consider her taken care of.

ACTOR 1

She'd better be. We have a billion-
dollar business to take care of, and
one woman isn't going to stand in
our way.

ACTOR 2

Even if she talked, so what? Who's
going to listen to her? She doesn't
have any proof.

ACTOR 3

How do you know? We can't be certain what Carl gave her. He could
have had backup files on everything.

ACTOR 2

Not a chance. We searched every-
where.

ACTOR 3

You'd better pray you're right, or
you know what's going to happen
to all of us.

31. CASTING: NOT FOR THE FAINT OF HEART

Now that you have your resumes, headshots, demo tapes, and your videotape of the open audition, it's time to get your hands dirty and start casting.
It's not easy to cast a movie. You suddenly realize that your friends aren't as
right for roles as other actors are. You may find that no one fits your vision
of the starring role. Even some of the supporting roles seem impossible to
cast from the list of actors before you.

Here's what you should do. First, cast the actors who fit the available roles
perfectly. Then cast the roles where a perfect fit doesn't matter (i.e., roles
where age, race, or sex is unimportant to the story). Then start trying to fit
the remaining actors into roles like a jigsaw puzzle. You may discover that
the casting process may prove easier for you if you combine several bit parts
into a larger supporting role, thereby decreasing the number of roles to cast.

If so, do it. Could a good actor become right for a role with a little rewriting? Once I rewrote my script and combined the roles of three burly male bodyguards into one wiry female bodyguard. It gave the relationship between my characters a completely new dynamic and was one of the best things in the movie. Ask yourself what it is about each actor that makes him or her wrong for a particular role. Is it merely that they don't fit your original concept? Would they fit your concept if they changed their appearance in some way? Have them audition again and see what they can do. See what that redhead looks like with a blond wig. See if the little guy can play a terrifying killer. See if the woman who looks like the girl next door can play a seductress. See if the nervous actor with the high voice can play a hero when he slows down the delivery of his lines and lowers his voice to make himself sound more masculine. You may find that these people, who wouldn't be your first choice, are perfectly acceptable for the roles you are casting. If you are still unsatisfied, then you will need to have another casting call. Another possibility is to ask the actors who you have already cast if they know of anyone who is right for the role. This often works quite well.

32. Do You Need a Star to Sell Your Movie?

Unless you have been living on the Moon for the past century, you know that stars can help sell your movie to the public. What you may not know is that they can also help sell your movie to a distributor, a video company, and an overseas buyer. The question you need to ask yourself is "Can I afford a star?" The answer is dependent upon the size of your budget. If you have a budget of ten to twenty thousand, then it may be possible to hire a recognizable actor to make your movie more commercial. If you have a smaller budget, it may be impractical. Please keep in mind that you can still sell a movie without a star, assuming the movie has *excellent* production values. The main value of a star is that they make the selling of your movie easier and the profit from that sale larger. A movie without a star is less likely to make as large a profit as a movie with one. The reason for this is that when a star has any particular audience that is loyal to him or her, this loyalty will be taken into account when the distributor debates whether to represent your movie. Even if the star has no particular box office appeal, the fact that you are using a recognizable actor/actress suggests to prospective distributors that you have made a union picture. This perception can increase your movie's value, due to the higher budgets of union movies.

When you start considering whether or not you should hire a star, you need to remember two things:

1. If you have enough money, make every effort to hire a star for your movie.
2. Even without a star, your movie *could* make a profit because your movie costs so little.

If you are still in the early stages of planning, it might be to your advantage to get a Letter of Intent from a star that states that he or she is interested in working on your film. Such a letter can encourage potential investors to put money into your project, as well as help motivate possible members of the cast and crew to become involved. This letter of intent will not constitute a binding contract but will demonstrate that the actor/actress has a serious interest in your film.

33. How Do You Get a Star?

Once you have determined that you want a star for your movie, you need to face the problem of finding a star that is affordable and willing to work on your film. When you make a low-budget movie like the one you are going to make, you won't be able to afford a major star, but you may be able to afford a recognizable actor or actress. There are several ways to contact a star. One of the best ways is to attend a sci-fi, horror, or nostalgia convention that will feature numerous stars signing autographs. Tell them that you are making a movie and ask for the phone number of their agent or manager. Also, ask if you can send them your script. Sometimes the actor/actress will give you a personal contact number to call. If you can't go to a convention, then make a list of actors and call the Screen Actors Guild's "Actors to Locate" number. The number for this service is currently 323-954-1600. When you call this service, they will tell you the phone number for the agent, manager, or some other contact number of up to three actors/actresses. Give the agent or manager a call and explain that you may be interested in hiring the actor/actress represented by them. Find out what the actor requires, which varies from person to person. Does the agent or manager need to see your script before they will consider the possibility of their client working with you, or do they have different needs? Ask yourself if you can live with the demands of that actor/actress. If their demands are reasonable to you, it then becomes a matter of negotiating a deal. Most will want at least SAG minimum, which at the time of this writing varies depending upon the budget of your movie. If an actor/actress knows that you are doing a non-union film, then they may ask for less. They may also turn you down flat, but it never hurts to ask. There may also be other matters that enter into the negotiation. Will their name be shown before the title in the opening credits? How big will their screen credit be? Will their credit be listed no farther than third after the title? Can their salary be union minimum plus ten percent of that minimum, so that the ten percent could go to their agent? Will you accommodate their special dietary needs? Will you pick up the expenses of their *companion*? There are as many requests, or "demands," as there are movie stars.

Sometimes the deal is all about ego. Sometimes it's all about money. Sometimes it's the work. Sometimes it is all three. No two actors/actresses want precisely the same things for the same reasons. Many actors/actresses, especially those who aren't working steadily, need to prove to the film industry that they are still alive and willing to work if given the chance. Remember this! An actor/actress who doesn't work for six months is an actor who will find it hard to get work. That's the nature of the film business, and almost every professional actor/actress is aware of this fact. When an actor/actress doesn't work, the word goes out through the grapevine. Rumors of "AIDS," "cancer," "drunkenness," "drug use," or an "unprofessional attitude" begin to circulate. Most actors/actresses will do almost anything to avoid the stigma of not working. Still, other actors/actresses may simply want to work on your film to get their hands on some quick cash for some personal reason.

There are a lot of recognizable actors/actresses in the world, so if one won't agree to a deal that fully satisfies your creative and budgetary needs, then move on to a star that will.

The real question is how do you afford an actor who is going to cost you some serious money? Logic would dictate that there would be no way possible for you to afford to pay them for the full two weeks of your shoot. So what's the solution? The answer lies in point 34.

34. THERE'S ALWAYS AN ARMCHAIR ROLE WITH A STAR'S NAME ON IT

In 1937, a serial was made called *Zorro Rides Again*. Its main villain was an actor named Noah Beery who had been a big star earlier in the decade.

Serials were low-budget affairs in which each dollar had to be squeezed until it begged for mercy. In order to afford a star like Noah Beery, the makers of the serial shot all of his scenes in one day. He played the chief villain who was always issuing orders, via radio, to his henchmen. Therefore, all his scenes took place in just one location, often in front of his radio. Because of this clever scheduling decision, Beery was seen in every segment of a twelve-chapter serial and enhanced the value of that serial immeasurably. I call these kinds of parts "armchair roles." In every script there is always a character (often seated in an armchair) who is seen throughout the movie and yet always appears in the same location. These roles are the ideal part in which to cast your star. It provides a *maximum* of exposure with a *minimum* of expense.

Go through your script to find these roles. It might be a good idea to expand a part to justify a star playing it. Whether you expand the role or not, you will be able to have a star in your movie that will add to its commercial value.

35. The Crew Is Crucial

It's possible to be so caught up in casting the actors that you neglect devoting proper attention to the hiring of the crew. If you do give it consideration at all, you might devote most of your time getting a decent camera operator and no one else. It's important to remember that your entire technical crew is as important to your production as any actor. Maybe more so. The crew will have to be there every day, whereas most actors only have a limited number of days to work on a movie.

Before we go any further, let's determine how large a crew you actually need. You need a director of photography/cameraperson, a sound person, a production assistant, a makeup artist, a prop person, and a wardrobe person.

The same people can handle many of these jobs. If you are working in a video format, then your director of photography/cameraperson can also be the sound person because the sound will record directly on the camera's videotape. The makeup artist and wardrobe person aren't vital to a production, but they are a good idea. The makeup artist can touch up actors so that they look consistent from scene to scene. The wardrobe person makes sure that everyone is given the right costume, then gathers those costumes at the end of the day's filming. It is also his/her job to fix costumes during production if need be. If you need to, you can have the actors handle their own makeup and wardrobe and thereby save yourself the cost of extra crewmembers, but this can be risky. Actors traditionally demonstrate notoriously bad judgment when it comes to their appearance. All too often their primary concern is how *good* they look rather than what the script says they should look like. The prop master is responsible for getting all the necessary props together and assigning the correct prop to the correct actor for each scene. They then take charge of all the props when filming ends for the day. This is a job you can do. It's burdensome, but it can be done. The production assistant does whatever jobs no one else has time to do.

This brings us to a possible crew of four, those four being the cameraperson/sound person, the production assistant, the makeup artist and the wardrobe person. As I said, you can cut out makeup and wardrobe, but it's not advisable. If you have to eliminate one of these jobs, then that job should be wardrobe. If you have to, you can do that job yourself.

Interview the applicants for these positions with the same scrutiny as you would the actors. Are they experienced? Are they reliable? Do they have references? Do they have samples of their work? This last question is somewhat moot in regards to the production assistant, but everyone else should have some sort of example of their work. Find out why they want to work on your project. It certainly won't be for the money, so what is their reason? Do they think it's going to be fun? Are they there to meet the stars? Is it for the fame? Is it because a buddy is working on the film? If they have these, or similar reasons, then don't hire them. The crew you want always has something to prove. They want to show what they can do, just as you do. They may want to be a part of something special, just as you do. If their reason and talent is sufficient, then, and only then, should you hire them.

36. Actors' and Crew's Contracts

Contrary to what many people think, a verbal agreement is a binding contract. The value of a *written* contract is that it can be more easily used as evidence in a court of law if one of the parties reneges on their agreement. Obviously, a clearly stated document will hold greater weight in a court of law than someone's perception of what the agreement meant. So you see, a contract is nothing more than a document illustrating that a meeting of minds took place between the two parties who have signed it, insofar as their business together is concerned. As such, a contract between you and your actors and crew is necessary. It is not, however, necessary to make that contact complex. A simple, understandable agreement is all that is normally needed. One of the few exceptions would be if you were hiring union talent, which usually necessitates contracts conforming to union regulations.

The following contract should give you an idea of how it would look. As always, it's a good idea to have an entertainment attorney check out any contract that you might use in order to ascertain its value as an agreement. Laws vary from state to state, and change from year to year, so always be careful with contracts.

Sample Actor Employment Agreement (Non-Union)

THIS AGREEMENT is made and entered into as of the day of _____ 2007, by and between _____, a California partnership (hereinafter "Producer"), and _____(hereinafter "Player").

A. Producer intends to produce a motion picture (hereinafter the "Picture") based upon the screenplay tentatively entitled "_____ _____" (hereinafter the "Screenplay") which Picture is intended for initial exhibition.

B. Producer wishes to utilize the services of Player in connection with the Picture upon the terms and conditions herein contained.

ACCORDINGLY, IT IS AGREED AS FOLLOWS:

1. PHOTOPLAY, ROLE, SALARY AND GUARANTEE: Producer hereby engages Player to render services as such in the role of _____ in the screenplay, at the flat fee salary of _____ dollars. Player accepts such engagement upon the terms herein specified. Producer guarantees that it will furnish Player not less than _____ day's employment.

2. TERM: The term of employment hereunder shall begin on or about _____ (the "Start Date") and continue until _____, or until the completion of the photography and recordation of said role.

3. PLAYER'S ADDRESS: All notices, which the Producer is required, or may desire, to give the Player may be given either by mailing the same addressed to the Player at the address listed at the end of this agreement, or such notice may be given to the Player personally, either orally or in writing.

4. PLAYER'S TELEPHONE: The Player must keep the Producer's casting office or the assistant director of said photoplay advised as to where the Player may be reached by telephone without unreasonable delay. The current telephone number of the Player is listed at the end of this agreement.

5. FURNISHING OF WARDROBE: The Player agrees to furnish all modern wardrobe and wearing apparel reasonably necessary for the portrayal of said role; it being agreed, however, that should so-called "character" or "period" costumes be required, the Producer shall supply the same. When Player furnishes any wardrobe, Player shall receive a reasonable cleaning allowance and reimbursement for any soiled or damaged clothes. Number of outfits furnished by Player:

_____ @ $_____
_____ @ $_____

6. NON-UNION PICTURE: Producer makes the material representation that it is not a signatory to the Screen Actors Guild collective bargaining agreement or any other union or guild agreement. Player warrants that Player is not a member of any union or guild, memberships in which would prevent Player from working in this picture.

7. PROMOTIONAL FILM: Producer shall have the exclusive right to make one or more promotional films of thirty (30) minutes or less and to utilize the results and proceeds of Player's services therein. Player agrees to render such services for said promotional films during the term of his/her employment hereunder as Producer may request, and Player further agrees to use by Producer of film clips and behind-the-scenes shots in which Player appears in such promotional films. Provided Player appears therein, Producer shall pay to Player the sum of _____ dollars ($_____) within ten (10) days after the first use of each such promotional film on television or before a paying audience.

8. NAME AND LIKENESS: Producer shall have the exclusive right to use and to license the use of Player's name, sobriquet, photograph, likeness, voice, and/or caricature, and shall have the right to simulate Player's voice, signature and appearance by any means in and in connection with the film and the advertising, publicizing, exhibition, and/or other exploitation thereof in any manner and by any means and in connection with commercial advertising and publicity tie-ups.

9. TRAVEL EXPENSES: Any right of Player to transportation and expenses pursuant to this Agreement shall be effective when and only when Player is required by Producer to render services more than seventy-five (75) miles from Player's principal place of residence. Any weekly expense allowance provided Player under this Agreement shall be prorated at one-seventh (⅐th) thereof per day. Player shall be reimbursed at the rate of _____ per mile for the use of Player's car to travel to distant locations.

10. INCLUSIVE PAYMENTS: All payments to Player hereunder shall be deemed to be equitable and inclusive remuneration for all services rendered

by Player in connection with the Picture and to be paid by way of a complete buy-out of all rights granted to Producer hereunder, and no further sums shall be payable to Player by Producer by reason of the exploitation of the Picture and all results and proceeds of Player's services hereunder in any and all media throughout the universe pursuant to any collective bargaining agreement, if any, or otherwise, by way of residuals, repeat fees, pension contributions, or any other monies whatsoever.

11. PUBLICITY: The Player shall not directly or indirectly circulate, publish or otherwise disseminate any news story, article, book or other publicity concerning the Picture, or employee's or others' services, without Producer's prior written consent, provided that the Player may issue personal publicity mentioning the Picture so long as such references are not derogatory. The Player has permission to show a videotape of Picture in connection with seeking future employment.

12. VHS TAPE/DVD: The Player will receive one VHS tape or DVD of the Picture within 90 days of completion of post-production.

13. CONFIDENTIALITY AGREEMENT: The Player shall hold in trust and confidence all information regarding the terms of this agreement. The Player hereunder agrees not to disclose any information concerning the terms of this agreement to any employee, consultant or third party under any circumstances whatsoever without the Producer's prior written consent.

14. ARBITRATION: Any controversy, claim arising out of, or claim arising out of or relating to this agreement or any breach thereof shall be settled by arbitration in accordance with the Rules of the American Arbitration Association; and judgment upon the award rendered by the arbitrators may be entered in any court having jurisdiction thereof. The prevailing party shall be entitled to reimbursement for costs and reasonable attorney's fees. The determination of the arbitrator in such proceeding shall be final, binding and non-appealable.

15. EMPLOYMENT ELIGIBILITY: All of Production Producer's obligations herein are expressly conditioned upon Performer's completion, to Production Producer's satisfaction, of the I-9 form (Employee Eligibility Verification Form), and upon Performer's submission to Production Producer of original documents satisfactory to demonstrate to Production Producer Performer's employment eligibility.

IN WITNESS WHEREOF, the parties have executed this agreement on the day and year first above written.

AGREED TO AND ACCEPTED:

(Player's Signature)

_____

(Print name)

_____

Player's Address:

_____

Player Work Phone Number:

_____

Player Home Phone Number:

_____

Player Social Security Number:

_____

AGREED TO AND ACCEPTED:

_____

[Name of your company],

By:

_____, Partner

The next contract is a simpler version of the previous contract. It is easier to understand because it is less detailed. It may be preferable to a more complicated contract if you are dealing with family or friends. However, given the fact that it is less detailed, it is possibly open to greater interpretation.

Sample Actor Employment Agreement (Non-Union) # 2

This contract shall serve as an agreement between the undersigned and [The name of your company].

In return for acting and/or technical services on behalf of the movie, *[name of your movie]*, said actor, or technician, shall receive screen credit, meals during production, copy of the video or DVD, and [whatever payment, if any, that is agreed upon; i.e., salary, deferred payment, points, etc.].

Said actor or technician agrees that failure to perform and/or deliver all which is expected of their duties shall render this agreement null-and-void. These duties shall include [list all the duties expected of the actor or technician].

_____

Signature of Producer

_____

Date
_____

Signature of Actor or Technician
_____

Date
_____

It should be noted that the latter sample contract, with a few minor modifications, could also be used as an agreement for securing locations, props, services, etc.

Please keep in mind that you will be less likely to have problems if you have some sort of contract for all of the business matters required by your film. People, as a rule, are more inclined to do business with you if you present them with a written agreement because it makes them feel more secure.

If you decide to do your film/video as a union project, you should be able to get a sample union contract/agreement once you have contacted the Screen Actors Guild and made arrangements to do your film/video as a SAG signatory production.

37. Insurance

There are three ways that you can deal with the issue of insurance. You can, of course, simply ignore purchasing any insurance. I don't advise this because an accident could financially ruin you. Also, many locations won't work with you unless you carry some form of insurance. You can choose to expand upon your current insurance policy to cover any and all locations in which you will be filming. This currently costs between one hundred and two hundred dollars. The costs, if any, will depend upon your existing policy. Finally, you can buy insurance to cover you for the duration of your filming schedule. Prices for this will vary. Whatever type of insurance you buy, it has to include some form of liability and accident coverage. There are companies who offer insurance designed specifically to cover the requirements of a film/video production. Over the next few pages you will find some basic information on what these policies cover.

Insurance for Filmmakers

Filmmakers can attach themselves to an existing policy and pay a small fee to obtain general liability insurance. Securing workman's comp is also a good idea. If you decide to get insurance specifically for you movie production, it should always cover the following:

1. Errors and Omissions.
2. Entertainment Insurance.
3. Other Incidental Coverages.

• **Errors and Omissions.** In the event of a lawsuit, this insurance provides your production company with a legal defense for covered liabilities within the limits of the coverage, protecting your production company from such liabilities as:

1. Invasion of privacy.
2. Copyright infringement.
3. Breach of implied contract — resulting from the alleged submission or acquisition of program, musical or literary material used by the insured.

• **Entertainment Insurance.** The types of coverage can include:

Negative Film or Videotape— This protects your production company when the physical loss of filmed negatives or videotape happens before a duplicate or protection print can be made, necessitating the abandonment, or re-shooting, of the production.

Faulty Stock— This protects your production company if you suffer due to a faulty camera, faulty processing, erasure of tape, etc.

Props, Sets, Wardrobe— This protects your production company if there is the physical loss of any prop or set or wardrobe, both owned or rented by your company.

Miscellaneous Equipment— This covers the physical loss of any camera or camera equipment that is owned or rented by your company.

Extra Expense— This covers additional expenses due to loss of or damage to any property.

Third Party Property Damage— This covers damage to the property of others while in the care of your production company.

• **Other Incidental Coverages.** Simply put, this refers to any coverage not included in your Errors and Omissions or Entertainment Insurance.

If for any reason you feel that the insurance company you would normally use isn't suitable to insure your movie, you may want to deal with an insurance company that specializes in Motion picture insurance. In Appendix C you will find a list of several companies; but additional insurance companies can be located in the yellow pages of a Los Angeles or New York City phone directory. Copies of these directories are normally found at your local library. You can also find these specialized insurance companies listed on the internet under the category of Entertainment Insurance or Motion Picture Insurance.

38. Do You Need a Completion Bond?

Unless you have tried to complete a project with other people's money, you may not be fully aware of what a completion bond is. If you aren't certain of the answer, then you need to read the following information. This should answer most of your questions concerning the *whys* and *wherefores* of a completion bond. Once you know more about getting a completion bond, you will need to decide for yourself whether you want it. If you want investors to finance your movie, then you will need it — but only if the investors require it. On the other hand, if you are self-financing your movie, then you won't need a completion bond. If it is determined that you do need a bonding company, they can be found easily in the yellow pages of any phone directory or on the internet. I suggest that you check to see if they have any experience in dealing with filmmakers before you consider doing business with them.

You may be wondering what a motion picture bonding company is. Basically, it is an insurance company whose specialty is the insurance of people with a financial interest in your movie who want a guarantee that it will be completed. You may not feel that you need a completion bond, but the people who are financing you movie may require it. In this way they are protected. If for any reason your movie is not completed, your investors can redeem the bond for a sum of money stated in that bond. In effect, this process is very much like the cash settlement received after an insurance case is resolved. Insofar as the movie itself, the insurance company does not guarantee its success or quality. It merely guarantees that it will be completed on time and on budget, and that it reasonably adheres to the screenplay.

The requirements for dealing with a Bonding company are pretty straightforward. They will need the following things in order to do business with you and your company:

1. A copy of your completed screenplay.
2. A budget breakdown.
3. A production schedule.
4. A payment/fee of six percent of the movie's budget to be paid to them.

It is very likely that they will want proof of each estimate in your movie budget. It is also possible that they may want references for those members of your staff in positions of authority. The bonding company may also want a list of production credits for each of these staff members.

It is very important to understand that your contract with a bonding company grants them a great deal of financial power over your movie. If they feel that it is in their, and your backers,' best interest, they may take over the issuance of all checks. A bonding company has the final say in all financial matters if they choose to exercise such control. They even have the ultimate right to fire you (or any member of your staff) if it is understood that you are the source of a serious financial problem. To make certain that the production runs smoothly, the bonding company will require written reports of the day-to-day progress of the movie, and may possibly have a representative do surprise spot checks on the set to assure them of that progress.

It is also important to understand that it is in the best interest of the bonding company that you finish your movie so they don't have to pay your investors any money on the issued bond. To that end they will require you have something called a *contingent cash reserve,* which is ten percent the movie's budget, set aside (supposedly for emergencies). This cash contingency can prove very uncomfortable for a producer who has a very low budget. There are, however, methods of dealing with the contingent cash reserve issue. For example, any costs incurred before you begin shooting your movie may be deducted from the reserve. This might include any "above the line" fees or costs. Just how much of these costs can be deducted will be determined by the bonding company. Another possible way to deal with this is to do a very efficient job as a filmmaker. As the completion of the movie draws near, it might be possible to convince the bonding company to allow you to have a portion of the cash reserve to use on the movie. If they agree to this, the money will be allotted to you in increments. Also, if you have been so efficient that you are ahead of schedule, under budget, and have completed at least sixty percent of the movie, it is conceivable that you might be able to renegotiate the deal with the bonding company and lower its six percent fee to four percent.

39. LOCATIONS AND SETS

It is a good idea to have at least one impressive location in your movie which is seen throughout the course of your film. The reason for this is that it enhances the production values, and therefore the marketability, of your movie. It could be an interior or an exterior, but it needs to be elaborate enough to be eye-catching and memorable.

The easiest way to deal with this issue is to check with the local film commission about available locations. Most film commissions are very helpful in this matter, and they may even have photographs of readily available locations. You also might ask the members of your cast and crew. They often have ideas about locations that could be ideal. The next step is to ask the person in charge of the location if you can film there. Sometimes they say no, but they are just as likely to say yes. Each owner of a location you want may have concerns you will have to address. Do you have insurance? Are you going to make a movie that they would disapprove of? Will their property be damaged in any way? Will your filming interfere with their daily personal or professional business? How long will you need it? When will you need it?

If for any reason you cannot get the elaborate location you need, then you need to break down the location into scenes and shots. It may be possible to film in several different locations and make them look like a single location through editing. For example, does one of your characters need to live in a big impressive house? Try filming it in the following way: obtain permission to film the exterior of a mansion for use as an establishing shot. Next, film some scenes in someone's large dining room, or film a scene at an expensive looking pool, or take everything out of someone's living room and redress it to look like a huge bedroom. You get the idea: piece together a mansion by using several different smaller locations. This method of filming is limited only by your imagination and the resources available to you.

Do you need to film in a forest? Maybe the local park will work as a location if you are careful with your camera angles and sound recording.

Do you need to film inside and outside of an impressive building? If you can't get access to both an interior and exterior, film an exterior and then shoot close shots in the long corridor of someone's home.

Need an office and yet don't have access to one? Move all of your furniture out of your bedroom, then bring in a borrowed office desk, chair, file cabinet and supplies.

Need a spaceship interior? Making one is easier than you might think. First of all, paint the walls of your garage black, then place oddly shaped pieces of black painted Styrofoam on those walls. Next, glue any high tech-looking "do-dads" to the walls as well. If you have a computer monitor, use it too. Build a control console out of some cheap plywood and then paint it black. Drill holes in the top and put clear marbles in those holes to simulate buttons. If you want, you can even put a light bulb inside the control panel so that the "buttons" look as if they are glowing. If you have an unneeded computer keyboard, remove its keys, paint alien letters on them, and then glue the keys to your console or one of the walls. If you can purchase some reflective tape at your local hardware store, cut large alien symbols out of the tape and strategically place those symbols on the walls of your set. When you film your scenes, these symbols will seem to radiate an eerie glow. The final touch is to coat a wire brush or scouring pad with minute amounts of silver paint and carefully and faintly trim the edges of the Styrofoam pieces to make it look like worn metal. If you use sinister lighting, keep your shots tight. You now have an unearthly spaceship and an impressive set.

Imagination and planning — the filmmaker's two greatest tools for sets and locations.

40. Planning a Logical Shooting Schedule

It's now time to make up your shooting schedule. There are two types of schedules. The first is *continual* filming or shooting when everyone is *available* over a period of weeks. The second is often the most feasible when you have very little money to work with. If the actors and crew are not being paid, or at least are not being paid much, then you may find that it's easier to work around other people's schedules. The advantage to this type of filming is that you can film a greater equivalent of days than on the continual schedule. Despite this, continual filming is often the preferable goal. You will find that many people simply lose interest over time. The shorter the period they have to work, the greater the enthusiasm, the greater the dedication, and the smaller the likelihood that they will quit before you are done filming. Whichever type of filming strategy you use, you will need an organized shooting schedule.

Since you are going to film a low-budget movie, it can't be a long schedule. Anything over two weeks for continual filming is probably impractical. It will depend on how much money you have to work with, and how much you have to pay people each day. Start with a fourteen-day schedule, then adjust the length according to your budget.

The first thing you need to do is to take into account any locations that are locked into specific days and/or times. Once they are placed into your schedule, you can tackle any scenes which are more flexible to scheduling. You do this by figuring out all your remaining locations to see how many of those locations can *reasonably* be accommodated at one time. You may be able to film in more than one location per day, but only if the second location is very close by. Keep in mind that each time you change the location, even if it's only to move across the street, you lose anywhere from thirty minutes to two hours, depending how far the other location is. This is because camera, lights, reflectors, the microphone, props, etc. all have to be packed, then set up again in the new location. This takes time, and time eats away at your schedule. Go through all the scenes in each location and figure out how many pages have to be shot. If it totals more than ten pages you will probably have difficulty in shooting all those scenes in one day. Try to anticipate all the technical difficulties that would logically occur, and allot extra time to those particular scenes. Continue this process until all your scenes are distributed over the fourteen days of your shoot. Are there scenes that can't be accommodated? See if they can be rewritten to take advantage of the locations that are already committed to the schedule. If that is not possible, and the scenes are truly important, then go over your list of scenes and see if something else can be eliminated so the other scenes can take its place on the schedule. One way or another, something will have to give. Either the scenes will have to go by the wayside or the budget will have to be adjusted to accommodate an additional day of photography.

The next step is to take into account the time of day of the photography. If there are night scenes, shoot all your interiors during the daytime with darkened windows to give yourself the scheduling advantage of day and night photography. Are certain actors on a tight schedule? Film their scenes first, if possible.

Later in this point is a fourteen-day shooting schedule for a non-existent movie. The format of this schedule is certainly not written in stone; you can decide for yourself how your shooting schedule should look. It can be much simpler if you like, but I recommend that you don't make it more complex, as it might become confusing. The important thing is that it clearly explains what scenes are going to be shot on which days, and who is needed for those days. I also recommend that the complete shooting schedule only be given to the crew and those actors with major roles. This is because they will be working on your movie for most, if not all, of the shoot, and therefore will need a complete schedule. Those with lesser responsibilities, working one or two days, can be given a shooting schedule that details only those days they will be needed. You save a little money on photocopies of the schedule this way, but there is a much more important reason to do this. Actors in small roles often forget the days that they are supposed to show up to work. The less complicated their shooting schedule, the less likely they will flake out on you.

The format for this shooting schedule is pretty simple. Centered and CAPITALIZED at the top of your page is your **TITLE**. Just below that, also

CAPITALIZED (to designate its importance), are the words "**SHOOTING SCHEDULE.**" Below that put the word "Issued": and the date it was given to the crew and members of the cast. In this way everyone has a written document demonstrating when and where he or she is expected to work. Below that you write "**Subject to script revisions.**" This let's everyone know that things may change, depending on the need of the shoot. Below that, on the far left in smaller type, you write this: "**Day of Week.**" This designates the day of the week that you will be filming. To the right of date is "**Set/Location.**" This doesn't necessarily refer to a built set. It refers to the specific scene location, or locations, described in the script in which you will be filming. To the right of location is the script **Scene #.** This allows each member of the production to know what specific scene, or scenes, will be shot on that day. To the right of Scene # is the heading "**Characters.**" This lets everyone know which character will be needed for that day's work. On the far right we put the heading "**Pages to Film.**" This let's everyone know how many pages will be filmed that day. This is mostly for the benefit of the director, the cinematographer, and their assistants. Below each of the headings you have a specific description that pertains to that scene. Below the "Day of Week" you must put the exact day of the month. Given that you will probably be filming for more than just a week, it will avoid confusion concerning which Monday (or whatever day of the week) you are referring to. Below the set description you have the heading "Needed." This is used to describe any special props, set dressings, or special effects that are vital to scene, or scenes, you are filming. If there are two or more locations being filmed on one day then you may need to list the names of characters twice, with the proper scene designation (unless the list of characters remain the same, regardless of location). At the end of the shooting schedule you place the heading, on the left-hand side of the page, "OMITTED SCENES." This is to help avoid confusion among the cast and crew when certain scenes are not filmed because you have chosen to cut out a scene prior to filming. Below OMITTED SCENES is the heading "PLEASE NOTE CHANGE OF —." This allows you to list any noteworthy changes in the current draft of your script which otherwise might cause confusion.

Sample Shooting Schedule

<u>(YOUR MOVIE'S TITLE)</u>
<u>SHOOTING SCHEDULE</u>

Issued: [Put the *specific date* when the schedule was assigned to cast and crew here.]
Subject to script revisions.

Day of Week. Date of Month	Set/Location	Scene #	Character	Pages to Film
Mon.	INT. VILLAIN'S HIDEOUT	1,3,5,7.	Villain Villain's Mistress	8½
	INT. HERO'S H.Q.	2, 4.	Hero	
	INT. CENTRAL HIGH SCHOOL	10, 75.	Heroine	
	Needed Police uniforms & badges. Computer & monitor. Black and white television set.			
Tues.	INT. POLICE STATION	12.	Policeman	7⅜
	INT. THUG'S APT.	16, 78.	Thug 1	
	INT. VILLAIN'S APT.	6, 8.	Villain	
	Needed Large computer. Rifle. Handcuffs.			
Weds.	INT. SCIENTIST'S HOME	22, 24.	Scientist	7 ½
	INT. BEN'S HOUSE	26, 28.	Ben Hero Thug 2	
	Needed Big screen TV. Dagger. Old newspaper. DVD player.			
Thurs.	HERO'S LAB	11, 13, 15, 20, 84.	Hero Heroine Sidekick	7
	INT. SCIENTIST'S LAB	9, 30, 99.	Scientist Hero Villain	
	Needed Tesla coil. 3 computers. 3 monitors. Notebook.			
Fri.	INT. SCIENTIST'S OFFICE	14, 17, 18, 21.	Villain Scientist	8

Day of Week.	Set/Location	Scene #	Character	Pages to Film
	Needed A safe. Documents. 7 test tubes. Red scarf.			
Sat.	INT. PRIVATE EYE'S OFFICE	19, 23, 25, 53, 61, 90, 93, 96.	Private Eye Hero Thug 1 Thug 3	6⅞
	EXT. PRIVATE EYE'S OFFICE	27, 29, 59.	Private Eye Hero Thug 2 Thug 4	8⅛
	Needed File cabinet. Files. Answering machine. A noose.			
Sun.	NO FILMING.			
Mon.	EXT. HEROINE'S HOME	32, 45, 66, 70, 81, 89.	Hero Heroine Thug 1 Thug 2 Jim	6⅝
	Needed Diary. Cell phone. Cup of tea.			
Tues.	EXT. SHACK.	31. 33, 36, 47, 58.	Hero Villain Policeman Thug 4	7⅜
Weds.	EXT. JIM'S HOUSE	37, 41, 50, 55, 73, 83.	Sidekick Jim Heroine Thug 4	8½
	EXT. SAM'S HOME	91, 95, 97.	Sam Sidekick Thug 2	
	EXT. VICTIM'S HOME	39, 51, 62, 98.	Hero Victim Thug 1 Scientist	
Thurs.	EXT. CORN FIELD	82, 87, 102.	Thug 1 Thug 2 Thug 4	8⅔

Day of Week.	Set/Location	Scene #	Character	Pages to Film
			Sidekick	
Fri.	EXT. VINEYARD	38, 40, 43.	Hero	7⅞
			Sam	
			Jim	
Sat.	EXT. DIRT ROADS	34, 44, 46,	Hero	7⁶⁄₈
		49, 55, 57,	Heroine	
		63, 67, 71,	Villain	
		79, 80, 85.	Thug 1	
			Thug 4	
			Sidekick	
OMITTED SCENES:		42, 54, 56,		
		64, 65, 68,		
		69, 72, 76,		
		77, 80, 86,		
		94, 100.		

PLEASE NOTE CHANGE OF CHARACTER NAMES:

Hero—in script as Protagonist.
Sidekick—in script as Little Buddy.
Villain's Mistress—in script as Shady Lady.
Henchman 3 and 4—in script as Henchman 3.0.

PLEASE NOTE CHANGE OF LOCATION:

High School—in script as Junior College.
Shack—in script as Cave.
Villain's Hideout—in script as Villain's Lab.
Scientist's Home—in script as Nuclear Scientist's Office.
Corn Field—in script as Wheat Field.
EXT. Heroine's Home—in script as INT. Heroine's Living Room.

You can place the address of each location in which you will be filming next to the Set/Location; or, if you prefer, you can list all the addresses on a separate sheet of paper to be given to your cast and crew. You may also want to give a time to show up to each address.

41. Product Placement

When a producer takes the opportunity to utilize product placement, you can expect to see a character in a movie using a well-known product or eating at a well-known chain of restaurants. This advertises that company's product, and, in turn, the filmmaker who uses that product in his or her movie receives certain benefits from that company.

Product placement can help make your movie more affordable. Does your character wear expensive shoes or drive an expensive car? Product placement can get you access to these things for free. Need extra food or drink for your cast and crew? Put those foods, drinks, or restaurants in your movie, and you will have saved yourself a lot of money.

There is absolutely no reason why product placement should compromise your movie. Go methodically through your script and see what your character wears, eats, and makes use of throughout the story.

There are, of course, conditions regarding whether or not a company might want to have their product appear in your film. Each company has it own requirements, and you should ask what they are. One universal rule is that a product should never be shown in a negative light. For example, a character that goes into to a bar and drinks a beer would be fine, but breaking a beer bottle over someone's head during a fight scene would never earn approval from a beer company.

Product Placement is handled through special advertising agencies whose sole job is to place their clients' products in movies. Each of these agencies handles many different products. In Appendix D you will find a list of product placement companies who are known for their high standard of professional conduct. Since their clients will change from time to time, you will need to contact each agency to find out which products are currently represented by them.

42. A CAST "READ THROUGH" IS IMPORTANT

When your movie has been completely cast, it's a good idea to gather all the principal actors and have them do a read through. A read through is where each actor/actress reads their part out loud as if they were playing their role before the camera. There are several reasons for a read through. The most important reason is that if there is anything wrong with the dialogue it will become blatantly obvious during the reading. You may also find that one of the actors may keep stumbling over a certain word or phrase. This enables you to work with the actor to find a replacement for that word or phrase which is satisfying to both of you. You also have the opportunity to explain any inherent nuances in the script that would enable each actor to play their role with greater veracity. If any actor has any concerns or questions, then you can address them on the spot rather than waste precious time on the set.

To put it simply, the read through is your opportunity to preemptively deal with problems so they won't need to be dealt with during production. On more than one occasion a thorough read through has saved time, money, and countless headaches due to everyone's greater understanding of what was needed.

43. It's Not Real Until It Happens

At this point, most new filmmakers think that they can now relax. All the preliminary work has been done, so there's nothing left to worry about, right? Unfortunately, the answer is no. Too many would-be filmmakers assume that once all their negotiations and deals are completed, everything becomes inevitable. In reality, something is going to go wrong. Someone is bound to back out on his or her deal with you. An actor might flake out. A location that was guaranteed is suddenly no longer available. A technician who agreed to work on your movie for a certain amount of money abruptly wants a lot more cash. There is nothing quite as fragile as a promise made to a filmmaker. So, expect the worst.

To help avoid this problem it is a good idea to have everyone doing business with you sign a contract. It doesn't matter if you are dealing with a good friend or a family member; you still need to protect yourself and your production. No reliable person will object to signing a contract. You also need to keep in mind that the best protection is to have a backup — a backup for actors, locations, sets, etc. It's also a good idea to consider "acts of God." What if it rains while you are filming an important exterior? Can you film it another time without compromising your movie? Can you rewrite the scene to take place indoors? Can you incorporate the bad weather into the scene?

It's best not to count on anything too much. If you do, you will be creatively paralyzed if it doesn't materialize. Be flexible enough to keep filming even if people you deal with, or forces of nature, let you down.

44. Practice Being Bad in Order to Be Good

If you are new to filmmaking, then you are definitely going to make amateurish mistakes no matter how talented you are. It's inevitable. The best way to avoid a lot of mistakes is to do a bunch of amateur filmmaking before you shoot your first professional movie. If you have the time, shoot a lot of short amateur films, edit them, do the titles, etc. With each film, take note of the mistakes you make and learn from them. Try to fully understand why you made each mistake and how you can keep from repeating it. If you can't shoot a batch of little films, then take a cheap video camera and shoot a version of your movie's most complicated scenes to figure out where the problems and solutions are. You don't have to use the real sets or locations. Use an empty room, if need be. Pick your camera angles as if the sets or locations were the real ones. Describe the background as you shoot each background, then play all the parts yourself. Next, edit all your shots on a cheap video editor or on a computer. This will tell you which shots work and which don't. Doing this can also save you time later because you will already have your camera angles worked out, thus saving you a lot of film or tape.

45. TEN HARD LESSONS ABOUT PRE-PRODUCTION

1. You don't need to write every single camera angle into your script. This only tends to confuse your cast and crew. Just describe the action as succinctly as possible. It's the job of the director to figure out which camera angles will be used.
2. Take into account that not every actor is needed *all day* long when you are filming. If an actor isn't needed until the end of a day's shoot, then don't tell him to show up at 8 A.M. Nothing will tick off an actor quicker than to have his day wasted due to incompetent scheduling.
3. Keep in mind that actors need to get into costume and make-up. Find out how long this process will take from those in charge of wardrobe and makeup, then allot the proper length of time in your schedule.
4. The initial setup of lights and other equipment also takes time. In addition, delays are more likely to take place when you first arrive on the set or location than any other time. As a result, don't expect to start filming until one to two hours after you first arrive at the location. Take this into account when planning your schedule.
5. Don't forget to plan time for meals and occasional breaks. There should be at least one hour planned for lunch and/or dinner. Breaks should be at least fifteen minutes long every four to six hours. Keep in mind that without breaks, your cast and crew will become exhausted and cranky.

6. Plan your locations around their close proximity to one another. If you have a short shooting schedule, your locations need to be centralized. This assures that a day's worth of filming, shot in different locations, can be realistically completed. This may require a rewrite to accomplish this if a particular scene cannot fit into your shooting schedule. The alternative to this may be to omit the scene in question.

7. It's a good idea to buy copies of various good movie scripts to get a better idea of what may be lacking in your own script. Study and analyze the structure and dialogue until it makes sense to you. There's a wealth of information out there, take advantage of it. Check out the local library or the internet for detailed information on scripts, contracts, talent agencies, locations, etc.

8. Video has less resolution than film, so if you are using a video camera to shoot your movie, be sure to minimize long shots and maximize close-ups. There is much more detail in a videotaped close-up than a long shot.

9. Don't be a fan boy. If a star or technician wants too much money to work on your movie, do not hire them. You cannot allow your admiration for that individual to cloud your good judgment. You hire people to help sell your movie, not to appease your ego.

10. Make sure that you have a little leeway in your budget to accommodate unexpected problems. When a situation arises that has to be dealt with, you will probably need a little extra money to help you handle the problem.

46. Flashback, Part Two

Have you ever heard of a producer named Whitney Ellsworth? Perhaps not, but then you *have* probably heard of the hit television show he produced called *The Adventures of Superman*. *The Adventures of Superman*, or *TAOS* for short, is, as of this writing, the longest running kids show in television history. It is also the longest running action, sci-fi, and dramatic series in television history. More to the point, *TAOS* was also produced on a *low budget*. How did Ellsworth do it? How could anyone produce a long running TV classic with very little money? Let me see if I can answer those questions.

Whitney Ellsworth was a writer of pulp fiction and a professional cartoonist throughout the thirties who had hopes of being a screenwriter. In 1938, he married Jane Dewey, a starlet under contract to Paramount studios. It was from Jane that he began to learn some of the professional ins and outs of moviemaking. When DC Comics bought out Malcolm Wheeler–Nicholson Comics, they took note of Ellsworth's remarkable organizational skills and hired him as their new editorial director. As time wore on, many of DC Comics' characters were licensed to movie studios. Given Ellsworth's position of importance, he was the logical choice to periodically go to Hollywood to act as a consultant on each of these projects. It was during this period that Ellsworth began to truly learn the craft, and business, of filmmaking.

In 1951, the producer of the *Superman* radio series was assigned the job of producing a TV series, with Ellsworth again serving as a consultant. Ellsworth, DC Comics and the sponsors soon became very concerned about the show, feeling that it was too violent and grim. Equally important was the fact that the producer kept going over budget. It was mutually decided that Ellsworth would produce all future episodes of the show.

Ellsworth took note of what had worked on the series and what hadn't. What worked had to be made to work even better. What had not worked had to be changed. He also knew that with a low-budget show like *TAOS*, organization, co-operation, and good will among all the workers were vital. As a result, Ellsworth initiated a great many changes. He hired the best technical talent that his meager budget would allow. He knew that even though the best might cost a little more, they would save him a lot of money in the long run because they were more efficient. The special effects were improved upon because he knew that if the trick shots looked inferior, the audience would quickly become bored. Cramped shooting schedules were lightened, making it easier on actors and directors, and thereby enhancing the quality of their work. All the members of the crew were encouraged to come up with ideas to make the show better. Parties were occasionally held to keep the atmosphere friendly and seem less like a 9 to 5 job. The individual wants and needs of his crew and actors were diplomatically listened to and, when reasonable, addressed. Several episodes were filmed at the same time to save money and make greater use of sets and locations. Scripts were made the focal point of the creative process because Ellsworth knew that without a good story the audience wouldn't care what took place on their TV screens.

Each season for the next five years Ellsworth would get together with another editor from DC Comics and plot out every episode to be shot that season. In this way the writers assigned to work on the teleplays needed less time to complete each script. More importantly, it meant that each episode could be tailored to the practicalities of the series. Budgetary considerations were taken into account. Stock footage could be incorporated, where logical, to lower costs. Characterizations could be made more consistent with previous episodes, as well as with the comic books. Ongoing supporting characters that had proven to be popular could be emphasized. Violence was played down to make the series more suitable for kids. Humor was utilized more often in order to lighten the action. Characters were more clearly delineated to make the show more understandable to viewers who had never read the comic book. The needs and preferences of the sponsor and comic book company were taken into account, creating a better working relationship. The carefully planned scripts allowed for greater production values, which made for a much better show.

The time that Ellsworth spent in pre-production solved many of the production and post-production problems that would have otherwise become expensive during each upcoming season. The result of all this hard work was a successful series that has entertained people for generations.

So you see, detailed *pre-production*, like *getting ready*, serves two very important purposes. It saves you money, and it permits you to make a better film.

That having been said, it's now time for production....

III. Production

47. SUDDEN OFFERS TO HELP

One of the more interesting things about this point in the filmmaking process is the fact that people who wouldn't give you the time of day before it became widely known that you were going to make a movie suddenly want to help. They may be actors, technicians, investors, or people who have a resource that could be of service to you.

You need to weigh the following two factors and consider which holds the greater importance for you. The advantage is that these people may in some way be able to enhance the look of your movie and thereby make it more valuable. The disadvantage is that these people who didn't believe in you or your film earlier may now only wish to be involved because of its current notoriety. Such people have been known to become flaky once the novelty of your project has worn off. There is, of course, the question of what this would mean to your cast and crew who believed in you from the start. Will they feel slighted?

There is a third factor to consider. You can always take advantage of any offers for locations and additional investors while rejecting offers from would-be actors and crewmembers. This lets you incorporate these resources into your film while not antagonizing your current cast and crew.

48. IF YOU DON'T KNOW YOUR CRAFT, YOU'D BETTER LEARN IT NOW

To be a competent low-budget filmmaker you need to learn a lot about many different cinematic skills. If you haven't learned the art and craft of cinematography, lighting, sound recording, and directing, then you'd better learn them awfully fast. These skills will be briefly explained in this book, but you will need to practice these skills in order to utilize them competently. Before you shoot a single frame of film or tape, I want you to test your level of competence in each of these areas in order to determine where your strengths and weaknesses are. In this way you can do your own camera work, lighting, sound work, etc., should you need to. Or, if you have others performing these duties, you will be able to relate to them on a level which they will readily understand. This informed relationship will enhance your movie.

There are many, many technical terms employed during the filmmaking process—so many that a book could be written just listing and explaining all of them. For this reason I will not attempt to list all these terms, but I *will* list those movie related terms that you would most likely need at some point during your production. Learn them if possible. At the very least, have this book on hand to refer to just in case one or more of these terms come up on the set. For easy reference, these terms appear in Appendix E.

49. Plan Your Shots

The easiest way to make your movie affordable is to never waste a lot of time and film (or tape) by shooting a lot of different camera angles of each scene.

Take your script and work out every camera angle ahead of time. Try to visualize how it would look once it has been edited, and make notes as to how each shot should look. For your own protection make sure that you shoot a master shot of each scene just in case these shots don't edit together as well as you had planned. Incidentally, a master shot is a long shot of the overall scene.

If you have difficulty visualizing your shots, then get together with an artist and work out the shots together so that each scene looks like the panel of a comic book. This is called storyboarding. If you don't have access to an artist, then do it yourself by drawing stick figures. This will help you picture each camera angle.

If for any reason you don't have time to storyboard the whole movie, then plan out those scenes which are the most complicated. Then, in your simpler scenes plan to shoot a master shot combined with specific inserts. Inserts are close shots designed to be *inserted* into your master shot to emphasize some particular dramatic point. An example of this would be a scene in which a killer commits a murder only to drop his wallet at the scene of the crime. A close-up of the killer's wallet slipping from his pocket, and another close-up of it falling to the floor, would constitute inserts.

50. CONTINUITY

Continuity refers to the manner in which shots are filmed so that they can be edited together in a seamless fashion. Normally a crew would have a continuity person (a.k.a. a script supervisor) who would be in charge of making sure that the actors do the same thing in each take. Without this, an actress might be holding her wine glass in her left hand in one camera angle and in her right hand in the next, making the two shots impossible to edit together. Unfortunately, since you are working with a tiny budget, it is unlikely that you will be able to afford a continuity person. This will necessitate the director do this additional job. The advantage of working on video is that the director can check the previous footage to verify what each actor was doing in the previous shot. This helps avoid mistakes in continuity and makes editing easier. If you are shooting your feature on film, then you will have to rely solely on your memory and the memory of your actors.

51. PERMITS

When it comes to shooting movies on city streets, there are two types of filmmaking: conventional filmmaking (shooting with permits) and guerrilla filmmaking (shooting without permits). In guerilla filmmaking, the director and crew shoot the scenes they need without permission and rely on their speed to get the footage they need in a public location before anyone knows what they are doing.

Given the fact that you will be working on a small budget, you may have no choice but to shoot a lot of your exteriors without permits. If you decide to work with permits, then you should contact the local Film Commission and inquire as to where you can find out about "shooting permits" in your community. In most cities the permits can be purchased at the City Hall. Unless there is a lot of filming done in your city, there may not be specific rules, regulations, and price guidelines for your film. The prices for shooting permits vary from city to city, but you had better count on it costing a few hundred dollars. It may cost less, but don't count on it. Depending on the city, it could conceivably cost thousands of dollars. However, such large prices are more typical of major cities than small towns.

In those areas not used to filmmaking it may be possible to obtain cooperation from the city without permits because they are not set up to sell them. Often they will only require that you co-insure the city for a million dollars as part of your insurance. By doing this, you may be able to film on city streets all you want.

Please keep in mind that those cities which require shooting permits have many rules and regulations that you will be expected to abide by. They can be very confusing, so be prepared to spend a little time trying to figure them out. If you can't fathom their meaning, ask for help from the local Film Commission.

52. Get a Good Production Assistant and Save Yourself a Lot of Aggravation

Production assistant is one of the most difficult jobs someone can have on a movie. Basically, the production assistant does anything that no one else has the time or inclination to do. It's hard work, with low pay and little respect. It's also one of the most vital jobs in a movie. The production assistant learns more about the filmmaking process by working on one movie than they could from a semester of film school because they have to work with nearly every member of the crew. A production assistant that becomes an associate producer by the end of the movie is not uncommon. Why? Because a good production assistant knows more about how to solve the day-to-day problems of film production than any other crewmember.

A good production assistant can make or break a low-budget movie. If they are good at their job, they will make the director's and producer's jobs much easier. If they are bad at their job, the movie can come to a screeching halt.

A "good production assistant" is diligent, quick, responsible, slow to anger, a problem solver, and has a reliable car in which to run errands.

It's difficult to hire a good production assistant because they often don't have a resume that showcases their talents. You will have to rely on your good judgment to hire someone who you believe embodies all the qualities mentioned above. The ideal situation is to hire someone that you already know and can trust. If your production assistant proves to be incompetent, then you have to replace him or her immediately. The job is too important to act otherwise.

53. A DIRECTOR IS A LEADER; BE ONE

The director sets the tone for the entire production. All the actors and crew take their cue from the director. If the director is weak, then the production will be loose and sloppy. If the director is tyrannical, then the cast and crew will be nervous and their creativity will be stunted. A good director, apart from being talented, is someone who projects a sense of being prepared as well as being in control. If the director has a tantrum, the cast and crew will believe that he is weak and unable to keep his emotions under proper control. They would, of course, be absolutely correct.

On the first day of the production it's a good idea to gather everyone together and concisely lay down the law to them. Let them know what your goals are and what you expect of them. Let them know that you welcome their input, but *you* are the one who decides what ideas will be used and what will not.

In the final analysis, it is not required that you have your cast and crew's friendship, nor their fear. It is only important that you have their *respect*. Once you have that, they will work like dogs for you because they will trust you to know what you are doing.

54. A DIRECTOR IS ALSO A PEACEMAKER

At some point an argument will occur on the set. It is inevitable when people work such long hours so closely together. It may be between members of the cast, the crew, or a member of the cast or crew and *you*. Matters can quickly escalate into a situation which will make working on the set impossible unless the matter is resolved. As I said in point 53, everyone takes their cue from the director. If the director cannot handle a situation like this, then that director will drop in the esteem of the cast and crew.

The best way to handle this kind of problem is to speak calmly and with authority to the parties involved. State that an argument *will not be tolerated* on the set. Any disagreement has to be resolved in a professional manner, away from the cast and crew. If those involved cannot conduct themselves in a professional manner, then you will have no choice but to chastise them. If this does not relieve the problem, then fire the source of the problem. This lets everyone know that you mean what you say, and that you don't consider anyone indispensable. Needless to say, this should be a last resort. Whenever possible, try to handle all problems with diplomacy.

As a rule, it's a good idea to deal with conflicts by taking the offending party aside and trying to resolve the problem. People often calm down if they don't have an audience. This manner of handling the situation doesn't embarrass the person, nor does it make them feel disrespected.

One last point. If the argument is between you and someone else, you must never allow your anger to override your good judgment. Always keep in mind that the important thing is to finish your movie on time and on budget, with the quality that it needs. The moment that you lose control of your emotions and argue with someone on the set, you are representing yourself instead of your movie. To do this in a situation dependent upon people's good will is nothing less than self-destructive.

55. THE THREE-QUARTER ACTOR

It is inevitable that you will come across a problem that I call the "three-quarter actor." The three-quarter actor is typically a personable actor/actress who is well liked by everyone in the cast. At least they are liked until three-quarters of their performance has been shot. At this point they become egotistical, argumentative, and generally act like a real jerk.

The reason for the three-quarter actor's radical change of character is due to the fact that they have figured out that with three-fourths of their work shot, it would be too costly and time-consuming to replace them.

Sadly, their reasoning is basically sound. It would often be very difficult to replace them. However, it is vital to remember that letting them get away with murder creates disharmony on the set. This leaves you with two alternatives, either one guaranteed to leave a bad taste in your mouth. You can ignore their unprofessional conduct, or you can fire them and re-shoot their scenes. Keep in mind that three-quarter actors have been known to wait until they have nearly finished shooting all of their scenes in the movie to make a sudden demand for a lot of money. Also, keep in mind that re-shooting the scenes of a particular actor or actress isn't always as difficult as it would first seem. If the three-quarter actor is playing a *supporting* role, it may be possible to re-shoot their scenes without losing too much time. Go through the script and see just how important their scenes are. Could you give their remaining scenes to another member of the cast? Quite often you can, with a little rewriting. Could you insert some of the close-ups you shot of that actor/actress for previous scenes into remaining scenes by rewriting the script so that their character doesn't have to speak?

A more drastic approach is to think of re-shooting the three-quarter actor's scenes in terms of individual shots instead of scenes. Just how many shots are actually required? Could that character be used in a series of close-ups that can be inserted into the previously filmed scenes? How many of the scenes will necessitate their being *completely* re-filmed? Could you eliminate some other scenes to accommodate the re-filming of those scenes that have to be completely re-shot? Will your crew be willing to work a few more days to re-shoot those scenes, or will you have to do it all by yourself? Usually the crew will be willing to pitch in and help out if it is truly necessary.

If you decide to re-shoot scenes, you need to understand that re-shooting scenes with an actor in a *leading role* can be very difficult. It may be easier to re-film your entire movie. This can be a very scary idea. It may also be your only practical choice.

It is also important to understand that the power of the three-quarter actor lies in your fear of firing them. Once they are fired and they understand that they can be replaced, their power is eliminated. It is not uncommon for this actor/actress to come back asking for a second chance. Naturally, it's up to you whether to rehire them.

56. ALWAYS HAVE ANOTHER ACTOR IN THE WINGS

As mentioned in the previous point, it may be necessary to replace an actor at a moment's notice. It's fairly common for an actor to become flaky during a production. It is also common for an actor to be unable to live up to the promise that they showed during the audition. Given all the possible reasons that an actor's role might have to be recast, it is a good idea to have a good actor available to step in at a moment's notice should it become necessary to replace one of the principal actors, or any other actor, for that matter.

You may be asking the question: "If so and so is such a good actor, why wasn't he or she cast in the movie in the first place?" There are various answers. They may not have been your first choice for a particular role. They may not have been originally available to work on the movie, but their schedule has changed. Perhaps they didn't want to play the kind of role that you wanted to cast them in, but are now willing to help you out if you are facing an emergency.

This actor/actress *has* to be someone who is not only talented but also reliable. Otherwise, you may face the same problem that prompted the firing of the previous actor/actress.

57. Keep a Tight Rein on Your Actors or They Will Stampede

Actors have a habit of disappearing when they are most needed. This is due to the fact that they spend most of their time waiting. As a result, they may decide to pop down to a nearby store to pick up something, or go for a walk, or do something else out of boredom. It's important that your cast and crew knows at the start of your production that no one is allowed to leave the set unless they have permission. If someone needs something, then a gofer or production assistant will get it. If they truly need to leave the set, then they need to let you or someone else in authority know where they will be and for how long. Most actors will understand the need for this and will accommodate this requirement of their job. If they balk at this rule, then it may be in everyone's best interest to replace them.

58. Release Forms

The release form is a document stating that an actor, having completed work on your film, gives you permission to use their image in a film. Legally, it prevents them from making the complaint later that they didn't know that you were going to use the footage that was shot of them, or that they didn't know how the footage would be used. The main targets of a release form are people who didn't know that they were being photographed, such as in a documentary. With a little modification, others loaning you the use of their property or services can use the same release form.

Sample Actor's Release Form

In consideration of value received, acknowledged as screen credit [plus whatever else you have offered them], as full payment for services rendered, receipt whereof is hereby acknowledged, I hereby give [Name of your company], it's successors, assigns, nominees, or designees, the absolute and irrevocable right and permission to copyright, rent, lease, sell, or publish motion pictures, photographic portraits, or pictures of me in which I may be included in whole or in part, or composite in character or form, in conjunction with my own or a fictitious name, in conjunction with [Your name and your partner if you have one] own or fictitious name of their designation, or reproduction thereof in black and white, color or otherwise, made through any media at their studios or elsewhere, for art, advertising, trade, display, editorial exhibition, television, motion pictures, or any purpose whatsoever without any limitations or reservations, without further compensation from him or his successors, assigns, nominees or designees, and to which photographs I hereby release and relinquish all right, claims and title.

I hereby release, discharge, and agree to save [Name of your company], it's successors, assigns, nominees or designees, from any liability by virtue of any blurring, alteration, optical illusion, or use in composite form that may occur or be produced in the taking of the pictures, or in any processing tending towards the completion of the finished product, or for any reason whatsoever.

NAME: _____ DATE: _____

59. KEEP FROM BEING SUED BY BEING CAREFUL ABOUT WHAT YOU FILM

When you have a huge budget you can afford to make mistakes because there is enough money to fix things after the fact. However, when you make a low-budget movie you have to be especially careful not to make a mistake that can get you in trouble later.

It's important to understand that while you are shooting a scene you don't accidentally use anything that is trademarked or copyrighted (unless you have permission from the owner of that copyright or trademark). If you film the name of a business, and they don't like the idea of their business being in your movie, they may sue you. If you mention a famous person or place in your movie, and they don't like the context in which they are mentioned, they might sue you. In other words, you can be sued if you intrude on someone else's legal rights. So what can you do to avoid a lawsuit?

When you are filming exteriors, try not to film anything displaying the name of a business.

Try to avoid any reference to a real person, place, or business in your script. If you have to make a reference, then make certain your reference is accurate and you can prove that it's accurate.

60. Let's Talk About Errors and Omissions

I referred to errors and omissions earlier, in point 37, which was about insurance. However, errors and omissions have a purpose beyond conventional insurance that you need to consider carefully. Basically, errors and omissions is a form of specialized insurance designed to protect your company, and movie, just in case you were to, for any reason, infringe on the legal rights of another person or business. A general example of this would be if you were to say something that could be considered derogatory about a person, living or dead, or a business. Another general example would be if you were to use a trademarked logo without permission from the owner of that copyright or trademark.

Let me give you some specific examples based upon the experiences of filmmakers that I know. A director I once worked with used two impressionists imitating a famous singing duo for a scene in his movie. When it came time to sell his movie to a television network, some TV executives became concerned that the "actual singers" might sue the network. As a result, they didn't want to buy the broadcast rights to his film.

A producer friend of mine made arrangements to use the CD of a new singer's song as the theme of her new movie. The singer, her agent, her manager, and her lawyer all assured her that the singer had the legal rights to the song and the recording. Contracts were signed, and it was used in the film. Just before the movie's worldwide release, a composer came out of the woodwork and announced that he, not the singer, owned the song. The producer was told that if she didn't remove the song from her movie she would be sued. It turned out that the singer, her agent, her manager, and her lawyer had all lied about the song's ownership. Fortunately for my friend, by working frantically for a week, she was able to replace the song with some stock music. If she hadn't been able to replace the song, she would have definitely been sued and would have definitely lost the case.

There is also the example of a movie producer who was sued because he filmed a nude seduction scene atop a real grave in a small-town cemetery. It turned out that the widow of the man in the grave felt that the scene disgraced the memory of her dead husband. Needless to say, this created a whole series of difficult problems for the producer and the distribution company, leaving both of them very unhappy.

One of the facts of life is that if someone can find a way to sue you, he probably will. This leaves you with two choices. You can be particularly careful not to infringe on someone's potential copyright and trademark, which may or may not work; or you can get errors and omissions insurance. It's up to you to decide which is the correct course for you.

Concluding this point you will see more specific information on what errors and omissions insurance covers. You can obtain errors and omissions insurance from any insurance company that sells insurance to companies and businesses.

Errors and omissions coverage provides protection against any third party liability claims and suits which might arise from any of the following:

1. Any infringement of trademark or copyright, whether under common law or statutory law.
2. Any forms of defamation, such as libel and/or slander.
3. Any unauthorized use of characters, plots, titles, ideas, formats, or performances of artists or other performers or other program material embodied in the insured production. This only applies to such claims such as those based upon infringement of copyright or common law property rights in literacy or musical material, plagiarism, unfair competition or privacy.
4. Any breach of contract, implied in fact or in law. This would include a breach of contract resulting from the alleged submission or program, musical or literacy material used by the insured, which has been committed or alleged to have been committed by the production in connection with the creation, performance, production, exhibition, broadcast, distribution, advertising or publicizing of the "insured production."
5. Invasion or infringement with the right of privacy or publicity, whether under common law or statutory law.

61. What You Do When Everyone Realizes That Filmmaking Is Hard Work

I have never worked on a film that was fun. Satisfying, yes, but never fun. Making movies is hard work, and the novelty of filmmaking can wear thin very quickly. This can prove quite detrimental to a production.

Since your cast and crew are working for small salaries, or perhaps deferred salaries, any negative feeling on their part toward your movie can prove destructive to its outcome. It is to your advantage to keep the set's collective mood light to offset the exhausting workload. And you can be certain that the work will become exhausting. Expect it. Plan for it to happen. When things go wrong and the actors get the giggles, take a break. In fact, take frequent breaks whenever it's practical.

If your cast and crew have a problem, be certain to address that problem promptly so that they know that their needs matter to you. When they understand that their professional problems and ideas will be addressed, they feel as if they are part of something special. This type of relationship is conducive to the filmmaking process and makes the work go much more smoothly and effectively.

62. Cameras

As discussed in point 15, there are three basic formats in which to shoot your movie: film, video, and digital tape. On film you can use either a 16-millimeter or a 35-millimeter camera. On video you can use High-Band 8, Super-VHS, Mini-DV, or Beta SP. On digital you can use Mini-DV or High Definition video. The question is how do you get a camera with your limited resources? Let's consider the possibilities.

Obviously, one possibility is for you to rent a camera that you feel is suitable. Simply look up any camera rental house in the yellow pages to check the prices. Also obvious is the fact that you will need to do this before you work up you budget, rather than during production. A good way to rent a camera, as well as other film or video equipment, is to rent it for use on a weekend. The value of this lies in the fact that most rental houses won't charge you for the Friday that you pick up the camera, thereby giving you three days of camera use for the price of two.

The odds are that you won't have the money to rent a 16-millimeter or

35-millimeter camera, in which case you will need to check out other possibilities. Look into local film schools and see if you can hire a film student who owns their own camera. If that isn't possible, then take a film class so you can make use of the cameras that are available to students. Do you know a filmmaker with a camera? Perhaps you can make a deal with him or her for that camera by giving them points in the movie. A similar possibility is to hire a professional cameraperson who owns his or her own camera. If you use a filmmaker or cinematographer, make sure that they also have all the lenses they need to do the job properly. A camera without all the necessary lenses is next to useless.

Acquiring a video camera is considerably easier. If you don't own one then you probably know someone who does. If you don't, then you can buy a High-Band 8, Super-VHS, or Mini-DV camera from a local department store for a few hundred dollars. Check to see if they have discounted cameras for sale. A discounted camera is normally one that has been returned for some reason but is still a perfectly good camera. Also, buying a camera toward the end, or beginning, of the year is a good decision. Stores usually want to move out some of their equipment to make room for newer models and often place their older models on sale. If you do purchase a camera, ask if they will give you a "loaner" if, for any reason, the purchased camera were to break down and need to be repaired. This can make a big difference if it were to break down during production. Also, check to see what the camera's "lux" is. The lux of a video camera refers to the sensitivity of that particular camera to light. The lower the lux, the less light you need to light your scenes. The ideal camera is one that is either a one or a zero lux. With a camera like this, you won't need as much illumination to light your set as you would with a less light sensitive camera.

Once you have the camera you are going to use, don't forget to spend some time getting used to it. Each camera works a little differently from every other camera, and it takes time to figure out all of its strengths and weaknesses.

63. Affordable Lighting Equipment

Assuming that you can't borrow what you need, it is possible to rent lighting equipment from the same sources that would rent cameras. You can also buy them for a fairly reasonable price, which usually ranges from 400 to 1,000 dollars. The two brands most widely used by low-budget filmmakers are Smith-Victor Lights and Lowell Lights, Smith-Victor being the least expensive. You can purchase or order either from any good camera shop.

There is also a cheaper alternative. You can put together your own lighting equipment by shopping at the local hardware store. First, buy four or five 120-watt floodlights. Then purchase an equal number of 100-watt bulbs. Buy three to five pink 75-watt bulbs, three to five blue 75-watt bulbs, three to five green 75-watt bulbs, and three to five amber 75 watt bulbs. These different colored bulbs can be used for dramatic effect. If available, buy two 200-watt bulbs. These types of bulbs can be of great help if you are illuminating a large room. Buy several adapters, along with two or three 50-foot extension cords. Also purchase seven silver clamp lights. These clamp lights will eliminate the need for light stands under most situations. Be sure to buy a surge strip. Buy one red sheet of cardboard, one pink, one blue, and one dull white. These colored pieces of cardboard can be used to bounce your light onto the actors for a pleasing dramatic effect. You might want to buy some large pieces of similarly colored tissue paper to use for similar lighting effect. In the case of tissue, you simply clothes-pin the tissue onto the front of the light clamp.

If you shop around to find equipment on sale, you should be able to purchase everything you need for about 250 dollars.

64. Sound: The Difference Between Success and Disaster

One of the things that can quickly give away the low-budget origin of your movie is its sound. Far too many low-budget movies have bad sound. Oddly enough, it doesn't have to be this way. Not if you know what you are doing.

Most people have the erroneous idea that purchasing one of the more expensive microphones automatically guarantees that your movie will have superior recorded sound. This is the opposite of the truth. The cheaper microphones usually work best. There are very good reasons for this. Expensive microphones are mainly designed for concert use. Because of this, these microphones pick up a lot of background noise when you are recording dialogue. This can create terrible problems in post-production. A good, inexpensive microphone can operate within a range of 100 to 10,000 Hz (or Hertz), whereas expensive microphones have a much wider Hertz range. The value of this information lies in the fact that the range of the human voice records more effectively within the narrow Hertz range of the cheaper microphone. This means that background noise, which records at a lower and higher Hertz range, is greatly reduced during the recording process, thereby making your post-production sound work much easier.

So what does this mean to you? It means that you should purchase a cheap uni-directional microphone that works within the Hertz range previously described. Your resulting sound will be much cleaner and distinct than what you will get with any other kind of microphone. A Shure or Radio Shack microphone is ideal for low-budget filmmaking. These microphones should cost you somewhere between twenty-nine and fifty-nine dollars.

If you are shooting on film, then there will be two methods of recording the sound: single system and dual system. Some cameras can record sound directly on film when that film is coated with a magnetic stripe. This direct recording of sound upon this magnetic stripe is called single system sound. Dual system sound is accomplished with a special sound recorder, often a Nagra recorder, which is linked to your microphone and your camera so that the audiotape used to record dialogue will always be in sync with the film. It is hard to find single system cameras nowadays, but they make the editing process easier if you transfer the film to tape and do the editing in a video format. Using a dual system, you will need to transfer the sound from the recorder to magnetic film, which can then run simultaneously with the processed footage of your movie. If you intend to do your editing on tape, then a single system camera would be the preferable choice. If you are intending to do your editing on film, which isn't cost effective on a small budget, you will need to use a dual system recorder.

65. Basic Camera Techniques That Every Actor and Director Needs to Know

The technique of acting in front of the camera is of vital importance if a competent performance is to result. Sadly, not every actor knows these techniques, so it will be the director's job to teach them to all the actors working on the film. These necessary basic techniques are as follows.

1. THE NEGATIVE VOICE. The negative voice occurs when an actor speaks their lines without conviction. Each actor needs to speak their lines as if they really mean what they say, and that what they say has importance.

2. LISTENING. There is an old expression which states that "acting isn't just *acting*, it's also *reacting*." Even when an actor isn't saying their lines, they should be listening to everything that's being said around them, as well as reacting to those lines being spoken.

3. A RESONATE VOICE. Having a resonate voice is very important if you expect that voice to be recorded properly on the set. A resonate voice is more distinct and impressive, and records with great clarity.

4. LESS IS MORE. Actors working before a camera, unlike actors on stage, don't have to play to the last role of the theater by acting broadly. They only have to play to the camera; therefore, their acting needs to be subtler than on the stage.

5. THE THREE-QUARTER POSITION. Actors photograph better in a three-quarter position. There are three positions in relation to the camera: full front, which has the actor facing the camera; profile, which has the actor turned sideways to the camera; and three-quarter, which has the actor in a position that is in-between the previous two. The three-quarter position is the most desirable because the actor photographs better with regards to modeling their face, creating a dramatic effect that is pleasing to the eye.

6. THE CLOSER THE SHOT, THE MORE THINGS ARE EXAGGER-ATED. In a close-up, an actor shouldn't move very much because the greater size of the image creates the illusion of greater speed and drama. An actor need only give the slightest reaction, with the least amount of movement, to get their point across.

7. THE ILLUSION OF DISTANCE. Film and video are two-dimensional; therefore, it is often necessary to position actors closer together than they would ever stand in real life. It may feel awkward to the actors, but it photographs better than a real stance would.

8. BLINKING/SQUINTING. Under bright lights, or a bright sun, most actors will have a hard time not blinking. Having the actor close their eyes, then look in the direction of the light source easily solves this. Gradually, the light will "soak" through their eyelids, and their irises will close down. When they open their eyes, the light will seem less bright, and they will be less likely to blink.

9. FIRST POSITION. First position refers to the specific place where an actor is standing at the beginning of the shot. If the actor is told to go "back to first" (also called back to one), it means that he/she needs to go back to the position they were in before the camera began rolling.

10. HITTING YOUR MARK. An actor's mark is the spot that an actor stands on during a scene. "Hitting your mark" refers to ending up

on exactly the right spot when an actor comes to a halt after walking. It's important that an actor can stop on the precise spot; otherwise, they will go out of focus or be off frame. There are two simple methods to help an actor hit their mark. The easiest is to put a small sandbag where you want them to stop. The instant their foot touches the sandbag they will know to stop. The most effective method is to have the actor stand next to the mark, then walk backward to their first position. The number of steps tells them when to stop. For some reason, walking backward and counting the steps works considerably better than walking forward and counting the steps.

If your actors employ these basic acting techniques, your movie will go a lot smoother and have a greater professional polish.

66. EFFECTIVE LIGHTING IS NOT THAT HARD

Good lighting doesn't have to be difficult when you know some basic rules. Once you know them you should be able to light your scene in just a few minutes. However, there are some terms that you need to know. *Key light* is the main source of lighting for your actors. *Fill light* is the lighting of lesser intensity on that part of the actor's face which is opposite the key light. *Cross lighting* is lighting which originates from the side of the set. *Backlighting* is a light source from behind an actor/actress which highlights their hair. Now that you know these terms, let's move on to the handful of rules you need to learn.

Interior Lighting

(a). Never light your actors from their front, or from a position near the camera. This creates an amateurish home-movie look to your lighting. It is much more effective to light your actors from the side, often called cross lighting, which is much more pleasing to the eye.

(b). Before you try to light your scene, figure out where the lighting would originate if it were coming from an actual light source within the scene (from overhead lights, lamps, a fireplace, etc.). This will help guide you as to how to set up your lights. Once you know the source of the scene's light, all you need do is light the scene as if the key light came from there (in a dramatic way, of course). If need be, change the set pieces to accommodate the dramatic lighting you choose to create.

(c). If your scene requires highly dramatic lighting, then light the scene from the side of your set, just out of camera range, with harsh lighting. This type of lighting is perfect for suspense, horror, and intense drama. If the scene isn't highly dramatic, or if the scene's mood is light in style, then use defused lighting by bouncing the light off a white piece of cardboard that isn't slick. You can also defuse the light by shining it through some white tissue paper, white silk or white gauze.

(d). The further back you cross light an actor's face, the more sinister and/or dramatic it becomes due to the greater amount of modeling.

(e). For a glamour effect, normally used to make women look more attractive, you should backlight your actress. By lighting the actress from behind and above, a halo effect is created. If it isn't possible to light the actress from above, then you can do it from below — but expect that it will be harder to achieve the look you want. This type of lighting also helps separate the actor from the background.

(f). For an ominous or horrific effect, light your actors from the front and upward toward their faces. The bizarre shadowing on their faces distorts their features. The closer the actor is to the light source, and the lower that light source is, the greater the distortion.

(g). If it is at all possible, light your actors' faces so their eyes are highlighted when in close-up. This will give a greater sense of life and vitality to their eyes. It also gives their eyes more detail.

(h). If you are shooting on film, then make certain you have a light meter, which can be purchased at any camera shop. When you have lit your set, take a reading on your light meter, then set the F-stop on your camera for the same setting as the light meter.

Exterior Lighting

Any artificial lighting done out of doors during the daylight isn't practical on a low budget. However, you can instead make the sun work for you by using a reflector. A reflector is a square piece of board with a surface that can reflect the sunlight onto the actors in the scene. Coating a large piece of cardboard with the dull side of some aluminum foil easily creates a reflector. Any lighting done at night will utilize the same lighting requirements used in lighting an interior. If the lighting is too harsh, then you can defuse the lighting by using a window screen. If you don't have access to a window screen, then a good substitute is a white sheet. You take the white sheet, pull it taut between four poles, and then place it near the actors in the scene.

67. CAMERA PLACEMENT

While there are a million and one angles from which to shoot a scene, there is usually one particular angle that is ideal for your master shot. A master shot is generally a long shot that photographs everything taking place in the scene. Before you pick your angle, remember that this is not a stage production. Consequently, the camera need not be "down stage center," photographing everyone entering and exiting from stage left and right. Make certain that the angle you use makes your visual composition interesting. Perhaps you can place your camera a little left or right of center. Or perhaps you can place the camera at a 45-degree angle to the set. Just remember to block all the action so that it will play to the camera in such a way that it can see everything that takes place.

As a rule, it's a good idea to place your camera about two inches below the eye level of your actors. This gives prominence to the actors and allows their features to photograph with fuller expression.

When you shoot your close-ups, don't utilize the same angle you used for your master shot. Move your camera to the side, several inches to a foot, from its original position. Since no actor/actress plays their scene precisely the same way twice, it will make the difference between the long shot and close-up less noticeable.

The easiest, and possibly best, way to figure out what to photograph in close-up is to do the following: watch the scene as it is rehearsed and take note where your attention goes at any particular moment. This will tell you what the audience will want to see in close-up.

There is a general rule in cinematography: do not break the invisible wall (also called the *action axis* and the *180-degree rule*)! What all these terms refer to is that once you have photographically established the side of something, or someone, do not suddenly set up another camera angle on the opposite side of that something or someone. In other words, if you photograph an actor on the right side, do not do another camera angle on that actor's left. The reason for this is that the effect can be rather jarring once the shots are edited together in post-production. Compose your shots so that they take place within the boundary of the "invisible wall" of the side you are filming.

68. Tips on Recording Effective Sound

Contrary to what most filmmakers believe, a boom is not always needed to record sound. For those who don't know, a boom is a pole-like device on which a microphone can be fitted so that individual actors can be recorded clearly. All you really need do is place your microphone a foot outside the frame of your camera. The uni-directional microphone described in point 64 should give you good clean sound even from several yards away. All you have to do is place it on a microphone stand and aim it toward the actors delivering dialogue. If you feel that you would obtain better sound by recording closer to the actors, you can place your microphone on the set and hide it behind a prop or set piece where it won't be seen. If you are bound and determined to use a boom, then you can jury-rig a boom by attaching a microphone to the end of a fishing pole. If you can't do it any other way, you can duct tape the microphone, at a 45-degree angle, to the end of the pole. The problem with this is that you will need a good boom operator to make use of this. An inexperienced boom operator will make noise each time they shift the angle of the boom and will ruin the scene.

Always record a minute or so of background sound when you finish a scene, just in case it might be needed in post-production to lay onto your soundtrack. Since background noise often changes from moment to moment, recording background sound can help make the sound seem more consistent when you insert your close-ups.

Make sure you duct tape your microphone cable to the floor. If you don't do this, actors and crew will continually trip over it, no matter how many time you warn them to be careful.

Make sure that you don't change the position of your microphone from shot to shot within a scene. If you do, your shots will not edit together properly in post-production because your actors will sound completely different in each shot. Do it only if it is absolutely necessary to hear everyone clearly. Just keep in mind that this may create problems later.

If you are shooting on film, your camera is likely to be too noisy to use without picking up its sound on your recorder. This is particularly problematic when filming in a confined space, such as a house interior. The simplest way to resolve this problem is to wrap your camera tightly in a sleeping bag, which muffles the sound.

69. Coverage, the Ultimate Protection

To most people the term "coverage" usually refers to some sort of insurance, but in cinematic terms it has a completely different meaning. To a director, coverage refers to all the various shots that photographically covers the scene and makes editing easier.

Generally speaking, the greater the variety of camera angles taken during a scene, the easier it is to edit that scene during post-production. As such, it's a good idea to get a wide variety of inserts and close-ups so that you are protected when you do start editing. This will allow you to fix mistakes and make improvements. This also lets you alter the "feel" of a scene if you choose to. You may wish to make the mood of the scene lighter, or more sinister, or make its pace faster or slower. Having a variety of shots to "cut to" allows you to make a number of choices in post-production. Such choices can make the difference between a mediocre film and a good one.

70. Photos on the Set Are Important

At some point you are going to want to do some promotion for your film. One of the promotion tools you will need are photographs of your actors. You will need these photos for the news media, as well as your poster. The best way to acquire these is to have a photographer on the set taking pictures. It's not a good idea to have them take photographs during an actual scene because they would probably distract the cast and crew, as well as get in the way. The photographer can, however, take photos of the rehearsals, as well as individual photos of any actor/actress who is not working on a scene.

You may find that you can't afford to have a professional photographer on the set for the whole production. If this is the case, then pick out those scenes that would best represent your movie, and have your professional photographer on the set only when you will be shooting those scenes. Another alternative is to have some member of the crew do it. Generally speaking, there is usually at least one member of the crew who likes to dabble in photography. If their job as a crewmember keeps them too busy to take photographs while you are filming, then set some time aside at the conclusion of the day's work to take the photographs you need.

71. Meals and Craft Service Can Save Your Production

Here's a fact to remember when it comes to your cast and crew: they will work their brains out for you if they are well fed. When your cast and crew are working for little or no money, they can become very cranky if they feel their stomachs are being neglected. When your craft service table is constantly full of snacks and drinks for them, they will be far less likely to become fed up with your production and quit.

Make certain that your meals are filling and satisfying. Take into account the tastes and dietary needs of your cast and crew. Do the actors/actresses have a favorite food or drink? Does anyone have some special dietary needs? Are there medical considerations to take into account? Find out, and try to accommodate those needs.

A well-stocked craft service table can also relieve the nervous energy that your cast and crew experience, as well as occupy them when they aren't working. On your craft service table try to have the following: soda pop (regular and diet), crackers, pastry, fruit (apples, oranges, grapes, bananas, etc.), instant coffee (regular and decaffeinated), sugar packets, sugar substitute packets, non-dairy creamer, nuts, little chocolate candies, Styrofoam cups, stir sticks, plastic spoons, an ice chest full of ice, and a percolator full of hot water. If it's winter, also include packages of hot chocolate, tea bags, and cough drops.

72. Special Effects on the Set

Special effects can be a major part of your movie's production values, and therefore can become a huge selling point to a distributor once the movie is completed. If you are planning to do your editing on tape or on computer, then you will be able to do a lot of effects that would normally cost a lot of money if you were doing optical effects on film. Despite this, doing special effects on the set can save you a lot of time and money during post-production. It should be noted, however, that you should not attempt to do special effects for your movie unless you can do it well. Any special effects proving to be inadequate will seriously compromise your movie.

There are a number of special effects that can be done cheaply on the set (or at least without complicated post-production) which look good when executed properly. Let's discuss these effects, which can be applied in a variety of ways.

The Cut

Perhaps the simplest special effect is the cut. By using it, something can instantly transform or disappear. It is accomplished by filming your scene up to the point where the effect is to take place, then stop running your camera. You make the change that you want by replacing something, removing something, or including something in front of the camera. Then you start up the camera again. Once the scene is played continuously, it will appear that something has instantly changed, vanished, or suddenly appeared. The camera, of course, cannot change its position or angle between shots.

The Perspective Shot

The perspective shot is when both the foreground and the background are in focus. This allows you to have a small object in the foreground camera appear much larger (a flying saucer, for example). It also makes anything in the background appear very small (for example, a leprechaun).

The Cutout

A variation of the perspective shot is to use a paper cutout as part of a perspective shot. If a paper cutout is glued to a pane of glass positioned before the camera lens, that cutout can look like it's part of the scene. A set can be made to appear larger and more impressive this way. Actors can seemingly enter a creepy old house that is not really there. In addition, if you slide the glass from side to side, you can make someone, or something, fly past the camera. The possibilities are limited only by your imagination. It is very important, though, that you never use a cutout photograph that legally belongs to someone else.

The Mirror Effect

If you place a mirror at a forty-five degree angle to your camera lens it will reflect whatever is off to the side of the camera. Therefore, it can create a split-screen effect in front of the camera. A variation of this effect is to use some clear glass instead of a mirror. On the opposite side of the camera you place whatever you would like to superimpose over the background. If you keep it dark over the image you want to superimpose, and then slowly illuminate it, whatever is there will appear over the background. This can be used to create such effects as ghosts or laser beams.

The Invisible Wire

Using some monofilament fishing line, you can move objects "invisibly" because the fishing line will be unable to be seen. You can also use regular thread that is the same color as the background, or something called invisible thread, to create the same effect. This special effect can also be used to support objects of moderate weight in front of the camera, such as a miniature rocket.

The Tilt Shot

If used correctly, the tilt shot, also called "dutching the shot," can heighten the drama of a scene. This effect is employed when the camera is tilted to one side. Used properly, this effect can make a small hill look like a dangerous cliff, or a concrete walkway look like the side of a building.

The Miniature

The miniature is a scale model used to create a location which would be impossible (or financially impractical) to film. Assuming that you are not an expert in making miniatures, you can find reasonably priced scale models at your local model train shop. With some careful construction, you can assemble and paint an effective recreation of a house, castle, mansion, etc. You will probably need to create backgrounds for the miniature as well. This is quite difficult for the inexperienced model builder, but you might be able to get a model train enthusiast to help. You need to film miniatures from a very low angle and at a higher film speed than in a regular shot, with that film speed generally being in relation to the size of the miniature. For example, if the miniature were one-tenth the size of the real object, then you would photograph it at a film speed at least ten times faster than normal. It is also a good idea to film the miniature outside to give your lighting a more realistic look. Please keep in mind that miniatures should only be used when you are shooting on film. Video is not a practical medium for this effect due to *most* cameras' inability to operate at high speed.

Pyrotechnics

While true pyrotechnics require a license, it is possible to fake explosions by substituting simple effects, such as a smoke bomb, sparklers, compressed air that blows out dirt and earth-colored cork chips, or the exhaust from a fire extinguisher. Simply place the smoke bomb, or whatever special effect that you prefer to use, where you wish the explosion to take place and set it off at the right moment. This particular effect is especially effective when it is followed up by an impressive stock shot of a fiery explosion.

The Stock Shot

Probably the simplest and least expensive special effect is the stock shot. Stock shots are footage culled from other movies, which are for sale. The cheapest way to obtain such footage is not through a business specializing in stock footage, which can be expensive, but through the use of public domain American movies. Check out the DVDs at your local video store. Make a list of the older color movies that contain the effects you need. Next, check the internet site for the Library of Congress to see if the movie's copyright has elapsed. If so, then you can legally use footage from that movie.

Make-Up Effects

Make-up effects for low-budget movies tend to fall into two categories: make-up that distorts features of the actor, usually for a horror film; and blood effects for use in horror and action movies. The following will explain the particulars of those effects most commonly used.

• **Blood.** You can, of course, buy stage blood from theatrical supply companies, which are easily found in the yellow pages, or from costume shops in your home town; but it is much easier and cheaper to make your own. Take a bottle of Karo corn syrup, add a little red food dye, then complete the mixture with a few drops of blue food dye. You may need to experiment a little with this mixture until it looks exactly the way you want.

• **Monster Face.** Normally, the distortion of features is accomplished by using specially made foam rubber appliances glued to the face with spirit gum. There is a cheaper way to achieve the same effect, however. Long before such appliances were common, Hollywood make-up artists used a combination of latex, spirit gum and cotton to create great make-up effects. This process requires six things: spirit gum, liquid latex or duo eyelash adhesive, cotton, castor oil, patience, and artistic ability. To distort an actor's features, or any other part of their body, you lightly coat the area with spirit gum, then let it dry to become tacky. You continue by laying small amounts of cotton onto the area you want to distort, and coat the cotton with liquid latex or duo eyelash adhesive. You repeat the process, building up the area to distort until that area is recreated into what you want. You then coat the area with castor oil to prevent any make-up being absorbed into the liquid latex. Finally, you coat the area, and surrounding area of skin, with a liquid make-up or grease paint to complete the make-up effect. To remove the cotton, latex, and spirit gum, use fingernail polish remover to dissolve them. Then use cold crème to remove any remaining grease paint or liquid make-up.

• **Bullet Hits.** Usually this is done with a squib, which is an exploding device worn under an actor's clothes. When detonated, it gives the impression of a bullet tearing through the clothes and body beneath. This legally requires a pyrotechnics expert and, as a result, can be expensive. A decent looking substitute for exploding a squib is to fire a paint gun filled with red paint "bullets" at the actor. The effect can be quite believable, especially when the shot is cut quickly in post-production editing. A bullet hit to the head, or to an exposed part of the actor's body, can also be done easily. Using mortician's wax or nose putty (available at costume shops or at Halloween stores), you create an open wound on the area to be "shot." You then use make-up to discolor the area within the fake wound to simulate the muscle beneath the skin. Then you place a small clothing button, with some invisible thread or monofilament attached, in the fake wound and cover it with a layer of nose putty. You then coat the area with make-up to match the skin. Then, while filming the bullet hit, you yank hard on the thread, which causes the button and fake blood to pop out violently — as if a bullet had ripped it open.

All of these effects can be very impressive when executed carefully. They can also be used in combination with one another. The opportunities for these effects are only as limited as your creativity.

73. PLAN FOR THINGS TO GO WRONG

It's time for a reality check. The fact of the matter is, no matter how much you plan things, something will inevitably go wrong. It may start raining. An actor or actor may not show up to work for some unknown reason. A location you counted on may suddenly become unavailable. A million things could go haywire. A good movie is not just the result of your good planning.

It is equally the result of you effectively dealing with the myriad problems that occur.

Many problems can be anticipated. Work out an alternative shooting schedule that takes into account the possibility of bad weather. In what interiors could you film if that possibility became a reality? Could you incorporate the bad weather into the dialogue without ruining the continuity of your movie? If an actor/actress doesn't show up, could you give his or her lines to someone else? If you can't use the location you want, can you rewrite the scene so that it can take place somewhere else?

As you are planning your film, ask yourself a question when you schedule each scene: "What could conceivably go wrong?" See if you can come up with several solutions to any possible problem. By doing this, you will be more fully prepared to deal with those problems when they arise.

74. TEN HARD LESSONS ABOUT PRODUCTION

1. The more you know about the intricacies of post-production, the easier it is to film technically complicated scenes. If you know how an action scene is to be edited, then it is much simpler for you to choreograph the action and film that scene. The more you know about visual effects, the easier it will be when you have to properly photograph scenes that employ those visual effects.
2. Keeping on schedule is vital when you are directing. A good director may have to change ideas midstream because there isn't time to film the scene the way he or she wants. A good director also knows when to stop trying to make the scene look perfect and move on to the next scene. A mediocre director tries to make every scene look perfect, and, as a result, never finishes the movie.
3. Always put your director's script in a specific spot and instruct the cast and crew never to touch it. If you don't do this, your script will continually go missing, costing you a lot of wasted time trying to find it.
4. Allow for shots that weren't planned on. Sometimes they can be the best shots in the movie. Please keep in mind that no matter how amazing an unplanned shot could potentially be, *don't* film it unless it fits into the continuity of those shots already filmed, and if it won't compromise those shots you still need to film.
5. If possible, film the actor's close-ups before you do any other camera angles. You will obtain better overall sound quality in close-up,

and if an actor becomes temperamental and storms off the set, you can film a double from behind in the master shot, thereby saving the scene.

6. Be very protective of your locations. Do not damage or misuse them, or you might lose access to them before you are finished filming there.

7. Assign someone the job of making certain that each actor knows his or her shooting schedule for the following day. If you don't, one or more of your actors will probably forget what time they are scheduled to show up and where they are supposed to appear.

8. Make sure that each actor and technician assigned to a day's work is given simple and clear directions to wherever you are filming; otherwise, they will get lost. One simple solution to this problem is to have the cast and crew meet at a centralized location that is well known, and then travel to new locations from there.

9. Be sure to have on hand at least two "six to eight" hour battery packs for your video camera. Procure more if you can afford them. Without these battery packs you will find it necessary to periodically halt your production in order to recharge your solitary battery. Extra batteries can also help you record better quality sound. How? If your camera's power pack is plugged into a wall socket, you will record an annoying electric hum on the sound track. Having multiple battery packs avoids this problem. An even better solution to this sound distortion is to use a video attachment called a "pin lift," which should be available at any good video retailer that sells video equipment.

10. Always keep several rolls of duct tape on hand during production. You will find that it has a million uses and will come in handy during a crisis. For example, it can seal an actor's ripped costume, tape down a set piece that won't stay still, and jury-rig equipment that has fallen apart.

75. Flashback, Part Three

The advent of sound, combined with the Great Depression, made the early thirties a difficult period for those low-budget production companies producing genre movies. Another problem they faced was the huge amount of competition. Companies like Liberty, Chesterfield, Lone Star, Monogram, Mascot, and countless others fought an ongoing battle with one another to get their films into those independent theaters not owned by the major studios. Herbert J. Yates, the head of Consolidated Film Labs, gathered several of the better companies together with a plan that would help solve their problem of too much competition. These companies would merge and pool all of their respective resources. The advantages of each company were evaluated and made more efficient. Each company's weaknesses were uncovered and corrected. Personnel, soundstages, and distribution connections were combined to form a new company called Republic Studios.

Republic was founded on the idea of producing action films, westerns, and serials with small budgets but high production values. Over the years, Republic produced countless successful movies with such stars as Gene Autry, Roy Rogers, and John Wayne. Their movie serials were so well produced that they are enjoyed — and studied — by film buffs today.

Republic kept their costs down by understanding the most important rules of low-budget production: *know your craft*; *don't be wasteful*; and *stress what you do best*. Republic knew that action was their biggest selling point, so they stressed stunt work and quick pacing. To accomplish this, they hired the best stuntmen in Hollywood and hired screenwriters who knew how to keep their scripts moving at a brisk pace. To aid in keeping their costs down, they hired the Lydecker brothers, who were an amazing special effects team specializing in miniatures. Their detailed models not only reduced costs but also enhanced production values. By using miniatures, Republic avoided costly post-production optical work; plus, Republic's movie heroes could have adventures in distant lands, fly to alien worlds, and escape from every kind of exploding building, tidal wave, burning oil field, or crashing plane that the screenwriters could conceive. Republic also hired creative and knowledgeable directors who knew how to plan shots that would maximize quality while minimizing the expense of shooting a lot of footage. Apart from the stars that Republic had under contract, they also hired actors capable of providing professional performances despite long hours, tiring working conditions, and little pay. In other words, if you couldn't do your job well, you didn't work at Republic Studios.

From its creation in the mid-thirties to its ultimate sale to NTA in the mid-fifties, Republic proved itself to be a successful master of the low-budget action film and carved a special place for the studio in cinematic history.

In conclusion: Republic kept its cost down by doing a good and efficient job *during production*. "Good" and "efficient"— words to remember.

IV. Post-Production

76. WHERE TO FIND AFFORDABLE EDITING

In the post-production process, editing can be your greatest expense, being as it involves technology that it is not easily accessible. Apart from hiring an editor, who can be very expensive, there are other means of affordable editing. This is particularly true when post-production is done on a video editing system or on computer. Before we go any further, it should be understood that all of the following suggestions would involve you doing the editing yourself.

Public Access

TV stations are supposed to set aside a few hours each week for public access to satisfy FCC regulations. This also includes local cable stations. Basically, Public Access means that the *public* has *access* to broadcast airtime and/or television technology. Most people use public access to put on their own talk shows, cooking shows, etc., while not taking advantage of the video editing possibilities that the station has available. Check with your local TV stations and find out what they have to offer. Also, find out if you can take classes in how to use the equipment. Keep in mind that there will probably be severe limits concerning the amount of time you may use the equipment, and how the technology may be used.

Schools

Many high schools and community colleges have film or audio/visual classes. Find out if you can access their editing equipment. If you have to become a student to use this equipment, so what? Take a class. It's worth taking a few tests to save thousands of dollars in editing fees.

Editing, Computer Programs

Computer programs enabling you to edit tapes are reasonably afford-able, but they have limits to consider. One important limit is that they eat up a lot of space on your computer, so it is unlikely that you will be able to edit an entire feature on your computer. Due to this limitation, you should edit only five to ten minutes of your movie, then transfer it to tape. Later you can properly assemble all the disconnected sections of your movie on rented video editing equipment. Since all the important editing has already been done, the assembling of these video sections can be accomplished at minimal cost.

Renting Professional Editing Equipment

In areas where a great deal of professional video work takes place (Los Angeles, San Francisco, New York, etc.), there are post-production facilities which will let you rent their video editing equipment. Every so often you will be able to find a business that rents their equipment at an affordable rate. Often there will be further discounts if you purchase your editing hours in blocks of ten. The problem here is that you will need to have a good work-ing knowledge of the editing equipment. It is also important to know that you will spend many weeks editing. Do not attempt this unless you have enough money to rent the equipment for at least a month.

Hiring a Professional Video Editor

Normally, hiring a video editor can be a very expensive proposition, but it's possible to find one at a reasonable price if you know how to negotiate a deal properly. Offer a percentage in your movie in exchange for their serv-ices. Odds are they will say no, but it can't hurt to ask. A greater likelihood is that they might offer their services at a discounted price in exchange for a percentage.

Editing Negative Film

If you are doing your post production on film, which I don't recom-mend on a very small budget, the best you can do is to call any and all nearby post-production facilities that deals with film. Then, in a manner not unlike the arrangement with the professional video editor mentioned above, you negotiate a deal for the sound and negative conformation costs. Negative conforming refers to the process by which the negative of your film is spliced together to make a master negative, a copy of which is needed to create the dupe negative needed make prints of your movie. It is conceivable that you might be able to hire a film student to do your post-production work for you with the equipment they have access to at their college. You may also be able to do the editing of the one-lite daily (raw footage printed from your negative which hasn't been color corrected) with a borrowed or purchased 16-millimeter splicer. Eventually, you will need to go to a film production facility to do most of the remaining work, since it is impossible to do anything more without the proper equipment. For this reason I recommend you transfer your film to video for the post-production work.

Keep in mind that, depending on the financial circumstances under which you have to do your post-production, it may be necessary to combine several of these methods in order to complete the editing of your film.

77. IN WHAT FORMAT SHOULD YOU EDIT?

There are varieties of formats in which you can edit, just as there are a wide number of formats to shoot in (see point 15). Of course, you can edit your movie in any particular format that you choose, but the ones I will be discussing here are those which will give you a superior image suitable for selling your film to distributors.

Three Quarter Inch

Of all the formats listed on this page, this is the one analog format which will probably be most readily available to you (analog referring to any format other than digital). Most of the post-production facilities that might be available to you will have editing equipment in either this format or S-VHS.

High-Band 8 and S-VHS

These are two perfectly acceptable analog formats for editing. You get an image very close to the slightly superior Beta SP, plus the advantage of affordability of tapes. Sadly, it is becoming difficult to readily purchase Super-VHS; consequently, High-Band 8 might be the more practical choice between these two formats.

Beta SP and M2

These formats are the two best analog formats. They are, unfortunately, rather expensive and usually only available from videotape distributors in major cities. Of the two formats, M2 is the superior format because it retains the integrity of its resolution better.

Digital

If you are editing with a special digital, non-linear editing computer, such as an Avid or a Casablanca, you can obtain an image that will probably be superior to what you would get in an analog format. However, you will need to transfer your film to some sort of tape format upon completion.

78. Editing Tips

Here are a few helpful tips for editing your movie.

(a) When editing, try to cut during an action. The differences between the two shots are less jarring that way.

(b) When cutting during an action, edit the second shot so that it takes place one to three frames earlier than the precise moment the previous shot ended. These overlapping frames allow the human eye to adjust to the change from one camera angle to the other.

(c) An effective way to make a transition from one scene to another without an expensive dissolve is to "cut to" the exterior of a scene's location where you can hear the dialogue taking place inside. Once established, you can cut to the scene taking place inside.

(d) Another way to accomplish a transition without dissolves is to use a J-cut, also called an L-cut. Just before the previous scene ends, you bring up some of the background noise, or a few words of dialogue, from the next scene. In this way the audience is more prepared for the shift from one scene to the next.

(e) Don't make a cut unless there is a good reason to make a cut. If there is no good reason for the cut, the audience will be visually jarred by the transition.

(f) If a scene has a lengthy piece of dialogue, it's a good idea to periodically cut to the reaction of someone listening to what is being said. This cross-cutting between actors helps keep the audience from becoming bored.

(g) If an actor messes up a line, cut out the bad portion of the line and cover the editing glitch with a cutaway of someone's reaction.

79. SOUND EFFECTS AND EFFECTIVE SOUND

Keep in mind the following things when you are doing the post-production sound work for your movie.

(a) When adjusting your sound levels, make them as loud as possible without causing distortion. If needed, you can lower the decibels of your sound track later when you mix in all the sound effects and music.

(b) Don't worry about perfecting each of your individual sound tracks as you are editing. You will have to adjust those sound levels once they are combined anyway, so don't focus all your energy on making any specific track perfect. It's how they sound mixed *together* that's important.

(c) It doesn't matter how "real" a sound effect is, it only matters how "real" the sound seems to the audience. Real punches don't sound like they do in movies, but the public has come to believe that they should sound a certain way. Lasers have no sound, yet they always make a weird futuristic noise in the movies. You have to use the kind of sound that your audience, and distributor, expects; otherwise, you will find that they will not accept your movie.

(d) If you have no other option, you can always use sound effects from *old* public domain American films. Just make sure that there is no music over the scene. You will find a wealth of punches, kicks, gunshots, etc. in old movies. Be absolutely certain that the movie is public domain, however. You can check on the Library of Congress website to verify that there are no current copyright holders. DVDs of American public domain movies are also a good source for stock footage when their resolution is good enough.

(e) If you are doing your post-production sound on film, then at some point you will need to "sound transfer" your taped dialogue. This will transfer your taped dialogue onto film, which will eventually need to be integrated onto your print when all the post-production work is done on your movie. Post-production on film is an expensive proposition, and I don't recommend it to a filmmaker with limited funds. What some filmmakers do to lower their costs, however, is to transfer their film to video and either do all their post-production there, or use it to do all the sound work and then transfer the integrated sound to film upon completion.

(f) If you find that there is a *minor* problem with the background noise in your scene, that problem can be disguised by laying some soft background music over the scene.

(g) If the background noise between two or more edited shots is so different that it reveals that they were done at separate times, you will need to add some similar background sound recorded independently of those shots. I referred to this in point 68. Fade-in the sound during the first shot, and fade-out the sound before the end of the last shot. The background differences between the shots will then become unnoticeable.

80. ADR, THE EASY WAY

ADR stands for "additional dialogue replacement." It refers to any dialogue dubbed during post-production (also called looping) to replace the original dialogue.

There are two basic reasons for ADR: to replace any unsuitable dialogue or to dub all the movie's dialogue.

Unsuitable dialogue could be the result of unexpected loud noises in the background at the time of the recording, a word or line mangled by an actor, or perhaps poor placement of the microphone. Dubbing the entire movie may be necessary when you are shooting your movie with a film camera. Film cameras can be rather noisy and often require the use of a device called a blimp. Essentially, a blimp is a fiberglass shell that houses the camera, minimizing the sound of the camera when it's in use. Rather than dealing with the continual problems of sound, the filmmaker may choose to film the scenes with the intention of replacing all the dialogue later. Dubbing an entire movie is difficult, time consuming, and can be expensive. As a result, I don't recommend this unless you have access to all the video recording equipment that you need free of charge, as well as actors who are willing to dub all their dialogue on a deferred salary.

Most ADR work includes the mistake of having an actor study the video or filmed image of their performance, then try to match an individual line by reading that same line into a tape recorder that works in synchronization with the dialogue of the movie or video. This process is repeated, line by line, until all of their dialogue is completed for the movie. The entire process of dubbing is then repeated again with each actor/actress in the movie. The problem with this is that it is very time consuming, and the actor is so focused with the precision of the lip-sync that they often lose a lot of the creative energy of their vocal performance. A more satisfying solution to the lip-sync problem is to have the actor in question "listen" to the dialogue that needs to be dubbed, then read their lines into a tape or video recorder. For some reason actors have an easier time matching the speed and rhythm of the original line when they are repeating what they have heard. This is very much like hearing a song on the radio, then singing that song with the same timing as the original recording artist. Rather than try to make each line a perfect match, get the sync as good as reasonably possible, then, whenever the dialogue doesn't match perfectly, cut away to someone's reaction. You can then return to the original lip-synced shot after the cutaway.

81. WHERE DO YOU FIND MUSIC?

There are two ways to obtain background music for your movie: have original music composed, or use stock music. Let's examine each possibility.

Original Music

You may be able to hire a local composer for your movie by offering him or her a small percentage of your film. The problem here is that most composers of music have little or no training in the composition of movie background music. Generally, such composers tend to be capable of writing songs and nothing else. Even if they are capable of composing background music, they may be slow and undisciplined. While it is possible to find someone who will meet your musical needs, it is, unfortunately, somewhat unlikely.

Stock Music

By checking the Hollywood yellow pages, or the internet, you will find many special businesses specializing in selling background music to producers needing music for their movie, video, or television projects. Payment for this music will vary, depending upon what rights you purchase. You will want to acquire worldwide rights for video, TV and theatrical showings *in perpetuity*. You can buy rights to individual pieces of music on a CD which may contain a number of stock musical pieces. By checking around, you will find quite a few businesses selling musical CDs at a very reasonable price. Sometimes they will charge as little as a hundred dollars a CD. Normally there will be a catalogue which will explain the mood and styles of music on each CD. It's a good idea to obtain a free sample CD to make sure the company's musical style will compliment your movie. You may want to buy several CDs to make certain you will have all the dramatic mood music you need.

82. MUSIC TIPS

Keep in mind the following suggestions when you are selecting stock music or suggesting ideas to your composer.

(a) When selecting music for a scene, study the scene in question until you have a strong sense of its rhythm. That rhythm will tell you what kind of beat the music has to have.

(b) Ideally, each of the main characters in your film should have a musical theme that is often heard when that character appears onscreen. This can help create immediate character delineation and heighten drama. It can also create a sense of foreboding, as in the case of the shark theme in *Jaws*.

(c) Don't have the sound level of the music so high that it becomes difficult to lower that level over dialogue in an unobtrusive manner. If there is no dialogue, this doesn't matter.

(d) Never assume that a piece of recognizable music is public domain simply because it's old. Musical copyrights last much longer than many other forms of copyrighted material. It is also possible that the music may be copyrighted overseas, which can have a longer copyright period than in America.

(e) If someone offers you the use of a song in exchange for screen credit in your movie, make certain that you can get documentation that they own full rights to that song. If they are merely the song's singer, they may not have any rights. If they are only one of the composers, then they do not have the right to make a deal without the consent of the other composer(s).

(f) No matter what kind of music you might have the rights to, don't use it unless it fits the mood of the scene in which it is inserted. If it doesn't match the mood of the scene, it will be counter-productive.

(g) If you have a piece of music that doesn't fit any scene, then see if there is a scene in which someone is listening to a radio or CD. If so, then a portion of the song can be played over this scene.

(h) The length on individual stock music varies. It can be quite short. Make sure that you purchase the rights to pieces of music that are three minutes or longer. This will give you greater latitude in fitting the music to the scene you are working on.

(i) It may be necessary to edit two or more pieces of music together to fit the length of your scene. To do this, you need to fade out one piece of music as you fade in the next. This will probably require some experimentation before the two pieces of music blend together without being noticed.

83. TITLES AND VISUAL EFFECTS

If you are doing your titles (a.k.a. credits) on film (hopefully by now you have realized that this is not a good idea), then you will have to go to a specialized post-production house called a "title house." Such companies not only do the titles for your film but often do visual effects as well. Creating your titles and visual effects on film can be very expensive. I suggest you do your titles and/or visual effects on tape or computer.

If you are editing on tape or computer then it is reasonably easy to do the titles. Keep in mind that editing on tape is linear — all the editing has to be done in sequence. For this reason, it is a good idea to transfer a couple of minutes of black footage onto the beginning of the movie, which can be replaced by your opening credits at the conclusion of the movie's editing process. It is important that your credits be the last piece of visual editing you do because your acknowledgements may change. This is less of a problem if you are doing your editing on a non-linear digital editor. Since this kind of editing can be non-sequential, the titles could be done later. It would be a good idea to check to see if this will work, though. On some digital editors, adding credits after you have finished the main body of your movie can shift your sound so that the music and sound effects would be out of sync.

There are a number of visual effects included in a video editing system that can be incorporated into your movie. The variety of effects available to you will depend upon the editing system you employ. Many systems are able to do dissolves (one scene gives way to another), wipes (one scene shifts position to replace another), fades (where a shot slowly become black or starts off black and slowly brightens until it is normal), and color fades (where a shot slowly becomes, or stops being, a color other than black). Some systems will be able to do many more effects. Digital editing systems can.

If, for some reason, your editing system can't do titles or the visual effects that you need, then it may be necessary to have someone create them on their computer and then transfer them to tape. You can then transfer the titles and effects to your video or digital editor. Make certain that these titles and effects are initially transferred to a superior tape format before you transfer them to your editor, otherwise the image will not have the necessary detail to generate a professional look. These superior video formats include S-VHS, Highband 8, Mini-DV tape, Beta SP, M2, and High Definition video.

One of the advantages of being able to generate your own credits is that if for any reason your movie falls short of the minimum 85 minutes needed to qualify it as a commercial feature, you can fill out the time with extra or slow-moving credits.

84. STOCK FOOTAGE

As mentioned in point 72, there are companies who sell stock footage to filmmakers. They can be located on the internet or in the pages of a Los Angeles phone book. This phone book can usually be found at your local library. Simply put, stock footage is film or video that can be purchased by a filmmaker to edit into their film/video in place of footage they can't shoot themselves. Stock footage can enhance your movie's production values by adding action scenes, special effects, or establishing location shots that would be impossible to film on your limited budget. The only problem with stock footage is that it can be slightly expensive to purchase. For this reason, you should be judicious in deciding how much footage you intend to use.

An alternative to buying shots from a stock footage company is to use footage from American public domain DVDs. It's vitally important, though, to make certain that the DVD footage is indeed public domain. This can be researched at the following web address for the Library of Congress: http://cocatalog.loc.gov/cgi-bin/Pwebrecon.cgi?DB=local&PAGE=First. If you'd rather not type such a long web address, or if their internet address has changed, type the words "Library of Congress" on your browser. At their website, click the "Copyright Office" icon, and you will be brought to the "Search Records" icon. Clicking it takes you to two icons, one being "Online Services." This will take you to a catalogue of materials copyrighted after 1978. Copyright searches of movies made before 1978 will require non-online research. This process can be explained in detail by clicking the second icon marked "Other Services." Once you click the "Online Services" icon, you will be taken to a catalogue search engine where you type in the title of the movie whose copyright you want to research. If there is no record of an existing copyright for the movie you are researching, or if its copyright hasn't been properly renewed, then the DVD is "probably" in the public domain, allowing free use of its footage. Please keep in mind that the use of footage featuring movie stars may be legally prohibited, being as their likeness may be trademarked. It is equally important never to use trademarked images, like corporate logos, without permission. You should also make certain to never use music from public domain DVDs because it will probably still be under copyright. It is also important that the public domain DVD be an American production because foreign movies will probable still be under copyright overseas.

85. TEN HARD LESSONS ABOUT POST-PRODUCTION

1. Only attempt to do post-production when you are mentally alert. When you are tired, you will make stupid choices, which you will only recognize when you recheck what you have edited on the following day.
2. Check your editing periodically. It will give you a much better sense of whether or not the shots are fitting seamlessly together as a scene.
3. Avoid draining a scene of its color in post-production. Overseas buyers hate anything in black and white, and aren't likely to purchase any low-budget movie that has such scenes. If you must have a scene that isn't in color, then make it sepia-toned instead of black and white.
4. If possible, when transferring your raw footage into your computer or video editor, be sure to use a fire-wire or an S-VHS connection. This way you will obtain a superior image because these video connections help maintain the integrity of your raw footage. If you have a choice between the two formats, go with the fire-wire. It keeps the video in digital mode and maintains its resolution better than an S-VHS connection.
5. Post-production takes a lot of time and patience. It can seem, at times, that you may never finish. Don't let the seemingly neverending work wear you down. You *will* finish as long as you don't lose sight of your goal.

6. Don't put in a visual effect unless it really looks good. Too often, amateurish computer effects or video effects are just thrown in for the sake of having the effect and end up cheapening the movie.

7. Make sure your movie title, plus your opening and closing credits, are easy to read. Too often, the "stylish font" of the title is favored over legibility.

8. It's easy to lose your objectivity when you are new to editing. Every so often have your work viewed by someone whose opinion you trust. They may pick up on mistakes you have overlooked and save you the grief of trying to make corrections once the movie is completely edited.

9. If the video format you are working in doesn't have enough audio channels to mix all the sound effects and music that you would like, then mix as much of the sound effects as you can, then transfer the mixed sound onto a tape, either video or audio. You can then erase the original mixed sound effects on your editor's audio track and replace them with the mixed sound effects that you transferred to tape. Since the transferred sound effects can go onto one channel, it will now qualify as one sound effect, freeing the other channels for additional sound work.

10. I would like to (re)emphasize the following point: *If you have a choice, don't do your low-budget post-production on film.* The reason is simple: it's too expensive, whereas post-production in a video or digital format can be affordable.

86. Flashback, Part Four

In 1997 I tried an experiment in digital filmmaking. This was done in cooperation with Charles Dichiera, a friend of mine, who was a documentary videographer specializing in restoring and distributing NASA videos. In-between our respective projects we would get together to plan a video which would make use of a newly developed digital camera and editing system that Charles had just bought. Since I had the video/film rights to several comic book superheroes published by Big Bang comics, I decided to do a short subject based upon a team of those characters. My, and Chuck's, purpose was to see how good a video we could make on a microscopic budget if we used this new digital technology.

The script was titled *Knights of Justice*, and concerned a group of two superheroes and two superheroines who had to save the world from a super criminal bent on its destruction. The numerous visual effects meant that the non-linear digital post-production technology was going to have to be taxed to its limit, and perhaps beyond. Since we had never used this equipment before, we really couldn't know precisely what those limits were. Over the course of many months, whenever our free time coincided, we'd work on *Knights*. Word began to leak out about what we were attempting, and soon we found ourselves obligated to have a premiere at a major comic book convention projected to have an attendance of at least fifty thousand people.

With an encroaching deadline staring us in the face, Chuck and I flung ourselves into the post-production of the video. While there was an anticipated learning curve to deal with, we soon realized that digital editing was much quicker than film or conventional video editing. The visual effects, so vital to a project like *Knights*, were much easier to create in a digital format than I'd originally thought. Whatever effects couldn't be done at first could eventually be accomplished by learning creative new ways to apply the post-production technology. The video was finished mere hours before the premiere, where it played to standing room only.

A few months later the *Knights of Justice* was marketed as a sell-through video, selling far more tapes than anyone expected and returning a sizable profit on our investment. More importantly, it had fully demonstrated what could be realized, despite limited funds, by using the right post-production technology.

Certain movies (especially science fiction, action and martial arts) only fully materialize during the post-production process. A video as visually complex as *Knights of Justice* only truly materialized in post-production. By doing the effects with a digital editor, we saved thousands, perhaps hundreds of thousands, of dollars. The special effects of *Knights*, which involved simulating laser beams, teleportation, human flight, explosions, super speed, super strength, an earthquake, hurricanes, digital view-screens, and much more, could only have been accomplished using digital post-production. Could the *Knights of Justice* have been made using conventional video post-production? Yes, but not as quickly. Could it have been accomplished on film using optical effects? Yes, but not as cheaply. When planning your movie, take into account the system on which you'll be doing your post-production work. If you are using a video editor, then give yourself a lot of time to do the editing. If you are doing your editing, sound work, music, titles and visual effects on film, then you will have to allot a larger portion of your budget to your post-production than you would for video or digital post-production.

Each professional filmmaker is very aware of the fact that their movie is made, or unmade, during post-production. A great film can be made to look terrible due to an incompetent or indifferent editor. On the other hand, a lousy film can be made to look perfectly professional through the skill of a creative editor. Minor errors can be fixed, and dramatic moments can be heightened. It all depends on the talent and dedication of those doing your post-production. In other words, post-production is as much a vital part of the filmmaking process as production, planning, or financing.

V. Distribution

Do I Hear the Crash of Art and Commerce Colliding?

87. YOU CAN'T MAKE DIME ONE UNTIL YOU UNDERSTAND HOW DISTRIBUTION ACTUALLY WORKS

It is important to understand the distribution process so you can deal with distributors on an informed business level. Distribution falls into the following divisions, each of which is handled differently.

Theatrical

Theatrical distribution is when a distributor places a movie in a theater. Hundreds, perhaps thousands, of prints are made of a movie, then special arrangements are made with chains of theaters to show that movie. Each theater agrees to share a portion of the profits from the sale of movie tickets with the distributor, who, in turn, shares a portion of those received profits with the producer. This type of distribution is very expensive and not very practical unless a major studio is releasing a movie. The advertising for a theatrical release is enormous and isn't practical for an ultra–low-budget movie. There is also a problem placing an independent movie in a theater due to the limited seasonal slots for such movies. The reason for this is that major studios dominate the schedules of nearly all theater chains during the months of May, June, July, August, October, November, and December. Only the remaining months are available to the smaller distribution companies releasing low-budget independent movies. Since the possibility of profit is more limited during these remaining months, it is unlikely that a theatrical release would occur if your movie doesn't have major stars in it. There is also a form of theatrical distribution called "four walling." Four walling is when the distributor rents the theater for one week. Because the theater has made

174

its profit, the distributor receives one hundred percent of the movie's profits resulting from the sale of tickets at that theater. Four walling is typically a slow distribution process and can be rather financially risky. Although less expensive than conventional theatrical distribution, it is still somewhat costly.

Overseas Sales

Overseas sales constitute a major market for low-budget movies. Between 48 to 90 percent of any low-budget movie's potential profit can come from overseas sales. Each year numerous film markets are attended by thousands of overseas buyers and distributors selling movies. The premise behind this "selling" is superficially simple. Each distributor arranges for a booth in which they meet buyers. The buyer then purchases theatrical, video, television, or internet rights for their particular territory. It is during this negotiation process that matters become complex. The distributor has to know what price to charge each buyer. This price depends upon the rights that the buyer wants and the economic conditions of their territory.

Domestic Video

Video distributors make individual deals with chains of video stores that rent and/or sell the movies they represent to the public. In a manner similar to the theatrical distributor, the video distributor has a hard time getting low-budget movies into video store chains because movies from major studios will always be that store's first choice. The video store owner knows that the video viewing of their potential customers is influenced by the millions of dollars in advertising provided by major studios, as well as the star value that such videos can provide. Movies sold directly to the public, called sell-through videos, suffer similar problems, but not to the same degree. A producer can expect to make a profit from their movie in one of two ways: the video distributor buys the video rights for a specific sum of money; or the producer gets a percentage from the sale of each video and/or DVD.

Cable/PPV/Free TV/Syndication/Airlines

Television has a voracious appetite for programming. Each week, hundreds of hours of time have to be filled by TV series, news, talk shows, commercials, and movies. Free TV makes its money by charging advertising agencies to air their commercials. To assure these agencies that there will be millions of people viewing their commercials, each TV network has to air programming that garners large numbers of viewers. This, of course, includes movies. Free TV will pay a negotiated sum for a limited number of broadcasts over a specific period. Since TV networks need to get viewers in the tens of millions, they tend to purchase movies distributed by major studios.

Cable TV pays for movies in much the same manner. The primary difference between cable TV and free TV is the means by which they make their profit. Cable TV makes its money by selling its programming airtime to local cable stations that, in turn, passes on the costs to the cable-buying public. Each cable TV network is designed for a more specific audience than free TV. As a result, it is easier to sell a low-budget movie to a cable company. Cable companies generally pay a single sum of money for a movie, that sum being determined by the period of time during which the movie may be shown, and whether or not the deal is exclusive or non-exclusive. "Exclusive" means that the movie will *only* be shown on their cable network, whereas "non-exclusive" means that the movie may simultaneously be shown on other networks as well.

Pay-per-view (PPV) charges a set sum to each member of the cable viewing audience wishing to watch their special event or movie. A producer whose movie appears on PPV generally gets a piece of the profits resulting from the fees collected from the broadcast of that movie.

Airlines, in an effort to entice potential customers, will purchase the right to show movies during their flights. Generally, they tend to show well-known movies that are suitable for people of all ages. This tends to preclude low-budget movies released by distributors who are not connected with a major studio.

Syndication refers to TV programming which is sold to individual TV stations, as opposed to appearing on free or cable TV. Profits received by the syndication company, shared with the producer, are the result of the negotiated fees paid by the local TV station for the right to air the programming in question. Generally, syndicated movies are sold in packages. These packages can contain anywhere from five to twenty-six movies, all of which share a commonality of genre.

88. The Important Film Markets

There are dozens of film markets for the buying and selling of movies. The following is a short list of those markets regarded as being most important.

The American Film Market

This market is believed to be the most important of the markets by many distributors and buyers. The American Film Market, or AFM, is an eight-day event which is currently held in Santa Monica toward the end of October or beginning of November. The AFM sells movies of all types to the worldwide theatrical, video, and television markets.

The Cannes Film Festival (a.k.a. Festival de Cannes, a.k.a. Festival International du Film de Cannes)

Held in May over the course of twelve days, the Cannes Film Festival is probably the most famous, or infamous, of all the film markets. While superficially a film festival, Cannes is also a market for the buying and selling of movies throughout the world. Cannes has become more of an *event* in recent years than a market for business. As such, buyers, distributors, and celebrities currently tend to use the festival for promotion instead of generating serious film sales.

MIFED (a.k.a. the Milan Film Festival)

Like the AFM and the Cannes Film Festival, MIFED is a major market, and has been called the most important of the annual overseas markets. Held in Milan in late October or early November over a five-day period, it sells movies to the worldwide markets.

MIPCOM

Mipcom is a five-day market held in Cannes in mid–May. It is devoted to the sale of movies and TV series to international video and television. Most buyers and distributors consider MIPCOM to be the most important market for TV programming.

L.A. Screenings

Like Mipcom, L.A. Screenings is a market for the buying and selling of TV series and movies to the international television market. It is normally held over a week's time at the Century City Plaza Hotel (and some neighboring hotels) in late May. It is affiliated with, and promoted by, *Video Age Magazine*. Of all the markets, it is the most low key and most easily accessible.

Unlike the other film markets, L.A. Screenings has no cost to interested spectators who want to attend the market. It is even possible to enter the booths of distributors at no charge. This is particularly unusual when you consider that most film markets can cost attendees hundreds of dollars for a badge that permits access to the entire market for its duration.

The lobby of the Loews hotel, where the American Film Market is usually held, also doesn't require a badge to enter. Due to this, many producers, directors, actors, buyers, and distributors often convene in the lobby to talk and do business. However, should you wish to enter any of the distributors suites, you will need a badge, which can cost from two hundred and fifty to seven hundred and fifty dollars.

89. What Kind of Distributor Do You *Really* Need?

Most people make the mistake of approaching famous major distributors when their film is ready to be marketed. This occasionally works, depending upon the type of film, but in most cases it is pointless.

If you are hoping for a theatrical release, you will probably need to approach a major studio. If you feel that your movie is more suited for the video/TV market, then most distributors will be suitable.

Before you decide upon which distribution company to contact, check out the videos at your local video store. Verify who the original distributor is and get a sense of what kind of movie they sell. Some distributors have a great deal of success with horror, others with action or science fiction, etc. Once you know which distribution companies have done well with movies similar to yours, you will be much more informed about which one you should approach to represent your movie.

There are hundreds and hundreds of distributors. Perhaps thousands. As such, there are too many distributors to fully list here, but the list in Appendix F of the better known distributors should help you locate the right distributor for your needs. Please keep in mind one thing. The movie business is constantly changing, and therefore the addresses, phone numbers, e-mail addresses, and websites are subject to change. When, and if, you contact any distribution company, make sure you ask for whomever is in charge of film acquisition, then inquire if they are currently seeking movies to distribute.

90. THE MARKETPLACES FOR YOUR MOVIE

You have to objectively consider the sales potential of your movie in order to know what sort of distributor you should deal with. Did you shoot in a video format, or on super 8-millimeter film? If so, then you probably have a movie suitable for domestic and international video/TV sales. A movie shot on 16 or 35 millimeter without big name stars has the possibility of a theatrical release, but is unlikely to be shown in theaters due to lack of a box-office attraction. If your movie is shot on 16-millimeter or 35-millimeter and edited on tape, it is still *possible* to obtain a theatrical release, assuming that the distributor is willing to foot the bill of re-editing your movie, or the cost of transferring the tape to film. However, without major stars, this is unlikely. The most likely marketplaces for your movie will be domestic video, cable TV, pay-per-view, and the overseas markets. The value of the overseas markets tends to fluctuate with the economic conditions of the territories that comprise these markets. At the time of this writing, the buyers who pay the largest sums of money for movies are the following (in no particular order): Germany, Italy, Australia, Spain, Japan, China, France, India, South America, and the United Kingdom. Most other countries will only be able to afford to pay small sums of money for an independent movie. Generally speaking, that sum will be somewhere between five hundred and eight thousand dollars. While the smaller territories can't afford to pay much individually, they can collectively pay a total amounting to hundreds of thousands of dollars. This is one of the major reasons it is important that your movie have a strong international appeal. If your movie can be sold to many territories, it has a much better chance of turning a good profit.

91. THE TWO-AND-A-HALF DISTRIBUTION DEALS

There are two primary deals that will be offered to you when you have finally settled on the distributor you want. Most distributors will offer you a percentage of any profit resulting from selling your movies. The size of your percentage would be dependent upon the deal you negotiate with the distributor. The other kind of deal is called a "negative pickup." This is when a distributor purchases the rights to your movie for an agreed upon sum of money. The specifics of those rights will vary, depending upon the deal made. These rights include, in part or in total, domestic and/or overseas, video, TV, and/or theatrical. There are advantages and disadvantages to each type of deal. If your movie makes a lot of money, then having a percentage deal is clearly an advantage, assuming you get the money due you. Unfortunately, it is not uncommon for a filmmaker to never receive *all* of the money their movie has earned. A negative pickup guarantees a profit for your film, but if your movie ends up making a great deal of money you will not be able to share in its success.

There is a third deal that is a combination of the other two. The distributor offers the filmmaker a percentage of the profits resulting from the sale of the movie, but also offers the filmmaker a small sum of money up front as an advance. The advantage to the filmmaker is that the filmmaker sees a little money right away while not giving up the possibility of a lot more money later on. The disadvantage is that, through creative bookkeeping, a distributor may never pay any further money to the filmmaker. This may mean that the filmmaker may make even less money than they would have from a negative pickup. Ultimately, the filmmaker has to decide which is more important: a guaranteed profit or the possibility of making a lot of money eventually.

92. PLAYING SCARED MEANS YOU'LL LOSE THE GAME

There's an old expression in gambling: "Don't play with scared money." What this means is that you should never gamble when you are not equipped to do what needs to be done without being emotionally crippled by fear. In gambling, this specifically refers to not having enough money to bet without being terrified of losing. This basic theory also applies to other aspects of professional life. When you are doing business, you cannot succeed if you are so afraid of failure that you make bad decisions. This can be especially deadly when dealing with a distributor. If you are facing a distributor who is used to playing hardball with his clients, then in one way or another you will be screwed. If you can detach yourself from your emotions and think logically, you won't be manipulated. If you aren't happy with everything in the contract you are offered, then haggle with the distributor to get what you want. If you don't get it, go to another distributor. You may not get what you want there either, or anywhere else, but signing a contract that doesn't completely meet your needs is foolish. Check with several distributors and obtain samples of their contracts to get a sense of what is normally offered. This way you have a much better idea of what is appropriate to ask for. If a distributor tries to force you to sign a contract immediately, refuse. Nine times out of ten they will wait. Carefully consider their offer and make a decision only when you have weighed all the ramifications. If a distributor tries to negotiate a disproportional good percentage for himself or herself by pointing out how bad your movie is or how it lacks box office stars or how it doesn't have lavish production values, etc., stand firm and demand a more equitable percentage deal. This is often nothing more than a ploy designed to intimidate you, making you more likely to sign a contract that is more advantageous to the distributor. There is no set percentage, but, as a rule, if the filmmaker receives less than fifty percent it's a bad deal.

As I stated earlier, if the deal doesn't "feel right" to you, turn it down. There are lots of distribution companies. If a particular distributor doesn't meet your needs, then go to another one. Most will give you a fair deal.

One last thing. I suggest bringing a small tape recorder to your initial meeting with a distributor. Tell them you want a precise record of what is said for business purposes. If the distributor balks at having a tape recorder in a meeting, then you may not want to do business with them. On the other hand, if the distributor does permit the use of the tape recorder, they will be unlikely to make promises that will be broken later. This is because a tape recording could serve as legal proof as to the intent of what was said and therefore does not leave room for interpretation, as someone's memory can.

93. Being Cheated by a Distributor

One of the realities of the filmmaking business is that while most distributors are honest, some cheat the filmmakers they represent. This is not only unfair and illegal, it is also an especially stupid business decision. It is stupid because a filmmaker who gets his or her fair share of the profits continues to do business with their distributor and therefore makes more profits for that distributor. It is partly for this reason that most distributors will comply with the letter of the contractual arrangement they have made with a filmmaker. The problem is that it is hard to tell the honest distributors from the dishonest.

The best defense you have to avoid being cheated is to be very careful in the early stages of dealing with a distributor. If you check out the distributor ahead of time to learn about their reputation, then you will decrease your chance of being cheated. You can get a good idea about what kind of distributor you might be dealing with by obtaining a list of names of those filmmakers who have had their films represented by the distributor. Once you have this list, contact these filmmakers and ask them how they were treated by the distributor. Was the distributor fair? Did the filmmaker receive their monies from that distributor at the proper time and for the proper amount? Did the distributor pad their expenses? If the distributor refuses to give you such a list, then you should think twice about doing business with him. Also, make sure that everything that you and the distributor agreed upon is clearly spelled out in your contract before you sign it.

Despite all the precautions you take, you still may find yourself cheated by a distributor. Sadly, there isn't too much you can do to get your money except take the distributor to court. This, of course, is dependent upon you having *proof* that the distributor has violated your contract. If you do, this might work. I say "might" for good reason. If you take the matter to court and prove your case, a dishonest distributor will occasionally comply with the court's ruling and pay the filmmaker his or her due. Too often, however, dishonest distributors merely wait until they have a lot of lawsuits filed against them and then declare bankruptcy to avoid paying all the people to whom they owe money. These distributors usually hide out for six months or so, then form a new distribution company, sometimes under someone else's name. Sadly, there is precious little you can do at this point except start all over again and find a new distributor. Before this becomes too depressing, let me say that there is a positive side to this, which I will discuss in point 103.

94. Ten Hard Lessons About Distribution

1. Don't let yourself get pressured into signing a contract right away. Take some time to study the contract. Let others, whom you trust, read it and voice their opinion. If you are confused by something in the contract, then make sure you thoroughly understand it before you sign.
2. Make sure you don't have to come up with *all* the promotional materials needed to sell your movie (e.g., VHS tapes, DVDs, posters, photos, etc.). If it is required in your contract, it could result in hundreds, perhaps thousands, of dollars of cost to you. On the

other hand, if you do come up with any, or all, of the promotional materials, then make sure you receive a much higher percentage of future profits resulting from the sale of your movie.

3. You may want to design a poster for a movie. It will probably end up being redone by the distributor, but at least it will show the distributor what you have in mind. A full-size poster can be costly, so just concentrate on the design and let the distributor absorb the cost of making it if they like it.

4. To learn how to design a poster, study the covers of comic books, not other movie posters. If all posters worked properly, all movies would make money. Effective posters, like comic book covers, are designed with simplicity in mind. Have one or two characters in the foreground that are posed against a background of a single color, such as black, blue, or perhaps a graduated red. A starry sky is often effective as well. This makes the poster stand out from all the busy posters on display, and makes people pay attention.

5. You may need to make a "slick" for your movie. A slick is a small-scale poster done in an 8½ inch by 11 inch format to advertise your movie at film festivals or film markets. To make the production of a slick easier on you, design it with a small computer using as high a resolution as you can, then print it out on a quality printer. Normally, the back of a slick features a synopsis, along with some credits stating the name of the company, the producer, director, and screenwriter, and the principal actors.

6. During post-production, make sure to have an "M and E track" made. Your M and E track is a version of the sound track that doesn't have any dialogue. This is needed for distribution to foreign territories for dubbing purposes. Normally this is put onto a DAT recorder, which is designed for this purpose. A simple alternative to this is to turn off the dialogue track when you make a video copy of your movie. Then you transfer your film to an appropriate video format, such as Beta SP, High-Band 8, or Super-VHS. ¾-inch tape and Mini-DV are currently not suitable because their tapes only run one hour in their highest mode of resolution.

7. One way to create a trailer for your movie, if you don't have any experience in making one, is to locate an effective trailer for a movie similar to yours and use it to make your own. Transfer the trailer to video. Next, using a video editing system, transfer the highlights of your film. Replace each shot in the original trailer with individual inserts of impressive shots from your movie. Then create a title and a closing credit for your trailer to replace the original's. Once the visuals are done, replace the narration and music with your own while maintaining a style and pace similar to the original.

8. If it's possible, attend the film markets where your movie is going to be sold. It will give you a much better sense of the distribution process. It will also help you develop some connections with buyers.

9. Don't bother the distributor any more than you have to during a film market. They will be much too busy to deal with you on a continual basis. When, and if, you visit their booth, be sure not to stay long. If a buyer sees too many people in a booth, they assume that the distributor is busy with another buyer, and any chance for a deal to be made has been lost.

10. Make an effort find out from your distributor *what* rights to your movie were sold to *which* territories, for *what* price, and under *what* conditions. In this way, you have a much more informed idea of what is going on with your movie.

95. Flashback, Part Five

The year 1954 was a bad year for distributors. Television was cutting into the onetime large moviegoing audience, and distribution companies were dropping like flies. Cinematic novelties like 3-D and Smellovision were tried, but audiences kept growing smaller and smaller. Amidst this cinematic chaos the company ARC was formed. ARC stood for the American Releasing Corporation. They studied the market and specialized in making well-made ultra low budget exploitation movies for the newly discovered teenage audience. A year or two later they changed their name to the more widely known American International Pictures. American International Pictures succeeded, despite an initial lack of working capital and double features whose posters promised more than the movies delivered, because they knew how to sell to their particular market. New World, American Cinema and Cannon Pictures would follow suit. Each company did extraordinarily well in domestic and overseas sales until they lost sight of their purpose. When they began to make movies with large budgets they floundered and ultimately failed. Their success and failures taught other distribution companies how to cater to the needs of their specific audience. Some chose to release martial arts films, some specialized in family films, some chose other genres. As long as they kept track of the changing markets and tailored their movies to meet the needs of those markets, they thrived.

To illustrate the value of distribution, I'll relate a professional experience of my own. Let me begin by saying that the worst movie that I ever produced, entitled *24 Hours to Midnight,* was a hit due to proper marketing. In 1988, a filmmaker friend of mine asked me to help him produce a movie. His situation was desperate. He had a contract to produce a film financed by an overseas distributor. He had started production on a martial arts movie, but the star had stormed off the set after a fight with the director. The film's completion deadline was coming due, and he now had no star and almost no money. I agreed to help my friend, and we quickly went to work to save his movie. The distributor agreed to purchase the 35-millimeter raw stock for us to use, and would pay for the post-production, but the production money would have to come out of my friend's pocket. Soon a new script was fashioned to explain the star's disappearance, and the director, who was incompetent, was let go. My friend became the new director and unofficial executive producer. I was made the producer, and it became my job to make sure everything ran smoothly. It didn't. Despite the fact that my friend was draining his credit cards in order to make the movie, he didn't especially care if the movie was good or not, merely completed. He brought in some buddies to help out who were equally disinterested in quality. Soon the director of photography was trying to rewrite the script to suit his personal taste. Performances were compromised due to the incompetence of a dialogue coach who seemed to think he was the director. Naturally, I objected, but my friend refused to address any of these problems. As long as the movie was completed, he was content. Since he was the executive producer, credited or not, I was in no position to override his decisions. One of the things I have learned in this business is that no matter how hard you try, you can't give people a sense of purpose. Either they are dedicated or they aren't, and there's nothing you can do to change them. They have to make that decision for themselves. When the movie went into post-production, things went no better. Plot points were edited out, and some scenes weren't placed in the proper sequence, making the movie confusing. The distributor, who had paid a lot of money to the star, decided that he wanted to see more of her in the movie. The script, which had explained the star's disappearance by having her character undergo plastic surgery to hide from killers (with the character then being played by a new actress), was ignored. Instead, the editor used the same footage, seen early in the movie, several times. When I finally saw the film, I was appalled. The movie now had been given the title *24 Hours to Midnight,* which had no connection to the picture's premise in any way. To say I had misgivings would be an understatement. Amazingly, the movie did quite well overseas. It was picked up for domestic video by a small company that understood how to market martial arts films. By the time they were done, nearly three hundred thousand dollars in video sales had been made. I later learned from various video store representatives that the movie proved to be so successful that Buena Vista Home Entertainment acquired the video rights and re-released *24 Hours to Midnight* nearly a decade later. About five years ago a new company called Draculina-Cine released the film again, as a sell through video. More recently, it was reported to me that *24 Hours to Midnight* was re-released on video for a fourth time by a distributor called Lion's Gate.

The fact of the matter is that *24 Hours to Midnight* had no business being a success. It was, at best, an uneven film whose potential was undermined by the indifference of too many people involved in its creation. Despite this, the distribution companies made it a success by marketing it based upon the needs of their buyers and the commercial strengths of the movie. Despite its flaws, *24 Hours to Midnight* was a fast-paced, action-packed movie loaded with enough martial arts fights, gun battles, and explosions to satisfy any undiscriminating moviegoer willing to turn off their brain for ninety minutes.

Obviously, I am not suggesting that anyone should make a bad movie with the expectation that it will still be a success. I wouldn't want such a thing on my conscience. In a very competitive marketplace, you need to produce the best film possible to maximize its sales potential. The point of this flashback is that the right distributor, selling the right kind of movie to the right market, can make nearly any movie profitable.

VI. It Ain't Over Till It's Over

The Credits Aren't Rolling, So Sit Back Down

96. MOVIES ARE A NEVERENDING PROCESS

Sometimes it seems that making a movie is like climbing a huge mountain. At that point you start to think you will never finish the journey. Since your movie is now being distributed, you may think that your climb is done. And why not? You planned everything properly, did your homework in pre-production, did a good job during production, managed to complete post-production without losing your mind, and survived your movie's distribution. Now it's over, right? Wrong! Your obligation to your film never really ends. You will find that you will be involved in the selling and/or promotion of your movie for as long as there is an interest in it. Every few years you will need to negotiate a new deal for its distribution. You, or your accountant, will need to pay your investors, and anyone else who owns a piece of your film, their percentage of any profit that comes in for as long as there are profits. There will always be something more to do.

The point of all this is that if you are not fully prepared to make a life-long commitment to your movie, don't make that movie. It is a responsibility that must never be taken lightly.

97. DO FILM FESTIVALS HAVE ANY REAL VALUE?

Each year there are thousands of film festivals. The primary purpose of these festivals is to honor the new work of filmmakers. Just about anyone

187

with enough money to pay the entry fee, and has a film or video meeting the festival's requirements, can enter. The value of these film festivals to a professional filmmaker is debatable. Most filmmakers use these festivals to help generate interest from distributors. For the filmmaker who already has a distributor, a film festival has lesser importance. These festivals can still help filmmakers if their movie wins some sort of award or critical acclaim that can be used for purposes of promotion. There is, of course, the inestimable personal value of the public acknowledgement that you have made a good movie. It's important to remember, however, that it can be expensive to enter your film in a lot of festivals. Entering your movie in many festivals in the hopes of drawing the attention of distributors could cost you thousands of dollars. Your best bet is to find a distributor on your own and save a lot of money. If the distributor thinks it would be a good idea to have your movie in a film festival, they can absorb the expense. If you still want to enter your movie in a film festival, I suggest you do your homework and check out all the festivals carefully. Once you have done this, you should only enter your film in those festivals that are appropriate for your type of movie. The following is a list of the better known film festivals (out of four thousand or more festivals) currently showcasing movies. You can find specific information on each festival on the internet.

Atlanta Film and Video Festival
Atlantic Film Festival
Austin Film Festival
Banff Film Festival
Berlin Film Festival
Black Film Festival
Boston Film Festival
Cannes Film Festival
Chicago Film Festival
Chicago International Film Festival
Chicago Underground Film Festival
Cinequest Film Festival
Comcast Film Festival
DC Independent Film Festival
Deep Ellum Festival
Des du Festival Film Monde
Detroit Film Festival
Digital Video and High Definition Festival
Edinburgh Film Festival
Fort Lauderdale International Film Festival
Hollywood Film Festival or Mill Valley Film Festival
Independent Film Festival
Indie Fest
Indie Memphis
International Film and Video Festival
International Film Festival
Kansas City Filmmakers Jubilee
Los Angeles Film Festival
Miami International Film Festival
Milwaukee International Film Festival
Montreal Film Festival
Montreal World Film Festival
Nashville Independent Film Festival
New York Film Festival
Northwest Film and Video Festival

Palm Beach International Film
  Festival
Palm Springs Film Festival
Philadelphia Video Festival
Sacramento Festival of Film and
  Music
San Diego Film Festival
Sedona International Film Festival
Short Film Festival
Slamdance Film Festival
Slick Rock Film Festival
Sonoma Valley Film Festival-Cinema
  Epicuria

Sundance Film Festival
Tallgrass Film Festival
Telluride Film Festival
Toronto Film Festival
Toronto International Film Festival
Traverse City Film Festival
Tribeca Film Festival
UNCG Carolina Film and Video
  Festival
Vancouver Film Festival
Vancouver International Film
  Festival
Woodstock Film Festival

98. PROMOTION, PROMOTION, PROMOTION

As I said in point 95, the financial success of any movie is largely dependent upon the skill of the distributor. It is also affected by the amount and quality of the promotion done on that film's behalf. You have probably heard the old story of a storeowner who, upon being asked why his business was such a success, replied, "Location, location, location." A variation of that same idea applies to the success or failure of a movie. To succeed it needs a lot of promotion, promotion, promotion! The more publicity you can obtain on behalf of your movie, the more likely people will pay to see it. So get reporters to write articles about it during production. Invite the press to the premiere. Appear on local radio or TV talk shows. Do whatever it takes to keep people interested in your movie.

99. DOING INTERVIEWS THAT WILL SELL YOUR MOVIE

At some point you will have to do an interview with a newspaper reporter, a writer of articles, or a TV or radio talk show host. Very few filmmakers give this aspect of promotion much thought because they assume it's just a matter of answering questions. If it were that simple, all interviews would be a success. There are many reasons an interview can go badly. The reporter or host asking the questions may be bad at their job, or they might have a hidden prejudice or agenda. It might also be that *you* are really bad at giving interviews.

To give a good interview you need to prepare yourself for it ahead of time. To begin with, you will have to come up with a very specific series of points that need to be stressed during the interview. Those specific points are as follows:

(a) *Your name.* Amazingly, sometimes people get so caught up in the process of being interviewed that they forget to mention who they are.

(b) *The title of your movie.* Make sure that it is accurately reported.

(c) *When is your movie available to be seen?*

(d) *Where will your movie be available to be seen?*

(e) *Why should the audience want to see your movie?*

Knowing these five points is just the beginning. Now you need to learn how to integrate your answers into the interview. This involves a form of improvisation that allows you to give the answers you want no matter what you are asked. Listen carefully to the questions you are asked and make a connection between those questions and the answers you want to give. For example, let's say you're being interviewed in Whateverville, USA, and you want to establish where your movie will be playing, but you have just been asked how you like their small town. Your answer *could* go like this: "I love the people here in Whateverville. One of the advantages of my movie playing at the Main Street Theater is that I get the opportunity to meet a lot of the great people who live in this town."

Or perhaps you are asked what you think of Charlie Chaplin films when you want to explain why people should want to see your movie. You might answer: "Chaplin's movies have stood the test of time because his films touched a cord in his audience. That's why I feel there will be a strong audience for my movie. The public has a special love for action films, and that's why I crammed so many stunts and fight scenes into my new movie. That's also why it's starring Dack Manly, the international martial arts champion. A lot of people think he'll be the new Bruce Lee."

With a little practice you should become proficient at promoting your movie no matter what question you're asked. A good way to practice is to have your friends ask you bizarre questions and see how well you deal with them. When you are able to give answers in a natural and easygoing manner, you will be ready for the toughest interview.

100. Keeping Track of Your Profits

As long as your movie makes money you will have to keep accurate records of your profits. This isn't as hard as it might seem. Most distributors will send you quarterly statements detailing specifically how much money your movie has made during each three-month period. If for any reason the distributor doesn't offer to send you such statements, ask for them. Demand them if you have to. These statements are very important because you will definitely need up-to-date documentation of your movie's profits for your business records. These records are especially important when dealing with your investors and/or the Internal Revenue Service.

Make sure that you keep all your financial records for at least seven years because there is always the chance of your company being audited by the IRS. While maintaining this ongoing paperwork is not especially difficult, it can become annoyingly time consuming, particularly if you are involved with making other movies. For this reason you might consider hiring an accountant to handle the responsibility of the ongoing paperwork, issuing checks, and filing tax forms.

101. Hold Onto Your Contacts

Over the course of time you will come into contact with a variety of influential people, such as overseas buyers, actors and actresses, producers and directors, and distributors other than the one that's representing you. Make sure you keep all the business cards given you. Also, write a note about the person who gave their card to you on its back. This will help refresh your memory as to your impressions of each person. Keep in contact with these people from time to time. You never know if the day will come when you might need the advantage of that person's expertise or resources. The important thing to remember is that you have to offer to whomever you're dealing with something that is proportionate to whatever they can offer you. This free exchange of resources assures a fair business relationship.

102. Flashback, Part Six

I want you to consider the two following stories.

Story number one. In 1991, an aspiring filmmaker made a 16-millimeter low-budget action film for a few thousand dollars. As he searched for a distributor, he got himself an agent who decided it would be to his client's advantage to do a lot of promotion for the movie. Soon, major studios were bidding for the right to distribute the movie. Once the distributor was chosen, the film was showcased at major film festivals, and the filmmaker found himself answering the questions of countless reporters. Soon, the movie and the filmmaker were famous. This motivated the major studio to blow the movie up to 35-millimeter and release it to theaters. All the publicity caught the public's attention, resulting in millions of dollars in movie tickets and videocassettes sold. The movie was titled *El Mariachi*, and the filmmaker was Robert Rodriguez. The success of *El Mariachi* led to Robert making such hit films as *Desperado*, *From Dusk Till Dawn*, *Sin City*, and *Spy Kids* and its sequels.

Story number two. In the late nineties some filmmakers decided to make a pseudo-documentary on video for very little money, with no stars and a largely improvised script. The odds of such a movie becoming a huge success were all but non-existent. Upon completion, the movie was cleverly promoted on the internet for nearly a year before it was released, thereby generating a growing curiosity among the public. When the move was shown at some film festivals its novelty intrigued a lot of film buffs. Critics all over of the country lavished praise for the movie's quirky style and unique premise. A distribution company bought the rights to the video, reportedly paying a million dollars to the filmmakers. The movie was transferred from video to 35-millimeter and played in theaters throughout the country, where it became a huge hit. That movie was *The Blair Witch Project*.

The one thing that these films had in common was the fact that each was creatively promoted as much as possible. To put it simply, with enough promotion, even a low-budget movie can become a box office champ.

VII. Final Thoughts

$\boxed{\textit{It's a Wrap}}$

103. Personal Observations

There are only three sure things in this world: death, taxes, and the fact that nothing else is a sure thing. Insofar as your movie is concerned, all you can do is make certain you have maximized both its quality and its potential for success. There is no way you can guarantee that your movie will make a profit. The only guarantee you can expect is that your movie will have the best possible chance for artistic and financial success if you have done your job properly.

If you have absorbed *all* the details of this book and followed *all* of its directions (and I do mean *all*), then you have a much better chance of success than ninety-nine percent of all the other aspiring filmmakers out there. Whether or not your movie makes dime one, you can take heart from two things. Making a feature film, even a mediocre one, is an achievement in which you can take pride. Countless would-be filmmakers complain to anyone who will listen that they want to make a movie. Only a handful of these filmmakers ever attempt to make a movie. Even fewer of these filmmakers ever complete one. Another thing to consider is the fact that no commercially viable movie ever truly loses money. Even if circumstances prevent initial success, a movie may make money in the long run due to a different distributor, different worldwide economics, and/or changing public tastes. It is also vital you remember that if for any reason your movie is not successful, it may still aid in your professional success. If your movie is good, you can still use it to demonstrate to film companies what you can accomplish on a low budget. One way or another you can still profit from your movie whether it makes money or not. So, let me be the first to say "Congratulations" on making your film and good luck with it. Lord knows you've earned it.

104. Recommended Reading and Viewing

In conclusion, I would like to recommend the following books and movies in the hope that they will aid in making you a more informed filmmaker, which in turn will make for a more successful career.

Books

Probably the greatest book on dramatic writing is *The Art of Dramatic Writing*, by Lajos Egri. Although it was published in the 1940s, its information concerning dramatic characterization, plot, and conflict is as valid today as it was sixty years ago. It will undoubtedly be at your local library or at a library in a neighboring city. You should also read *The Independent Filmmaker's Guide to Writing a Business Plan for Investors*, by Gabriel Campisi. Gabriel, who used me as a source of information on movie production and distribution in his book, explains, in much greater detail than was possible in this book, how to do business with investors by creating a detailed business plan. Lastly, the book *In a Door, Into a Fight, Out a Door, Into a Chase*, by movie serial director William Witney, details the process of making low-budget movies (or serials) under extremely trying conditions. It is also a fascinating read about the early days of the movie industry.

Movies

I assume that any potential filmmaker has already seen such classic movies as *Citizen Kane, The Searchers* and *Casablanca*, so I will concentrate on lesser-known low-budget movies. If possible, try to see the following two movie serials from the 1940s: *The Adventures of Captain Marvel* and *Spy Smasher*. *The Adventures of Captain Marvel* because of its tight editing and clever special effects, which belie its low-budget origin. *Spy Smasher* should be seen for its breathtaking pace and impressive stunt work. You should also study the horror films *Night of the Living Dead* and *Carnival of Souls* for their dramatic use of lighting and creative camera work. While you're at it, listen to the DVD commentary track of a crime thriller called *Danger: Diabolik*. Directed by Mario Bava, it is a fascinating study in how wide-angle lenses, plus paper cutouts and miniatures, can make the sets of a low-budget movie look big and expensive. If you like martial arts movies, you should take a close look at *Revenge of the Ninja*. This movie has remarkable martial arts choreography despite its very small budget. It would also be a good idea to see the

Spanish action film *El Mariachi* to study its audacious camera angles, quick pacing and fluid use of the camera. Its commentary track is also very informative insofar as learning how to cut corners without sacrificing quality. There is also a cult classic from 1945 entitled *Detour* that you should check out. Directed in six days by Edgar G. Ulmer on a reported budget of $20,000 dollars using only three primary sets, it is a minor masterpiece of film noir. Additionally, it is a great study in how clever direction and clever writing can overcome serious budgetary constraints. At the insistence of some of my peers, I will recommend (albeit somewhat reluctantly) one final movie. I suggest that you take a look at a direct-to-video movie produced and directed by yours truly — *Battle Beast*. This feature is a martial arts/horror movie that I made as an experiment to determine whether consumer digital cameras were good enough to use for professional purposes. Because it was an experiment, I had to keep the budget very, very low in order to minimize the financial dangers inherent in such an experiment. Said budget ended up being a little under six thousand dollars. While it certainly does not represent my best work, *Battle Beast* is a good example of how the use of digital technology, during production as well as post-production, can make a technically complex movie financially feasible. It also demonstrates how the creative use of camera angles, combined with equally creative editing, can make a variety of divergent locations look like one huge, impressive, and therefore expensive, location.

And now it's time for me to say ... FADE OUT.

Appendices

A: Script Coverage Companies

Act One Program http://www.actoneprogram.com/Critique.htm
Anna Piazza http://colorpro.com/chadwick-gros
Beverly Hills Literary Consultants, Inc. http://beverlyhillslit.com
Big Deal News http://www.bigdealnews.com
Bigger Picture Films http://www.thebiggerpicturefilms.com
Blank Slate Script Consulting http://blankslatescriptconsulting.com
Chicagoland Script Works http://www.chicagolandscriptworks.com
Comedy Screenplay Coverage http://www.voy.com/7710
The Complete Screenplay & More http://www.completescreenplay.com
Coverage, Inc. http://www.hprodev.com/coverageinc
CoverScript.com http://www.coverscript.com
Creativescreenplay.com http://creativescreenplay.com
Dave Trottier http://davetrottier.com
Flea Bitten Productions http://www.fleabittenproductions.com/; scriptdoctoring.html
Got Ya Covered http://www.apokolips.com/gotya
Hollywood Script http://www.hollywoodscript.com
Hollywood Script Analysis http://www.hollywoodscriptanalysis.com
Hollywood Scriptwriting Institute http://www.Moviewriting.com
James P. Mercurio http://www.jamespmercurio.com
Jon Nalick http://home1.gte.net/res09dkv/ays/index.html
LSC: Literary & Screenplay Consultants http://www.scriptzone.com
LynBark http://home.earthlink.net/%7Elynbark?; index.html
Maggie Prescott Script Consulting http://mprescott2.tripod.com/id3.htm
Making It in Hollywood http://www.victorya.com
Manuscript Development http://www.manuscriptdevelopment.com
Masked Man http://www.atelierpix.com/maskedman
Off Camera Productions http://www.offcameraproductions.com
On the Page http://www.onthepage.tv
Planet Shark Productions http://www.planetsharkproductions.com/; about/index.
   html#hireus
Pro-Read Extreme Script Consultation http://www.pro-read.com
Red Inkworks http://www.redinkworks.com
Reviews 4 Less http://www.geocities.com/Hollywood/Agency/6471/spp.html
Richwood Script Consultants http://www.scriptnotes.com
Scr(i)pt Magazine Coverage Services http://www.scriptmag.com/pages/mb/services.
   shtml
Screen Brokers http://www.galaxymall.com/services/screenbrokers
Screenwriter.comhttp://www.screenwriter.com/sc.html
Screenwriting Consultant http://www.lpscripts.net
Script Analysis http://www.keanewords.com

The Script Analyst http://www.thescriptanalyst.com
Script Feedback http://funwriter.tripod.com/scriptfeedback
Script Genie http://hometown.aol.com/heavann/ scriptgenie.html
Script Muse http://www.scriptmuse.com/services.html
Script Pimp http://www.scriptpimp.com
Script Services http://www.scriptservices.com
Script Shrink http://www.scriptshrink.com
Script Surgery Film Script Consultants http://www.scriptsurgery.com/services.shtml
Script Viking http://www.scriptviking.com
Scriptapalooza Coverage Service http://www.coverageservice.com
ScriptDoctor 911 http://www.scriptdoctor911.com
ScriptFLY Coverage http://scriptfly.com/coverage
The ScriptMaster http://home.earthlink.net/~mcheda/fees.html
ScriptPIMP http://www.scriptpimp.com/script_coverage/ home.cfm
Scripts That Sell http://www.scriptsthatsell.com
ScriptShark.com http://www.scriptshark.com
Smart Girls Productions http://smartgirls.com
Smoke 'n' Mirrors Entertainment http://www.geocities.com/smoke_n_mirrors_
    entertainment
Stephan Gray http://www.bevhillslitconsult.com
Story and Script Development http://www.storyandscriptdevelopment.com
Story Conference http://www.storyconf.com
Story Factory http://www.scriptessentials.com
Story Sense http://www.storysense.com
StoryNotes http://storynotes.com
Storytech http://thewritersjourney.com
StudioNotes http://www.studionotes.com
Tanglewood Productions http://www.tanglewoodfilms.com/coverage.htm
TriggerStreet.com http://www.triggerstreet.com
The Ultimate Screenplay Analysis http://usaa3.tripod.com/ theultimatescreenplay
    analysisanywhere
Writer 2 Writer http://www.w2wnetwork.com
Writing a Screenplay http://members.aol.com/nala456
Xandy's Script Service http://www.xandysscriptservice.com

B: Screen Actors Guild Local Branches

ARIZONA
(602) 383-3780
E-mail: dlivesay@sag.org
Arizona, Idaho, Utah

BOSTON
(617) 262-8001
Fax: (800) 737-6105
Maine, Massachusetts, New Hampshire,
    Rhode Island, Vermont

CHICAGO
(312) 573-8081
Fax: (312) 573-0318
Illinois, Indiana, Iowa, Minnesota, Missouri,
    North Dakota, Ohio, South Dakota,
    Wisconsin

COLORADO
(800) 724-0767
Fax: (323) 549-6886
Colorado, Kansas, Nebraska, Wyoming

DALLAS
(972) 361-8185
Fax: (972) 361-8186
Arkansas, Northern Texas, Oklahoma

DETROIT
(248) 351-2678
Fax: (248) 351-2679
Michigan

FLORIDA
(305) 670-7677
Fax: (800) 844-5439
Alabama, Florida, Louisiana, Mississippi, North Carolina, Puerto Rico, South Carolina

GEORGIA
(404) 239-0131
Fax: (404) 239-0137

HAWAII
(808) 596-0388
Fax: (800) 305-8146

HOUSTON
(800) 724-0767
Fax: (800) 311-3216
Southern Texas

NASHVILLE
(305) 670-7677
Fax: (800) 844-5439
Kentucky, Tennessee

NEW YORK
Connecticut, New York and North New Jersey

NEVADA
c/o Hrair Messerlian
(323) 549-6475
Fax: (323) 549-6460

NEW MEXICO
Same as the Colorado office

ORLANDO
(407) 788-3020
Fax: (407) 788-3080

PHILADELPHIA
Same as the New York office
Delaware, Pennsylvania, Southern New Jersey

PORTLAND
Same as the Seattle office
Oregon

SAN DIEGO
c/o Hrair Messerlian
(323) 549-6475
Fax: (323) 549-6460
Southern California

SAN FRANCISCO
(415) 391-7510
Fax: (415) 391-1108
Northern California

SEATTLE
(206) 270-0493
Fax: (800) 378-6741
Alaska, Montana, Washington

UTAH
Same as the Arizona office
Idaho, Utah

WASHINGTON DC
(301) 657-2560
Fax: (800) 253-9730
Maryland, Virginia, Washington DC, West Virginia

Appendix C: Motion Picture Insurance Companies

Allen Financial Insurance Group, Inc.
P.O. Box 9957
Phoenix, Arizona 85032

(800) 874-9191
(602) 992-1570
www.eqgroup.com

AON/Albert G. Ruben Insurance Services
48 West 25th St., 12th Floor,
New York, NY 10010
http://www.aon.com/default.jsp

Also

1080 Whilshire Blvd., Suite 700
Los Angeles, CA 90024-4108
(310) 234-6821
(310) 234-6851

Arts & Entertainment Insurance, LLC
Location: Marblehead, Massachusetts
Phone: (800) 676-9374
www.videoinsurance.com

C & S Int'l Insurance Brokers, Inc.
New York, New York
(212) 406-4499, ex. 302
www.csins.com

Ford Insurance Agency, Inc.
2 Harold Dow Highway Eliot, Maine 03903
(207) 439-2500
(207) 439-6805
Toll Free: 800-537-7843

Frankel & Associates
9233 W. Pico Blvd., Suite 226
Los Angeles, CA 90035
310-552-3349
800-696-3023

Gaslamp Insurance Services
1111 6th Ave., 3rd Floor
San Diego, California 92101
(800) 920-4125
(619) 238-4367
www.gaslampinsurance

Marshall Entertainment Insurance
10879-A Alice Dr., #325
Sumter, South Carolina 29150
(877) 363-1539
www.marshallentertainment

Also

2000 Universal Studios Plaza, Ste. 625
Orlando, Florida 32819
(407) 363-1537
(407) 363-1537
www.marshallentertainment.com

Premier Class Insurance Service, Inc.
10002 Pioneer Blvd., #104
Santa Fe Springs, California 90670
(562) 821-0321
(866) 441-0321
www.firsttower.

Zeboray(r) Insurance Services
P.O. Box 1044
San Clemente, CA 92674
(949) 498-7017
Toll Free (Outside California):
    800-829-8445

Appendix D: Product Placement Companies

A List Entertainment, Inc
1064 Hi Point Street
Los Angeles, CA, 90035 USA
323-939-2045
Fax: 323-933-8298
Contact Person: Marsha R. Levine
ML@alistentertainment.com
www.alistentertainment.com

Above the Line Placements
214 Main Street, #270
El Segundo, CA, 90245 USA
310-796-9536

Fax: 310-796-9546
Contact Person: Milt Lane
mlane@atlplacements.com
www.atlplacements.com

Anheuser-Busch, Inc.
16830 Ventura Blvd., Suite 506
Encino, CA, 91436-1721 USA
818-906-1242
Fax: 818-906-1251
Contact Person: Michael Gianino
michael.gianino@anheuser-busch.com

Baldoni Entertainment, Inc.
"The Product Integrators" TM
706 Crest Drive
Manhattan Beach, CA, 90266 USA
(310) 372-2191
Fax: (541) 770-8034
Contact Person: Jay Gleason
jaygleason@productintegrators.com

**Bragman Nyman Cafarelli Public
    Relations and Marketing**
9171 Wilshire Blvd., Suite 300
Beverly Hills, CA, 90210 USA
(310) 274-7800
Fax: (310) 274-7838
Contact Person: Kevin Jackson
kjackson@bncpr.com

Courtlemagne Communications
11601 Wilshire Blvd., Suite 1800
Los Angeles, CA, 90025 USA
(310) 914-8700
Fax: (310) 914-8710
Contact Person: Melissa McSorley
mmcsorley@courtlemagne.com
www.courtlemagne.com

Creative Entertainment Services
1015 N. Hollywood Way, Suite 101
Burbank, CA, 91505 USA
(818) 842-9119
Fax: (818) 842-9568
Contact Person: Stacy Jones
stacy@acreativegroup.com
www.acreativegroup.com

Davie-Brown Entertainment
2225 South Carmelina Ave.
Los Angeles, CA, 90064 USA
(310) 979-1980
Fax: (310) 820-7277
Contact Person: Stephanie Green
sgreen@davie-brown.com
www.davie-brown.com

Eclipse Worldwide
955 Fremont Street
Menlo Park, CA, 94025 USA
(650) 325-9029
Fax: (650) 325-9027
Contact Person: Jon Holtzman
holtzman@eclipse-worldwide.com
www.eclipse-worldwide.com

Feature This!
5784 Venice Blvd.
Los Angeles, CA, 90019-5018 USA
(323) 935-2997
Fax: (323) 935-7186
Contact Person: Jay May
jay@featurethis.com

Fuji Film
1141 N. Highland Avenue
Hollywood, CA, 90038 USA
(323) 957-8823
Fax: (323) 465-8279
Contact Person: Ken Schaffer
    kenschaf@aol.com

Hadler Public Relations, Inc.
801 N. Brand Blvd., Suite 620
Glendale, CA, 91203 USA
(818) 552-7300
Fax: (818) 545-9116
Contact Person: Robert Handler
bob@hadlerpr.com

HERO Product Placement
10777 Sherman Way
North Hollywood, CA, 91352 USA
(818) 764-7414
Fax: (818) 764-7415
Contact Person: Ms. Julie Weinhouse
jw@heropp.com
www.heropp.com

Hilton Hotels Worldwide
5757 Century Blvd., Suite 410
Los Angeles, CA, 90045 USA
(310) 665-1388
Fax: (310) 641-2721
Contact Person: Maria Berkovitz
maria_berkovitz@hilton.com

Hippie Skivvies LLC
793 Foothill Blvd., Suite A-118
San Luis Obispo, CA, 93405-1615 USA
(805) 544-5566
Fax: (805) 544-2235
Contact Person: Paige Covell
paige@hippieskivvies.com
www.hippieskivvies.com

Hollywood International Placements
8507 Washington Blvd.
Culver City, CA, 90232 USA
(310) 204-1180

Fax: (310) 204-1171
Contact Person: Tami Glenn
tami@hollywoodprops.com
www.hollywoodprops.com

International Promotions
10725 Vanowen Street, Suite 113
North Hollywood, CA, 91605 USA
(818) 755-6333
Fax: (818) 755-6444
Contact Person: Linda Swick
Linda@intlpromotions.com
www.productplacements.com

L.A. Dolce Vita
924 Ninth Street, Suite #6
Santa Monica, CA, 90403 USA
(310) 394-1588
Fax: (310) 394-8092
Contact Person: Anne Iverson LADOL
   CEUSA@aol.com

Lets Go Hollywood
4500 N. Thatcher Ave., P.O. Box 56159
Norridge, IL, 60656-0159 USA
(708) 456-5900
Fax: (708) 456-5986
Contact Person: George Simkowki
primetimesim@aol.com

Midnite Express
300-301 N. Oak Street
Inglewood, CA, 90302 USA
(310) 330-2300
Fax: (310) 330-2359
Contact Person: Milton Reyes
mreyes@mnx.com

Motion Picture Magic, Inc.
17337 Ventura Blvd., Suite 120
Encino, CA, 91316 USA
(818) 905-9814
Fax: (818) 905-8560
Contact Person: Diane A. Lolli — Mark
   Mills
moviediva@aol.com
www.motionpicturemagic.com

New Media Group PLC
The Old Post House, 18 London End
Old Beaconsfield, Bucks, HP9 2JH
   England
(01) 494-672-492
Fax: (01) 494-671-644

Contact Person: John Barnard or Gareth
   Dobson
the.chairman@newmediagroup.co.uk
www.newmediagroup.co.uk

Norm Marshall & Associates, Inc.
11059 Sherman Way
Sun Valley, CA, 91352 USA
(818) 982-3505
Fax: (818) 503-1936
Contact Person: Devery Holmes
Devery@normmarshall.com
www.normmarshall.com

Pier 3 Entertainment
811 N. Catalina Blvd., Suite 1308
Redondo Beach, CA, 90277 USA
(310) 376-5115
Fax: (310) 318-5858
Contact Person: Beth Zager
beth@pier3entertainment.com

Premier Entertainment Services, Inc.
366 Adelaide Street, #102
Toronto, Ontario, M5A 3X9 Canada
(416) 363-0274
Fax: (416) 363-0275
Contact Person: David Newton
clientservices@pes-global.com
www.pes-global.com

PRO.P.AG.AND.A
3767 Overland Avenue, Suite 115
Los Angeles, CA, 90034 USA
(310) 202-2300
Fax: (310) 202-2303
Contact Person: Lisa Precious
lisa@propagandagem.com
www.propagandagem.com

Production Profiles Limited
164 Waldegrave Road, Strawberry Hill
Twickenham, Middlesex, TW1 4TD
United Kingdom
(02) 08-891-5194
Fax: (02) 08-404-2181
Contact Person: Joe Keenan and Delena
   Keenan
joe@productionprofiles.co.uk
www.productionprofiles.co.uk

Rogers & Cowan U.S.
1888 Century Park, Suite 500
Los Angeles, CA, 90067 USA

(310) 201-8875
Fax: (310) 201-8884
Contact Person: Tara Walls
twalls@webershandwick.com
www.productionprofiles.co.uk

The ROSS Group
2222 Neilson Way, Suite 202
Santa Monica, CA, 90405 USA
(310) 396-0035
Fax: (310) 396-9905
Contact Person: Mary Hall Ross or Alison
   Jellicoe maryhallross@thereelrossgroup.
   com www.thereelrossgroup.com

Set Resources, Inc.
3015 Main Street, Suite 360
Santa Monica, CA, 90405 USA
(310) 450-9779
Fax: (310) 388-3057
Contact Person: Aaron Gordon
aaron@setresources.com
www.setresources.com

Sheri Sendra
7841 Talbert Street, #6
Playa del Rey, CA, 90293 USA
(310) 578-9067
Fax: none
Contact Person: Sheri Sendra

Showcase Placements, Inc.
2890 Empire
Burbank, CA, 91504 USA
(818) 526-0788
Fax: (818) 840-0132
Contact Person: Richard Briggs
rbriggs4@ford.com
www.showcaseplacements.com

Six Continents Hotel
3165 Corinth Avenue

Los Angeles, CA, 90066 USA
(310) 915-7515
Fax: (310) 915-9677
Contact Person: Judith Pruett
judy.pruett@6C.com

Spotlight Marketing
833 W. Chicago Avenue, Suite 603
Chicago, IL, 60622 USA
(312) 829-1800
Fax: (312) 829-1886
Contact Person: Karen Mellman
karen@spotlightmarketing.com

Studio Services, Inc.
14817 Bessemer Street
Van Nuys, CA, 91411 USA
(818) 782-4074
Fax: (818) 782-2970
Contact Person: Howard Buck
hdbuck@pacbell.net
www.studioservices.com

UPP Entertainment Marketing, Inc.
3401 Winona Avenue
Burbank, CA, 91504 USA
(818) 526-0111
Fax: (818) 526-1466
Contact Person: Barbara Maultsby
blm@upp.net
www.upp.net

Vista Group
805 S. San Fernando Blvd.
Burbank, CA, 91502-1534 USA
(818) 840-6789
Fax: (818) 840-6880
Contact Person: Eric Dahlquist, Sr.
ericsr@vistagroupusa.com
www.vistagroupusa.com

Appendix E: Filmmaking Terms

ABOVE THE LINE and BELOW THE LINE. This refers to the two divisions of your budget that separates the artistic elements of the budget (above the line) from the technical elements (below the line). The writer, producer, director, and actors are listed as above the line, and everything else—the crew, equipment costs, etc.—are considered below the line.

ABOVE THE TITLE. A name in the credits that appears before the title of the movie. This is normally reserved for a star with major box-office appeal or an important director.

ACTION. The word, called out by the director, signaling the actor to begin his or her performance.

ACTORS EQUITY. The union for actors who work in professional theater.

AD-LIB. This is any dialogue or action that is not in the screenplay, often resulting from an improvisation.

ADJUSTMENT (a.k.a. BUMP). This refers to an upgrade in the status of an actor due to some additional business or dialogue given to them. This normally results in additional money paid to that actor.

AFTRA. American Federation of Television and Radio Artists. This union represents professional performers working in radio and/or television.

ART DIRECTOR. The person who designs the sets used in the movie.

BACK-STEPPING. This refers to the method by which an actor hits his or her mark without looking at that mark by stepping out of frame backwards and counting the steps.

BANANA IN/BANANA OUT. Blocking, used by an actor to enter or exit a shot, which has a slight arc to the path.

BEST BOY (a.k.a. FIRST ASSISTANT ELECTRICIAN). The supervisor of the lighting on a set, as well as other electrical technology employed on that set.

BIT (a.k.a. SCHTICK). Typically, a visually funny gag used in a comedic scene.

BIT PART. A small role that makes a contribution to the scene, often with a little "bit" of dialogue, such as one or two lines. It can also be a role in which a brief piece of action is portrayed.

BLOCKING. The physical movements of actors and/or the camera, choreographed by the director for a scene.

BOOM. A contraption similar in appearance to a "fishing pole" which holds the microphone above the actor's head so that the actor's voice can be recorded.

BREAKDOWN. A list of all the roles in a script, with a description of each character, the number of that character's scenes, and how many lines that character has.

BOOM OPERATOR. The technician who operates the microphone boom. This technician also helps the sound mixer in the attachment of miniature microphones to actors.

BRIGHTNESS. A directorial reference wherein an actor is told that additional personality and energy is needed in their performance.

BRUSH CAMERA. Directorial blocking wherein an actor is instructed to exit a shot by "brushing" past the camera.

BUSINESS. An actor's physical action during a scene which contributes in some way to the dramatic intent of that scene.

CALL. The precise time when an actor and/or crewmember is expected to arrive for work on the movie.

CAMEO. A role of small size, often with only a few lines.

CAMERA REHEARSAL (a.k.a. WALK-THROUGH). A rehearsal of a scene for the benefit of the camera operator and crew so that the technical requirements of the scene can be accomplished in harmony with the blocking of the actors.

CGI. Contraction for Computer Generated Image. A form of special effect in which an image is created on a computer and then transferred to film or video.

CHEAT. To "cheat a shot" or "cheat your look" is to look in a direction which, while pleasing photographically, would not be the direction the character would actually be looking.

CHROMA-KEY. A video process by which it is possible to electronically combine two separate images.

CLEAN ENTRANCE or CLEAN EXIT. An actor's entrance onto the shot from off frame, or an actor's exit completely off frame at the conclusion of their performance.

CLOSE-UP. A camera angle wherein the subject of that angle is seemingly close to the camera. Variations of the close-up are the ECU, which stands for extreme close-up, and the MCU, which stands for medium close-up.

COLOR CORRECTED. A technical reference to film footage that has had the color of its image corrected in some way. Since it is quite common for the color of newly processed footage to be slightly off, it is necessary to have this fixed before a print can be made of the movie.

CONTINUITY. The crewmember who is responsible for continuity makes sure that each shot is visually consistent with the preceding shot or shots, as well as those shots that will follow it, so that they will edit together smoothly. This may involve taking snapshots of the actors on the set to use as a reference later. You will find a more thorough explanation in point 50.

COSTUME DESIGNER. As you may have guessed, this is the person who designs the costumes.

COVERAGE. The amount of camera angles "covering" a scene is referred to as "coverage." The use of this term implies that a large variety of camera angles were used to photograph a scene.

CRAFT SERVICES. A business who has the responsibility of supplying snacks, food, and beverages for the actors and members of the crew on the set of a motion picture.

CREW. The group reference for all on-set movie technicians.

CRI. The contraction for Color Reversal Intermediate, which is the end result of a film duplication process rarely used today. When a 16-millimeter feature film is blown up to 35-millimeter, the new 35-millimeter negative is called a CRI.

CUE. The moment an actor knows to say their line. That moment is based upon a specific word spoken by another actor, a sound, an action, or a piece of business.

CUT! The word called out by the director to signify that all filming is to stop.

DAILIES (a.k.a. RUSHES). This refers to the processed footage of the previous day's filming.

DAY-FOR-NIGHT. A means of filming a scene in the daytime that gives it the appearance of being shot at night. It is normally accomplished by the image being darkened and a bluish tint being added.

DAY-PLAYER. A union actor who works on a movie for a daily rate. This is a reference normally associated with the amount of money that the Screen Actor's Guild requires an actor to earn each day.

DEVELOPMENT. A term to indicate a movie studio's interest in a possible production, even though they have yet to commit to a start date.

DGA. Short for the Directors Guild of America, the union that represents the professional interests of movie directors, assistant directors and production managers.

DIRECTOR OF PHOTOGRAPHY (a.k.a. the DP). The camera person primarily responsible for the look of the cinematography.

DISSOLVE. A transition in which one shot gives way to another shot.

DOLLY (a.k.a. PUSH-IN). A "dolly" is the name for any wheeled support for the movie camera. This support can be something as inexpensive as a shopping cart, a wheelchair, or, if the budget is high enough, the standard four-wheeled mechanized platform generally used on motion pictures.

DOUBLE. An actor who temporarily replaces another actor in a shot where it is impossible to recognize the original actor. For example, a character seen in a long shot or in a close-up of his hands.

DRIFT. When an actor moves off their mark, thereby compromising the photography, it is called "drifting" or to have "drifted."

DUBBING (a.k.a. LOOPING). To dub something is to substitute a voice in post-production that matches the lip movements of the original actor, or, in the case of a foreign film, matches the vowel pronouncement of that actor.

DUPE NEGATIVE. Once the negative of your movie has been edited, it is necessary to protect that negative from harm (such as scratches), so a duplicate of that negative is made. It is via this "dupe negative" that a print of your movie is made.

DUTCHING THE SHOT. This refers to the tilting of the camera, creating a slightly off-balanced look to the image.

ESTABLISHING SHOT. A shot which "establishes" the exterior of the location in which a scene is about to take place. For example, a long shot of an exterior of a restaurant, inside which the principal characters are having dinner.

EXECUTIVE PRODUCER. The producer who locates the money for the budget of the movie.

EXTRAS (a.k.a. BACKGROUND ARTISTS, a.k.a. ATMOSPHERE). Actors who play a role without dialogue and do not make a significant contribution to the scene, yet whose absence would compromise the look of that scene. For example, the crowds of people walking down the sidewalk when a car chase is taking place.

FADE IN/FADE OUT. A fade is a transition. A FADE IN is where we go from black to a screen image. A FADE OUT reverses the process.

FEATURED (FEATURED PART or FEATURED ROLE). A small acting role, but one of consequence to the plot.

FILL LIGHT. Light used to "fill in," or brighten, the dark areas of an actor's face, creating a more pleasing visual appearance.

FIRST ASSISTANT DIRECTOR and SECOND ASSISTANT DIRECTOR (a.k.a. 1st AD and 2nd AD). The 1st AD is the assistant to the director and helps the production manager with the shooting schedule. The 2nd AD tends to works with crowds and extras.

FIRST TRIAL COMPOSITE (a.k.a. FIRST TRIAL PRINT). The first color-corrected print of the movie ready for showing in a theater.

FLAT. A constructed section of a fake wall used to create a set.

FOLLOW SHOT. A Follow Shot is a combination of camera movement and focus adjustment which permits the camera to "follow" the subject being photographed.

FOREGROUND. Whatever is in front of the person or object you are photographing is called the foreground. Whatever is in back of what you are photographing is called the background.

FRAME. The rectangular image representing what will be photographed by the camera once the scene begins.

FROM THE TOP (a.k.a. BACK TO ONE). To begin the scene again, which requires the actors to return to the spot where they were standing at the start of their performance.

FX. An abbreviation for special effects. It refers specifically to those special effects that are performed on the set, as opposed to those placed into the movie during post-production.

GAFFER. Remember the technician I mentioned in the preface? A technician who sets up lights under the control of the director of photography.

GOLDEN HOUR. The period just before sunset that is especially pleasing photographically because the sunlight casts a golden color over everything. Not to be mistaken for the term "golden time."

GOLDEN TIME. Golden time refers to the period of time after a normal 8-hour work day when union actors are paid double their normal salary.

GREEN LIGHT. To "green light" a movie project is to officially state that the movie project is ready to go into production.

GRIP. A crewmember who moves things on the set, with the exception of anything electrical.

HAIRDRESSER. The person responsible for the look and style of the actors' hair and/or wigs.

HAND PROPS. This refers to all props which are held or handled by the actors on camera.

HONEY WAGON. The trailer or RV that contains dressing rooms and bathrooms for actors. On very low budget movies it may refer to a portapotty.

IN THE CAN. When a scene is completely finished, it is referred to as being "in the can" because all the footage can now be put into the film can to be processed.

KEY MAKE-UP ARTIST. The person who is responsible for the look of all actors' make-up, and oversees its application.

MARK. The spot on which an actor must stand to stay within range of the camera or to remain in focus. A mark is usually represented by two pieces of tape forming a "T," on top of which the actor places his or her feet.

MOS. To film without sound.

NEGATIVE CONFORMATION (a.k.a. NEGATIVE CONFORMING, a.k.a. CONFORMATION OF NEGATIVE). When the editing of your movie is completed (using your dailies), it is then necessary to edit the negative of your footage, thereby conforming that negative to the specific cuts already used on the daily footage. This is done to assure that no damage is done to the negative during the creative process of editing.

ONE-LITE DAILY (a.k.a. ONE-LIGHT DAILY). When the raw footage is processed by a film laboratory, you receive "dailies" or "rushes." One type of rushes are one-lite dailies, which is footage that has not been color corrected.

POINTS. Another word for a percentage of a movie.

PRINCIPAL. A role of large size. Normally a major role in a movie.

PRINT. A print is a film-based copy of your movie.

PRODUCTION MANAGER. The person who organizes the budget, coordinates the shooting schedule, and is responsible for keeping everything within budgetary limits.

PROPERTY MASTER. The person who is responsible for keeping track of all properties (better known as props), as well as their upkeep.

ROLLING! The word called out to signify that sound should begin recording.

SAG. Screen Actors Guild, the union representing actors who work in motion pictures.

SCREEN TEST. A filmed "test" of an actor's audition designed to inform those doing the casting as to whether that actor is cinematically suitable for the part.

SCRIPT SUPERVISOR. This crewmember writes in-depth information concerning each take, and also makes certain that each shot fits into the continuity of those shots that preceded it.

SET DECORATOR. The crewmember who, under the guidance of the production designer, chooses the props. The set decorator also places those props, along with all set dressing, throughout the set.

SET DRESSER. The set dresser helps both the set decorator and the prop master in the performance of their duties.

SET-UP. A camera reference describing a new camera angle or position to be "set up" for the next shot.

SHOT. The image that is recorded by the camera. It's also called a "take."

SKIP-FRAME. If the decision is made to speed up the action of the scene after that scene is shot, the footage undergoes a post-production process wherein the negative is re-photographed minus individual frames of action (usually every other frame). This speeds up the action dramatically when that scene is projected.

SOUND MIXER. The crewmember who operates the recording equipment and "mixes" the sound being recorded by the microphone.

SPEED! A word called out to signal that the sound recorder and the cameras are working in synchronization.

STAND-IN. A stand-in is a person who "stands in" for an actor while lights are adjusted. Occasionally they fill in for an actor while the director figures out the blocking of a scene.

STORY BOARD. When the potential shots of a scene are portrayed in a series of comic strip-like drawings during pre-production, it is called storyboarding. It is normally used to figure out an action- or special effect-laden scene.

STRIKE. When a set or piece of movie equipment is no longer needed, it is time to "strike," or remove, that set or piece of movie equipment. Its removal is referred to as the set or equipment having been "struck."

TREATMENT. An outline of a movie script that has yet to be fully written as a screenplay.

UNDERCRANKING. To speed up the action by altering the movie camera's film speed to a lesser frame rate per second. By doing this, the filmed action, when projected at normal speed, appears to move faster. This is most often used to speed up fight scenes, car chases, or create a comic effect.

VIDEO-TO-FILM TRANSFER. As the name suggests, this is a process wherein a video-taped image is transferred to film so that the movie may be projected in a movie theater for a public showing.

VO (a.k.a. VOICE OVER). This refers to dialogue that is not spoken on-camera. It is usually added in post-production.

WARDROBE MASTER. In charge of keeping track of everything in the wardrobe department, as well as its upkeep.

WILD TRACK. To record sound minus an image.

WORKPRINT. A print of the movie that is technically unfinished, usually missing special effects, titles, and/or sound effects.

WRAP. To finish a specific body of work on a film. For example, to finish filming at a location or to complete all work on a movie.

WRAP PARTY. The name of the party put together for the benefit of the cast and crew once filming is finished.

ZOOM. Contraction for Zoomar lens. To zoom means to enlarge the image from a long shot to a closer shot, or to do the reverse.

Appendix F: Distributors

A & E (Arts and Entertainment) Home Video
125 Fifth Ave., 15th Fl.
New York, NY 10011

(708) 328-6700,
(800) 423-1212
http://www.aetv.com

Academic Media Network
(Educational Video Network)
acameda@pioneer.net
http://www.acameda.com

Acorn Media
7910 Woodmont Ave., Suite 350
Bethesda, MD 20814
(800) 999-0212
(301) 907-9049
info@acornmedia.com
http://www.acornmedia.com

African American Videos
PO BOX 14590
San Francisco, CA 94115
(415) 346-2055
aveprsf@best.com
http://www.amvideos.com:80/index.html
Distributes videos about the black expe-
    rience.

Allied Entertainment Inc.
8899 Beverly Boulevard, Suite 911
West Hollywood, CA
(310) 271-8684
info@alliedentertainment.com

Altschul Group Corporation
1560 Sherman Ave., Suite 100
Evanston, IL 60201-9971
(800) 323-9084
(708) 328-6700
(708) 328-6706
http://www.agcmedia.com

Ambrose Video Publishing Inc.
145 W. 45th St., Suite 1115
New York, NY 10036
(800) 526-4663
(212) 768-9282
http://www.ambrosevideo.com
Distributes documentaries and educa-
    tional videos.

American Film Foundation
1333 Ocean Avenue
Santa Monica, CA 90401
(310) 459-2116
(310) 394-1260
http://www.americanfilmfoundation.com

American Portrait Films, Inc.
P.O. Box 19266

Cleveland, OH 44119-1545
(800) 736-4567
(216) 531-8355
http://www.amport.com
Distributes videos that address Christ-
    ian concerns.

Anchor Bay Entertainment
1699 Stutz Drive
Troy, MI 48024
(248) 816-0909
Fax: (248) 816-3335
questions@anchorbayent.com
http://www.anchorbayentertainment.
    com

Andrea International
President: Shirin Drost
(310) 546-1239
Fax: (310) 546-9551
http://andrea-int.com

Anthology Film Archives
32 Second Avenue
New York, NY 10003
(212) 505-5181
http://www.arthouseinc.com/anthology

Ark Media Group, Ltd./New Era Media
PO Box 410685
San Francisco, CA 94141
(415) 863-7200
salesweb@arkmedia.com
http://www.arkmedia.com/xcart/home.
    php

Arthouse, Inc.
154 Grand Street, Suite 208
New York, NY 10013
(212) 334-6165
(212) 334-6273
arthouse@arthouseinc.com
http://www.arthouseinc.com
Distributes avant garde and experimen-
    tal films.

Athos Films Distribution
Husemannstr. 5, 10435
Berlin, Germany
49-30-449-9769
www.athos-films.com

Baker & Taylor Entertainment
2709 Water Ridge Pkwy.
Charlotte, NC 28217

(800) 775-1800
http://www.btol.com

Bandana Productions
909 E. Glendale Ave.
Shorewood, WI 53211
(414) 964-3742
(414) 964-5484
bandana@uwm.edu

Benchmark Media
569 No. State Rd.
Briarcliff Manor, NY 10510
(800) 438-5564
(914) 762-3838
(914) 762-3895
benchmedia@aol.com

Berkeley Media LLC
Saul Zaentz Film Center
2600 Tenth Street, Suite 626
Berkeley, CA 94710
(510) 486-9900
(510) 486-9944
info@berkeleymedia.com
http://www.berkeleymedia.com

Blackside, Inc.
486 Shawmut Avenue
Boston, MA 02118
(617) 536-6900

Budget Films
4590 Santa Monica Blvd.
Los Angeles, CA 90029
(213) 660-0187
http://www.budgetfilms.com

Buena Vista Entertainment
500 S. Buena Vista St.
Burbank, CA.
(818) 560-1000
http://www.disneygo.com

Cambridge Documentary Films, Inc.
PO Box 390385
Cambridge, MA 02139-0004
(617) 484-3993
(617) 484-0754
mail@cambridgedocumentaryfilms.org
http://www.cambridgedocumentary
   films.org

Canyon Cinema
145 Ninth Street, Suite 260

San Francisco, CA 94103
(510) 626-2255
films@canyoncinema.com
http://www.canyoncinema.com
Distributes avant garde and experimental films.

Carousel Film & Video
250 Fifth Avenue, Suite 204
New York, NY 10001
(800) 683-1660
(212) 683-1662
carousel@pipeline.com
http://www.carouselfilms.com

Christiancinema.com
130 N. Kelsey Suite C, Visalia, CA 93291
(888) 527-2388
(559) 651-9898
Distributes Christian videos.

Cinnamon Productions
19 Wild Rose Road
Westport, CT 06880
(203) 221-0613
Distributes movies concerning Native American issues.

Clearvue/eav
Formerly: Centre Productions, Inc. & Churchill Films, Inc.
6465 North Avondale Avenue
Chicago, IL 60631-1996
(800) CLEARVU
CustServ@clearvue.com

Also

1560 Sherman Avenue, Suite 100
Evanston Il 60201
(888) 892-3484
Fax: (847) 328-6706
clearvueservice@discoivery.com
http://www.clearvue.com

Cloud Ten
PO Box 1440,
Niagara Falls, NY 14302
http://www.cloudtenpictures.com
Distributes Christian movies.

Collision Course Video Productions
(Paradigm Productions)
2600 Tenth Street, Suite 611
Berkeley, CA 94710

(510) 883-9814
info@paradigmproductions.org
http://www.paradigmproductions.org

Colombia/Tri-Star Pictures
10202 W. Washington Blvd.
Culver City, CA 90232
(310) 244-2332
feedback@sonypictures.com

Crown Video
15397 117 Ave.
Edmonton, AB
T5M 3X4
Canada
(708) 471-1417
Distributes Christian films and wholesome
   family movies.

Davenport Films
11324 Pearlstone Ln.
Delaplane, VA 22025
(800) 804-7466
(540) 592-3717
davfilms@crosslink.net
http://www.oz.net/~davfilms/index.html
Distributes documentaries and movies
   centering on folklore and American
   folk culture.

Direct Cinema Ltd.
PO Box 10003
Santa Monica, CA 90410-1003
(800) 525-0000
(310) 636-8200
(310) 396-3233
info@directcinemalimited.com
http://directcinemalimited.com

Disney Studios
(See Buena Vista Entertainment)

Electronic Arts Intermix
535 West 22nd St., 5th floor
New York, NY 10011
(212) 337-0680
(212) 337-0679
info@eai.org
http://www.eai.org
Distributes avant garde and experimental films.

Environmental Media Corporation
1008 Paris Ave.

Port Royal, SC 29935
(800) 368-3382
(800) 368-3382
(843) 986-9093
bpendergraft@envmedia.com
http://www.envmedia.com

Film Artists Network
PO Box 323
Canoga Park, CA 91305
(818) 344-0569
fand@artistsnetwork.com

Film Ideas
308 N. Wolf Road
Wheeling, IL 60090
(800) 475-3456
(847) 419-8933
filmid@ais.net
http://www.filmideas.com

Filmic Archives
The Cinema Center
Botsford, CT 06404
(800) 366-1920
(203) 268-1796
custsrv@filmicarchives.com
http://www.filmicarchives.com

Filmmakers Collaborative
99 Moody Street
Waltham, MA 02154
(781) 647-1102
(781) 647-1140
info@filmmakerscollab.org
http://www.filmmakerscollab.org

Filmwest Associates, USA
300 West Second St.
Carson City, NV 89703
(775) 883-8090
(800) 570-5505
sales@filmwest.com
http://www.filmwest.com

Filmwest Canada
2400 Hayman Road
Kelowna, B.C.
Canada V1Z 1Z8
(250) 769-3399
(800) 570-5505
info@filmwest.com
http://www.filmwest.com

Fineline (merged with New Line Pictures)

First Run Features/Icarus Films
32 Court Street, 21st Floor
Brooklyn, NY 11201
(800) 876-1710,
(718) 488-8900
(718) 488-8642
info@frif.com
http://www.frif.com

Flower Films (Les Blank)
10341 San Pablo Ave.
El Cerrito, CA 94530
(800) 572-7618
(510) 525-0942
(510) 525-1204
blankfilm@aol.com
http://www.lesblank.com

Galan Incorporated Television and Film
5524 Bee Caves Road, Suite B-5
Austin, TX 78746
(512) 327-1333
(512) 327-1547
info@fullcir.com
http://www.galaninc.com

Giorno Poetry Systems
222 Bowery
New York, NY 10012
(212) 925-6372
http://www.brainwashed.com/giorno

Globalvision
575 Eighth Avenue, Suite 2200
New York, NY 10018
(212) 246.0202
(212) 246-2677
roc@igc.org
http://www.globalvision.org
Distributes informational, educational, and entertainment programming for worldwide markets.

Hallmark Home Entertainment
6100 Wilshire Blvd., Suite 1400
Los Angeles, CA 90048
(213) 634-3000
(213) 549-3760

HBO Video, Inc.
1100 Ave. of the Americas
New York, NY 10036
(212) 512-7400
(800) 648-7650
(212) 512-7458
http://hbohomevideo.com

Independent Television Service (ITVS)
501 York Street
San Francisco, CA 94110
(415) 356-8383
(415) 356-8391
itvs@itvs.org
http://www.itvs.org

Insight Media
2162 Broadway
New York, NY 10024
(800) 233-9910
(212) 721-6316
(212) 799-5309
custserv@insight-media.com
http://insight-media.com

International Film Circuit
301 East 22nd Street
New York, NY 10010
(212) 686-6777
(212) 545-9931
ifc@internationalfilmcircuit.com
http://www.internationalfilmcircuit.
  com

Janson Associates, Inc.
88 Semmens Road
Harrington Park, NJ 07640
(201) 784-8488
(201) 784-3993
steve@janson.com
http://www.janson.com
Distributes special interest documentaries, plus family and children's films.

Ken Crane's DVDs/Laserdiscs
http://www.dvdplanet.com/main.asp

KET, The Kentucky Network Enterprise Division
560 Cooper Dr.
Lexington, KY 40502-2279
(606) 258-7205
(800) 354-9067
(606) 258-7396

Landmark Media
3450 Slade Run Dr.
Falls Church, VA 22042
(800) 342-4336
(703) 241-2030
(703) 536-9540
landmrkmed@aol.com
http://www.landmarkmedia.com

LCA (c/o New World Video)
1440 S. Sepulveda Blvd.
Los Angeles, CA 90025
(310) 444-8100
(310) 444-8101

Library Bound, Inc.
200 Forbisher Dr.
Waterloo, Ontario
Canada N2V 2A2
(800) 363-4728
(519) 885-2662
duncan@librarybound.com
http://www.librarybound.com

Library Video Company
P.O. Box 580
Wynnewood, PA 19096
(610) 645-4000
(800) 843-3620
(610) 645-4040
lynn@libraryvideo.com
http://www.libraryvideo.com

Library Video Network
320 York Rd.
Towson, MD 21204
(800) 441-TAPE
lvn@bcpl.net
http://www.lvn.org

**Lions Gate Entertainment, Inc.
(in USA)**
2700 Colorado Ave., #200
Santa Monica, CA 90404
(310) 449-9200
(in Canada)
1055 W. Hastings St., Suite 2200
Vancouver, BC 62
http://lionsgatefilms.com

Long Bow Group, Inc.
55 Newton St.
Brookline, MA 02445
(617) 277-6400

(617) 277-6843
lbowinc@aol.com
http://www.tsquare.tv/longbow.html

Madera Cinevideo
311 South Pine, Suite 102
Madera, CA 93638
(559) 661-6000
(559) 674-3650
maderacvc@pacbell.net
http://www.mcinavideo.qpg.com
Distributes videos concerning Latino
    life.

MasterVision
969 Park Ave.
New York, NY 10028
(212) 879-0448

Media Basics
16781 Chagrin Boulevard, Box #130
Shaker Heights, OH 44120
(800) 542-2505
(781) 481-9042
matt@mediabasicsvideo.com
http://www.mediabasicsvideo.com
Distributes educational videos for
    schools.

Media for the Arts
P.O. Box 1011
Newport, RI 02840
(800) 554-6008
(401) 846-6580
artmfa/@art-history.com
http://www.art-history.com

MGM/UA
2450 Broadway St.
Santa Monica, CA 90404-3061
(310) 449-3000
http://mgmua.com

Midnight Ramble Video
PO Box 11522
Portland, OR 97211
(503) 287-0318
MidnightRV@aul.com
http://midnightramble.com
Distributes movies with all-black casts.

Mongrel Media
1028 Queen St. West
Toronto, Ontario

Canada M6J 1H6
(416) 516-9775
(416) 516-0651
info@mongrelmedia.com
http://www.mongrelmedia.com

Moriah Films (Simon Wiesenthal Center)
9760 West Pico Boulevard
Los Angeles, CA 90035
moriah@wiesenthal.com
http://www.wiesenthal.com/moriah

Moving Images Distribution
402 West Pender Street, Suite 606
Vancouver, B.C.
Canada V6B 1T6
800-684-3014
(North America) 604-684-3014
(local) 604-684-7165
mailbox@movingimages.ca
http://www.movingimages.ca
Largest distributor of Canadian documentary, animation, and educational films and videos in Western Canada.

MPI Media Group
16101 South 108th Ave.
Orland Park, IL 60462
(800) 777-2223
(708) 460-0555
(708) 460-0175
http://www.mpimedia.com

MTI Home Video
14216 SW 136th St.
Miami, FL 33186
(305) 255-8684
http://mti@mtivideo.com

Mystic Fire Video
P.O. Box 422
New York, NY 10012-0008
(800) 292-9001
(212) 941-1443
ordering@mysticfire.com
http://www.mysticfire.com

National Black Programming Consortium, Inc.
68 East 131st Street, 7th floor
New York, NY 10037
(212) 234-8200
(212) 234-7032

info@nbpc.tv
http://www.nbpc.tv

National Women's History Project
3343 Industrial Dr., Suite 4
Santa Rosa, CA 95403
(707) 636-2888
(707) 636-2909
nwhp@nwhp.org
http://www.nwhp.org/

New Day Films
22-D Hollywood Ave.
Hohokus, NJ 07423
(888) 367-9154

Outside continental USA:

(845) 774-7051
(845) 774-2945
orders@newday.com
http://www.newday.com

New Dimension Media
A Questar Company
680 N. Lake Shore Drive, Suite 900
Chicago, IL 60611
(800) 288-4456
(312) 642-9805
Info@NDMquestar.com
http://www.ndmquestar.com

New Line (Merged with Warner Brothers)
Paramount Studios
5555 Melrose Ave.,
Los Angeles, CA 90030
(323) 956-5000
(323) 462-1977

PBS Video
1320 Braddock Place
Alexandria, VA 22314-1698
(800) 344-3337
(866) 274-9043
www@pbs.org
http://www.pbs.org
http://www.shoppbs.org

Phoenix / BFA Films & Video
Affiliate: Coronet / MTI Film & Video
2349 Chaffee Dr.
St. Louis, MO 63146
(314) 569-0211
(800) 221-1274

(314) 569-2834
http://www.phoenixlearninggroup.com

**The Poetry Center and American
Poetry Archives**
San Francisco State University
1600 Holloway Avenue
San Francisco, CA 94132
(415) 338-1056
(415) 338-0966
newlit@sfsu.edu
http://www.sfsu.edu./~newlit/welcome.
htm

POPcinema
(973) 838-3030
Bruder@brivideo.com

Porchlight Entertainment
11050 Santa Monica Blvd., 3rd Floor
Los Angeles, CA 90025
(310) 477-8400
http://info@porchlight.com

P.O.V. (Point of View)
(PBS Video)
http://www0.pbs.org/pov

Professional Media Service Corp.
Baker & Taylor
1160 Trademark Drive, Suite 109
Reno, NV 89511
(800) 223-7672
(800) 253-8853
btinfo@btol.com
http://www.promedia.com

Pyramid Media
(Pyramid Films)
P.O. Box 1048/WEB
Santa Monica, CA 90406-1048
(310) 828-7577
(800) 421-2304
(310) 453-9083
info@pyramidmedia.com
http://www.pyramidmedia.com

Questar Video, Inc.
P.O. BOX 11345
Chicago, IL 60611-0345
Mailing address: 680 N. Lake Shore Dr.,
Suite 900
Chicago, IL 60611
(800) 544-8422

(312) 266-9400,
(312) 266-9523
http://www.questar1.com

Rhino Home Video
10635 Santa Monica Blvd., 2nd Fl.
Los Angeles, CA 90025-4900
(310) 474-4778
(800) 843-3670
(310) 441-6575
http://www.rhino.com

Richter Productions, Inc.
330 W. 42nd St./32
New York, NY 10036
(212) 947-1395
(212) 643-1208
Richter330@aol.com
http://www.RichterVideos.com

Salt City Book and Video
2807 Brewerton Rd.
North Syracuse, NY 13212
(315) 454-0629
Distributes low-budget horror and special interest videos.

Schlessinger Media
P.O. Box 580
Wynnewood, PA 19096
(800) 843-3620
(610) 645-4000
lynn@libraryvideo.com
http://www.libraryvideo.com

S.I. Video Direct
PO Box 968
Englewood, FL 34295
(941) 473-2601
(941) 473-2701
stann@sivideo.com
http://www.sivideo.com

Something Weird Video
P.O. Box 33664
Seattle, WA 98133
(888) 634-3320
(425) 290-5830
(206) 364-7526
somweird@ix.netcom.com
http://www.somethingweird.com

Starlight Home Entertainment
6222 Whilshire Blvd., Suite 200

Los Angeles, CA. 90048
(323) 932-7000
info@starlightfilm group
http://www.starlightfilmgroup.com

Tempe Entertainment
PO Box 210
Uniontown, OH 44685-0212
http://tempevideo.com

Terra Nova Films
9848 South Winchester Ave.
Chicago, IL 60643
(800) 779-8491
(773) 881-8491
(773) 881-3368
tnf@terranova.org
http://www.terranova.org

THA Media Distributors
1200 West Pender, #307
Vancouver, BC
Canada V6E 2S9
(Canada only): (800) 661-4919
(604) 687-4215
(604) 688-8349
tha.sales@thamedia.com
Information: tha.info@thamedia.com

**Thin Air Video (Contemporary Poetry
    Archives)**
58 East 4th St., #3
New York, NY 10003
(212) 254-2803
thinairvideo@earthlink.net
http://www.thinairvideo.com

**Third World Newsreel/Camera News,
    Inc.**
545 Eighth Avenue, 10th floor
New York, NY 10018
(212) 947-9277
(212) 594-6417
twn@twn.org
http://www.twn.org

Troma
36-40 11th St.
Long Island City, NY 11106
(718) 391-0110
htpp://www.troma.com

Twentieth Century–Fox
10301 W. Pico Blvd., #100

Los Angeles, CA 90064
(310) 369-3050

Universal Pictures
100 Universal City Plaza,
Universal City, CA 91608
(818) 777-9775

Alternate Address:

70 Universal City Plaza,
Universal Plaza, CA 91608
(818) 777-4300
(818) 733-0226
http://universalstudios.com

Upstream Productions
6850 35th Ave. NE, Suite #11
Seattle, WA 98115
(206) 526-7122
(206) 524-8879
uproduct@aol.com

Video Arts International, Inc.
6-7 St. Cross Street
London EC1N 8UA
United Kingdom
44 (0)20 7400 4800
44 (0)20 7400 4900
http://www.videoarts.co.uk

Video Project
PO Box 77188
San Francisco, CA 94107
(800) 4-Planet
(415) 284-0600
(415) 821-7204
video@videoproject.com
http://www.videoproject.net
http://www.actnowproductions.com

Villon Films
c/o Peter Davis
4040 Ontario St.
Vancouver BC
Canada V5V 3G5
(604) 879-6042
(604) 879-6042
By e-mail: peter@villonfilms.com
http://www.villonfilms.com

Vision Maker Video (VMV)
P.O. Box 83111
Lincoln, NE 68501
(800) 835-7087

(402) 472-8675
http://www.visionmaker.com

Warner Brothers
4000 Warner Blvd.
Burbank, CA 91522
(818) 954-6000
wbsf@warnerbros.com

Weston Woods Studios, Inc.
PO Box 2193
Norwalk, CT 06852-2193
(800) 243-5020
(203) 845-0498
http://teacher.scholastic.com/products/
   westonwoods

WETA
2775 South Quincy Street
Arlington, VA 22206
(703)998-2600
(703) 998-3401
http://weta.capaccess.org/wetaweb/web_
   email.shtml
http://www.weta.org

William Greaves Productions, Inc.
230 W. 55th St.
New York, NY 10019
(212) 265-6150
(800) 874-8314
(212) 315-0027

Women Make Movies
462 Broadway
New York, NY 10013
(212) 925-0606
(212) 925-2052
distdept@wmm.com
http://www.wmm.com

Zeitgeist Films
247 Centre St., 2nd Fl.
New York, NY 10013
(212) 274-1989
(212) 274-1644
mail@zeitgeistfilm.com
http://www.zeitgeistfilm.com

Zia Film Distribution
360 Montezumz Ave., #320
Santa Fe, NM 87505
(505) 438 9299
http://www.ziafilm.com

Zipporah Films (Frederick Wiseman)
One Richdale Ave., Unit #4
Cambridge, MA 02140
(617) 576-3603
(617) 864-8006
zfilms@world.std.com
http://www.zipporah.com

Bibliography

Books

Albright, Hardie. *Acting, the Creative Process*. Belmont, CA: Dickenson Publishing, 1967.

Alton, John. *Painting with light*. Berkeley, CA: University of California Press, 1995.

Burns, Bob. *It Came from Bob's Basement*. San Francisco, CA: Chronicle Books, 2001.

Caine, Michael. *Acting in Film: An Actor's Take on Movie Making*. Milwaukee, WI: Applause Books, 1987.

Campisi, Gabriel. *An Independent Filmmaker's Guide to a Business Plan for Investors*. Jefferson, NC: McFarland, 2004.

Corman, Roger, and Jim Jerome. *How I Made a Hundred Movies in Hollywood and Never Lost a Dime*. New York: Da Capo Press, 1990.

Egri, Lajos. *The Art of Dramatic Writing*. New York: Touchstone Books, 1946.

Eisenstein, Sergei. *The Film Sense*. (Trans. Jay Leyda). New York: Harcourt, 1942.

Fielding, Raymond. *The Technique of Special Effects Cinematography*. New York: Communications Arts/Hastings House, 1972.

Glut, Don. *I Was a Teenage Movie Maker*. Jefferson, NC: McFarland, 2007.

Glut, Don, and Jim Harmon. *The Great Movie Serials: Their Sound and Fury*. New York: Doubleday, 1972.

Goldner, Orville, and George Turner. *The Making of King Kong: The Story Behind a Film Classic*. Taylorville, IL: Oak Tree Publications, 1975.

Grossman, Gary. *Superman: Serial to Cereal*. New York: Popular Library, 1976.

Harter, Chuck. *Superboy and Superpup: The Lost Episodes*. Loma Linda, CA: Cult Movies, 1997.

Heald, Tim. *The Making of Space: 1999*. New York: Ballantine Books, 1976.

Heitland, Jon. *The Man from U.N.C.L.E.: The Behind the Scenes Story of a Television Classic*. New York: St. Martin's Griffin, 1987.

Keaton, Buster, and Charles Samuels. *Buster Keaton: My Wonderful World of Slapstick*. New York: Da Capo Press, 1960.

Kerr, Walter. *The Silent Clowns*. New York: Knopf, 1975.

MacKay, Harvey. *Swim with Sharks*. New York: Morrow/Avon, 1988.

Pudovkin, Vsevolod. *Film Technique and Film Acting*. Jackson, TN: Grove Press, 1958.

Roddenberry, Gene, and Stephen E. Whitfield. *The Making of Star Trek*. New York: Ballantine Books, 1968.

Rodriguez, Robert. *Rebel Without a Crew*. New York: Plume, 1996.

Smith, Dick. *Dick Smith's Do-It-Yourself Monster Make-Up Handbook*. New York: Warren Publishing, 1965.

Stanislavski, Constantin. *An Actor Prepares*. (Trans. Elizabeth Reynolds Hapgood.) New York: Theatre Arts Books/Metuen, 1936.

Weiss, Ken, and Ed Goodgold. *To Be Continued*. New York: Crown, 1972.

Witney, William. *In a Door, Into a Fight, Out a Door, Into a Chase*. Jefferson, NC: McFarland, 1996.

Articles

"The Abduction of Grog." *Cinemagic*, Issue 5, Winter 1976.

Carlson, Gary S. "History of Big Bang Comics, Volume One." *Image Comics*, Issue 24, 1998.

_____. "History of Big Bang Comics, Volume Two." *Image Comics*, Issue 27, 1998.

Fisher, Dennis. "An Outspoken Interview with the Sultan of Speculation: Curt Siodmak." *Filmfax*, Issue 5, November/December 1988.

Hitt, Jim. "Underrated Serials." *Serial World*, Issue 31, Summer 1982.

Leavitt, Sam. "Brainstorm; Moody Camera Holds Suspense in Thriller." *American Cinematographer*, Issue 6, June 1965.

Loring, Charles. "Pictorial Composition — Key Element in Cinematography." *American Cinematographer*, Issue 8, August 1962.

Macelli, Joseph V. "A Word to the Wise." *American Cinematographer*, Issue 7, July 1966.

"Movie Highlights." *Karate World*, Issue 2, Summer 1993.

"Professional Super-8 Issue. Special Issue: The State of the Art." *American Cinematographer*. Issue 11, November 1975.

"Robert Wise Talks About the New Hollywood." *American Cinematographer*, Issue 7, July 1976.

"Shazam." *Famous Monsters of Filmland*, Issue 101, September 1973.

Silke, James. "The Cast: The First Principles of Motion Picture Acting." *American Cinematographer*, Number 6, November/December 1963.

"Sinister Spider and His Celluloid Web." *Screen Thrills Illustrated*, Issue 8, May 1964.

Skotak, Robert. "Behind the Scenes on *The Time Travelers*." *Filmfax*, Issue 60, April/May 1997.

_____. "Worlds, Wars & Wonders: The Amazing Career of Ib J. Melchior." *Filmfax*, Issue 56, May/June 1996.

Weaver, Tom. "The Mogul, the Man, the Fan ... Sam Sherman." *Filmfax*, Issue 27, June/July 1991.

Wildi, Ernst. "Peterson's Bolex Guide to 16-mm Movie Making." *Photographic Magazine*. Los Angeles: Peterson Publishing, 1973.

"Wizard of Speed and Time." *American Film*, Issue 8, June 1988.

FILMS

The Adventures of Captain Marvel. Dirs. John English, William Witney. Perf. Tom Tyler, Frank Coghlan Jr., Louise Currie, William Benedict. 12 Chapters. Republic Pictures, 1941.

The Adventures of Superman. Based upon characters appearing in DC comics. Perf. George Reeves, Phyllis Coates, Noel Neill, Jack Larsen, John Hamilton, Robert Shayne. 104 Episodes. Flamingo Films, 1951–1957.

Battle Beast. Dir. Philip R. Cable. Perf. Lorin Taylor, Lisa Todd, Charles Dierkop, Allen Wade, James Willis. Draculina-Cine, 2001.

The Blair Witch Project. Dirs. Daniel Myrick, Eduardo Sánchez. Perf. Heather Donahue, Joshua Lenard, Michael C. Williams. Artisan Entertainment, 1999.

Carnival of Souls. Dir. Herk Harvey. Perf. Candace Hillgoss, Frances Feist, Sidney Berger, Art Ellison, Stan Levitt. Herts-Lion International, 1962.

Danger: Diabolik! Dir. Mario Bava. Perf. John Philip Law, Terry Thomas, Marisa Mell, Michel Piccoli, Adolfo Celi. Paramount, 1968.

Detour. Dir. Edgar G. Ulmer. Perf. Tom Neal, Ann Savage, Claudia Drake, Edmund MacDonald. Producers Releasing Corporation, 1945.

Invasion of the Body Snatchers. Dir. Don Siegel. Perf. Kevin McCarthy, Dana Wynter, Larry Gates, King Donavan, Carolyn Jones. Allied Artists, 1956.

It Conquered the World. Dir. Roger Corman. Perf. Lee Van Cleef, Peter Graves, Beverly Garland, Sally Fraser. American International Pictures, 1956.

Knights of Justice. Dir. Philip R. Cable. Perf. Allan Woodman, Lorin Taylor, Sandra Kuhn, Mike Constantin, Dan Layne, Tom Wells, Sandi Tipton. Diamond Distribution, 1999.

Little Shop of Horrors. Dir. Roger Corman. Perf. Jonathan Haze, Jackie Joseph, Mel Welles, Dick Miller, Jack Nicholson. The Film Group, 1960.

The Making of Paragons Paragon. Practical Cinema Productions, 1982.

Mariachi, El. Dir. Robert Rodriguez. Perf. Carlos Gallardo, Consuelo Gomez, Jaime de Hoyos, Peter Marquardt, Reinol Matinez. Colombia Pictures, 1992.

Night of the Living Dead. Dir. George Romero. Perf. Duane Jones, Judith O'Dea, Karl Hardman, Marilyn Eastman, Keith Eastman, Judith Ridley. Walter Reade Organization, 1968.

Plan 9 from Outer Space. Dir. Edward D. Wood Jr. Perf. Bela Lugosi, Maila Nurmi (Vampira), Lyle Talbot, Gregory Walcott, Mona McKinnon, Tor Johnson. American International Pictures, 1959.

Revenge of the Ninja. Dir. Sam Firstenberg. Perf. Sho Kashugi, Keith Vitali, Virgil Frye, Arthur Roberts. Cannon Pictures, 1983.

Spy Smasher. Dir. William Witney. Perf. Kane Richman, Marguerite Chapman, Sam Flint, Hans Schumm, Tristram Coffin. 12 chapters. Republic Pictures, 1942.

24 Hours to Midnight. Dir. Leo Fong. Perf. Cynthia Rothrock, Myra Cothran, Bernie Pock, Stack Pierce, Mike Hamilton. Sunny Films, 1989.

WEBSITES

Academy of Arts and Sciences. http://www.oscars.org/nicholl/format.html.

Adventures of Superman Message Board. http://disc.yourwebapps.com/Indices/40415.html.

American Film Maker — Home of the Independents, http://www.ifta-online.org/afm/home.asp.

Before CGI, There Was the Lydedeckers, Glass House Presents. http://www.glasshousepresents.com/jan_alan_henderson.html.

Christian Media — All Things Spiritual. http://allthingsspiritual.com/Christian Media.php3.

The Entertainment Resources and Marketing Association. http://www.erma.org/web.

The H.P. Lovecraft Archive. http://www.hplovecraft.com.

Homemade Special Effects. http://www.mightycoach.com/articles/specialeffects/index.html.

LA's Only Qualified Film, TV & Commercial Production Resource. http://www.la411.com.

Library of Congress, Copyright Office. http://www.copyright.gov.

Movie Industry Marketing. http://www.movieindustrymarketing.com/exec/gt/tpl.h,content=15.

Movie Studios, Distributors and TV Stations. http://www.imdb.com/studios.

National Right to Work Legal Foundation. http://nrtw.org.

Producers Masterguide: Film Markets, TV Markets, Exhibitions & Trade-Shows. http://www.masterguide.com/globalmedia/markets.html.

Project Gutenberg Australia, a Treasure-Trove of Literature. http://gutenberg.net.au/plusfifty-a- m.html#letterD.

Public Domain Books. http://www.authorama.com.

Sample Business Contracts. http://contracts.onecle.com/dreamworks/universal.moa-distrib.1995.06.shtml.

Screen Actors Guild. http://www.sagindie.org.

Simply Scripts, Writers Resources. http://www.simplyscripts.com/WR_format.html.

Superman Comes to Television, by Michael J. Hayde. http://www.geocities.com/MikeH0714/Superman1.

The Video Distributor Database. http://dpg.lib.berkeley.edu/webdb/mrc/distrib?type=Studio.

Voyage to the Bottom of the Sea, Special Effects Central. http://www.vitbots.com/special_effects_central.html

Index